Saint Peter's University Library
Withdrawn

# EDUCATING
# HOMELESS
# CHILDREN AND
# ADOLESCENTS

# OTHER RECENT VOLUMES IN THE
# SAGE FOCUS EDITIONS

# EDUCATING HOMELESS CHILDREN AND ADOLESCENTS

## *Evaluating Policy And Practice*

**James H. Stronge**
**editor**

**SAGE** PUBLICATIONS
*International Educational and Professional Publisher*
Newbury Park London New Delhi

Copyright © 1992 by Sage Publications, Inc.

All rights reserved. No part of this book may be reproduced or utilized in any form or by any means, electronic or mechanical, including photocopying, recording, or by any information storage and retrieval system, without permission in writing from the publisher.

*For information address:*

SAGE Publications, Inc.
2455 Teller Road
Newbury Park, California 91320

SAGE Publications Ltd.
6 Bonhill Street
London EC2A 4PU
United Kingdom

SAGE Publications India Pvt. Ltd.
M-32 Market
Greater Kailash I
New Delhi 110 048 India

Printed in the United States of America

**Library of Congress Cataloging-in-Publication Data**

Educating homeless children and adolescents: evaluating policy and
practice / edited by James H. Stronge.
p. cm—(Sage focus editions: 144)
Includes bibliographical references.
ISBN 0-8039-4424-1.—ISBN 0-8039-4425-X (pbk.)
1. Homeless children—Education—United States. I. Stronge,
James H.
LC5144.2.E38    1992
371.96'7'0973—dc20                                    92-23013

92  93  94  95  10  9  8  7  6  5  4  3  2  1

Sage Production Editor: Judith L. Hunter

# Contents

# *Preface*

Homelessness, an immensely complex and multidimensional sociological problem, can be found throughout America's history. Nonetheless the specter of homelessness in contemporary American society seems strange indeed. One of the more enigmatic issues of contemporary homelessness is that of schooling. The phenomenon of homeless families with school-age children, as well as a growing population of independent school-age youth, has served to focus homelessness as an issue of concern for both educational policy makers and practitioners.

*Educating Homeless Children and Adolescents: Evaluating Policy and Practice* serves to highlight the issues related to the provision of an education for homeless children and youth. Specifically the book offers background information relative to the problems of homelessness and education, provides an analysis of educational policy as it relates to this special population, offers practical strategies for effectively serving homeless students, and features a review of emerging homeless education programs that appear to be successfully addressing the educational needs of homeless children and youth. The book is organized into three major sections composed of 13 chapters.

Part I, Homelessness in America: The Educational Context, includes five chapters that focus on background issues related to educating homeless children and youth. Chapter 1, "The Background: History and Problems of

Schooling for the Homeless," by James Stronge, offers a historical overview of homelessness in America, discusses the sociological context of contemporary homelessness, and identifies barriers to the education of homeless students. Chapter 2, "The Legal Context: From Access to Success in Education for Homeless Children and Youth," by Virginia Helm, provides an analysis of legal issues drawn from applicable case law and the Stewart B. McKinney Homeless Assistance Act. Chapter 3, "The Psychosocial Context: Supporting Education for Homeless Children and Youth," by Cynthia Crosson Tower, discusses the psychosocial effects of homelessness on children and provides educational recommendations for dealing with these effects. Chapter 4, "The Context of Family: Implications for Educating Homeless Children," by Meredith van Ry, focuses on the nature of homelessness in families, including the characteristics of homeless families and the effects of homelessness on family life. Chapter 5, "The Reality: The Status of Education for Homeless Children and Youth," by Patricia First, details the current status of state and local implementation of the McKinney Act.

Part II, Education for the Homeless: Overcoming the Barriers, includes four chapters that deal directly with the provision of appropriate educational opportunity for particular segments of the homeless student population. Chapter 6, "Children and Homelessness: Early Childhood and Elementary Education," by Anne Eddowes, highlights the needs of young children and the delivery of age-appropriate educational programs for homeless children. Chapter 7, "Adolescence and Homelessness: The Unique Challenge for Secondary Educators," by Jane Powers and Barbara Jaklitsch, discusses reasons for youth homelessness and offers implications for educators in dealing with the problems posed by these students. Chapter 8, "Educating Special Needs Homeless Children and Youth," by Lori Korinek, Christine Walther-Thomas, and Virginia Laycock, defines special needs students among the homeless, discusses organizational obstacles to service delivery, and identifies essential elements of successful programs for the special needs homeless population. Chapter 9, "Educational Support Services for Homeless Children and Youth," by Joseph Johnson, delineates the types of support services that are vital to making education appropriate for homeless students and discusses how these services can be provided.

Part III, Education for the Homeless: Access and Equity Issues, includes four chapters that relate to policy and practice concerned with educational opportunity and appropriateness for homeless children and youth. Chapter 10, "Ensuring Access to Education: The Role of Advocates for Homeless Children and Youth," by Joan Alker, discusses trends in national advocacy for homeless people, the enactment of the Stewart B. McKinney Act, and issues for advocates at the state and local levels. Chapter 11, "Educational Climate for the Homeless: Cultivating the Family and School Relationship," by María Luisa González, identifies a supportive model for homeless family and school cooperation and offers strategies for cultivating a healthy family-school relationship. Chapter 12, "Educating the Homeless in Rural and Small School District Settings," by Doris Helge, identifies unique factors that inhibit service delivery to homeless children and their families in rural settings and provides specific recommendations and planning considerations for addressing those factors. Chapter 13, "Programs With Promise: Educational Service Delivery to Homeless Children and Youth," by James Stronge, provides a service delivery model for characterizing homeless education programs and identifies emerging educational programs that offer a promise for successfully addressing the educational needs of homeless children and youth.

The contributing authors to this book have, through their combined talents, made an effort to articulate fairly the dimensions of homelessness as they relate to education and to offer conceptually sound, practical advice to academicians, evaluators, policy planners, and practitioners who may be concerned by this most noxious and persistent problem. We perceived our role in developing this book from the outset as one in which we would focus on the needs of homeless students, describe the obstacles to their education, and provide policy and programmatic initiatives that may be of value in overcoming those barriers.

It is our collective hope that in developing *Educating Homeless Children and Adolescents: Evaluating Policy and Practice,* we have brought to bear some greater measure of understanding of the plight of homeless students and possibilities for their education. We recognize full well, however, that a text devoted to educating homeless children and youth is not a solution: It is merely an accommodation to reality—a stopgap measure. The solution lies not in the institutionalization of homeless education but rather in the elimination of the factors in society responsible for pervasive homelessness. As a nation, we have always had some level of homelessness, and we may continue so. The contemporary boon in homelessness, however, should be deemed unacceptable. A decent place to live, a decent job, and an opportunity to achieve our personal and societal goals—the American Dream—should be within reach of us all. Let us therefore dedicate our efforts to the extinction of the purpose for which this text was written.

James H. Stronge, Editor

# PART I

# *Homelessness in America*

## The Educational Context

# 1

# The Background

## History and Problems of Schooling
for the Homeless

JAMES H. STRONGE

The specter of homelessness in contemporary American society seems strange—an anomaly in a land of plenty. "Homelessness in the midst of affluence and relatively low unemployment runs counter to public expectations" (Levitan & Schillmoeller, 1991, p. 5). But homelessness does exist and is a growing concern across America.

Homelessness is an immensely complex and multidimensional social problem: It has no single cause; it has no simple solutions. Albeit *homelessness* means the absence of a permanent place to call home. But "being homeless means more than not having a secure place to sleep. Being homeless means having no place to store the things that connect you to your past; it means losing contact with friends and family; it means uprooting your child from school; it means having to endure the

AUTHOR'S NOTE: Chriss Walther-Thomas's comments and suggestions for improving this chapter are gratefully acknowledged. Background research and the initial draft for portions of the section regarding the history of homelessness is attributed to Cheri Tenhouse. The organization for the section "Problems Associated With Educating the Homeless" is adapted from Stronge and Tenhouse (1990); for additional details regarding educational barriers for the homeless, refer to this monograph.

shame of what is still perceived as personal failure" (National Coalition for the Homeless, 1990, p. 1).

One of the more enigmatic issues of contemporary homelessness is that of schooling. Schools were generally insulated from the concerns of homelessness in earlier periods of our history. Today, however, with the phenomenon of homeless families with school-age children, as well as a growing population of independent school-age youth, homelessness has been brought to the schoolhouse door. It is this issue that serves on the focus of this book: educating America's homeless children and youth.

To discuss education for the homeless outside of the broader sociological context would be a sterile exercise. The overwhelming nature of the problems, either brought on or concomitant with homelessness, can force parents to concentrate on such basic necessities as adequate food, proper clothing, and safe shelter. Consequently the issue of education no longer may hold the same priority for those families. While the focus of the book is the delivery of educational services to homeless children and youth, issues relative to the broader sociological perspective are also addressed. Moreover this introductory chapter raises several questions pertinent to this discussion: What is the history of American homelessness? What is homelessness, and what subgroups are reflected in the broader homeless population? How extensive is homelessness? What are the factors related to homelessness in contemporary society? What are the unique educational challenges posed by homelessness? What policy implications for educating homeless children and youth can be derived from a societal context?

## History of Homelessness in America

> And then the dispossessed were drawn west—from Kansas, Oklahoma, Texas, New Mexico; from Nevada and Arkansas families, tribes, dusted out, tractored out. Carloads, caravans, homeless and hungry; twenty thousand and fifty thousand and a hundred thousand and two hundred thousand. They streamed over the mountains, hungry and restless—restless as ants, scurrying to find work to do—to lift, to push, to pull, to pick, to cut—anything, any burden to bear, for food. The kids are hungry. We got no place to live. Like ants scurrying for work, for food, and most of all for land. (Steinbeck, 1939, p. 317)

Obviously homelessness in America is not new. While ebbs and flows have occurred in the story of homelessness, it is one that is at least as old as Colonial America. Levitan and Schillmoeller (1991) noted that local poorhouses and almshouses were provided for the frail, elderly, and orphans and that asylums housed the mentally ill. In addition, vagrancy laws, developed in the 1800s, jailed the homeless, removed them from the locality, or put them to work, thus removing them from sight of the general public. This is a far cry from the highly visible status of contemporary homelessness. Hombs (1990) noted that visibility is perhaps the most identifiable attribute of contemporary homelessness.

Wallace (1965) reported that the period surrounding the Civil War caused the first real incidence of massive homelessness in America. As early as 1857, soup kitchens were organized in New York for the relief of the distressed. After the war, many civilians and veterans were forced from their homes; some could not find jobs in the aftermath and wandered from town to town, looking for employment.

Hoch (1987) noted that "since about the mid-eighteenth century, the number of homeless has been tied to changes in economic conditions, increasing with economic downturns and declining with the return of prosperity (or the outbreak of war)" (p. 17). Several other factors have influenced the ebb and flow of homelessness, including industrialization and immigration. The expansion of industrialization led to the growth of cities, with the concomitant migration from rural to urban areas, resulting in large concentrations of people, a large number of them poor, in areas not equipped to house them. Further complicating matters, industrialization substituted machines for human workers by the late 1800s, forcing many of the displaced workers into a quest for work and new places to live.

Immigration, particularly from Europe, increased dramatically during the latter half of the 19th century and early part of the 20th century and played a role in American homelessness. Many of these people arrived poor in America and soon joined the other American homeless (Wallace, 1965). Approximately 60,000 homeless men and women were to be found in New York City alone by 1890 (Giamo, 1989).

By the early 1900s, many cities had an area where homeless men would congregate (a time described by Hoch [1987] as the "Deviant" era of homelessness). These areas, often referred to as "skid rows," provided cheap lodging in hotels, with inexpensive meals provided by missions. "The number of homeless men remained relatively constant until 1927 when wages first began to decline and 1929 when the Great Depression hit the nation" (Wallace, 1965, p. 21).

The Great Depression resulted in a dramatic increase in the ranks of the homeless. Individuals and entire families were uprooted, out of work, and forced to leave their homes and to seek refuge elsewhere. By 1933, the homeless population in America was estimated at approximately 1 million. President Roosevelt's New Deal offered support and opportunity for the homeless; such programs as the Work Progress Administration provided public jobs, temporary shelters, and an opportunity for hope of leaving the ranks of the homeless. It was not until the outbreak of World War II, however, that the grip of the Depression finally was broken.

In the 1940s, World War II and its aftermath provided an almost unlimited supply of jobs and returned the country to economic prosperity. As dramatically as it had increased a decade earlier, the homeless population declined during the war. Unlike previous wars, the end of World War II did not place large numbers of men back into the ranks of the homeless. New federal programs and benefits, including the GI Bill of Rights, helped most World War II veterans return to society and avoid homelessness.

During the three decades following World War II, it appeared that the homeless population was disappearing. During this time of economic stability, it only seems sensible that homelessness would decline. While less apparent, however, the population of skid rows still existed. The identifiable occupants of skid row during this period were, for the most part, older alcoholic white men.

Throughout the 1970s, a change in the demographics of the homeless occurred. The homeless population began to include younger people, more women, and more members of minority groups. The number of homeless who were drug abusers or mentally ill increased (Ropers, 1988). Hopper and Hamburg (1984) claimed that the 1970s set the stage for what was to come, concerning the condition of the homeless. "It was during the 1970s that the distinctive forces making for contemporary homelessness took shape and the first signs of nascent crisis surfaced" (Hoch, 1987, p. 21).

During the 1980s and continuing into the current decade, a rapid increase in the "new" homeless has riveted national attention on their plight. For the first time, the homeless include in significant proportions all ages and races, as well as both sexes. Hoch (1987) noted that "although more socially diverse than their skid row predecessors, the new homeless share a similar marginality." The new homeless are "near the bottom of the economically weak and politically disenfranchised underclass" (p. 30).

## *Defining Homelessness*

### Narrow Versus Broad Definitions

Defining *homelessness,* an important early step in developing appropriate service delivery strategies, is an elusive task. Identifying an individual as homeless appears to be straightforward: Either a person does or does not have a place to call home. Definitions range, however, from ones that follow a strict interpretation of homelessness to ones that encompass a much broader perspective (Stronge & Helm, 1991). A sampling of more restrictive definitions include the following:

> A condition wherein an individual on a given night has no place to sleep and is forced to be on the street or to seek shelter in a temporary facility (Kaufman, 1984)
>
> Persons without an address that assures them of at least the following 30 days of sleeping quarters that meet minimal health and safety standards (Caro, cited in Rivilin, 1986)
>
> Someone sleeping or living in (a) limited or no shelter for any length of time, (b) shelters or missions run by religious organizations or public agencies for any length of time, (c) cheap hotels or motels when actual length of stay or intent to stay is 45 days in length, (d) other unique situations that do not fall into categories a-c (Hope & Young, 1986)

While most would agree that someone who sleeps on the street or in an emergency shelter is homeless, Peroff (1987) noted that restrictive definitions of this type raise several legitimate questions:

> If a person can live with a relative and chooses not to, is that person homeless? Are those who live in "doubled up" overcrowded conditions homeless? What about battered spouses who decide to leave their homes temporarily to live in a group home until they find alternative permanent housing or move back to their home when their domestic situation improves? Finally, are those living in permanent housing but with such low income that they might become homeless to be included? (p. 34)

The National Coalition for the Homeless (1990) provided the following definition of homelessness, reflecting a more expansive view:

> Homelessness, broadly defined, means lack of a fixed residence. Thus, the concept embraces anyone whose day-to-day living arrangements are precar-

ious. Obviously, this includes those people whose primary nighttime residence is a public or private shelter, or emergency housing placement (such as the motels or hotels used by local welfare agencies), or an abandoned building, as well as people living on the streets, in parks, transportation terminals, automobiles, or campgrounds. Less apparent are the "invisible" homeless, those who move from one improvised setting to another, doubling up with friends and family, and making use of emergency lodging only on rare occasions. (p. 1)

As with more narrow conceptions of homelessness, broader definitions have their own set of problems. Broad-based definitions tend to overstate the population, thus obscuring the ability of policymakers to match scarce resources with the most needy service areas.

**McKinney Act Definition**

In an effort to bring clarity to the meaning of homelessness, and for purposes of federal assistance, the Stewart B. McKinney Homeless Assistance Act of 1987 (P.L. 100-77) provides a definition of a homeless person as one who (a) lacks a fixed, regular, and adequate nighttime residence or (b) lives in a shelter, an institution (other than a prison or other institutionalized facility), or a place not designed for or ordinarily used as a sleeping accommodation for human beings.

While the McKinney definition provides a general guideline for identification of and subsequent service to homeless individuals, it does not fully satisfy the debate over who is to be considered homeless. A recent review of state plans for the education of homeless children and youth revealed that, of the 35 states included in the analysis, 9 devised definitions broader than the McKinney definition, including children who were doubling up or living in tents or camps, in foster homes, in runaway shelters, and in a variety of other settings. Six of the 35 states simply did not include a definition in their plans (Jackson, 1990).

**Categories of Homeless**

Perhaps a useful tactic for making sense of who are the homeless would be to identify categories of homeless. As Magnet (1987) aptly summarized, "the homeless are not a unified mass but rather several distinct subgroups at the margin of society" (p. 170). Numerous categories for the homeless are suggested in the literature—categories based on type of shelter, primary identifiable characteristics of homeless individuals or primary reasons for becoming homeless, and severity (likelihood of remaining) of homelessness. Wright (1988) offered a categorization based on shelter type: (a) on the street (actually living on the street), (b) quasi-homeless (living in cars, tents, abandoned buildings, etc.), (c) shelters (living temporarily in public/private shelters), and (d) doubling up (living with friends or relatives in dwellings due to having no other place to live). Hagen (1987) suggested grouping the homeless by the primary identifiable characteristics or major reasons for their becoming homeless: alcohol/drug abuse, mental illness, and so on. Several authors (see, for example, Rossi, Wright, Fisher, & Willis, 1987; Rivilin, 1986; Wright & Lam, 1987) suggested a model based on severity of homelessness, reflecting the likelihood of remaining homeless (e.g., chronic homeless, marginally housed, periodic homeless).

Providing a direct answer to the question of who are the homeless is a challenging one. Whether an operational definitional approach or a categorical methodology is applied to the problem, the result may be to obfuscate the issue more than to clarify it. Despite the lack of agreement regarding what constitutes homelessness, however, the evidence undeniably supports the existence of a population of individuals that can be characterized primarily by their lack of a place to call home.

### *Extent of Homelessness*

How many homeless men, women, and children are in America today? The answer, simply put, is no one knows. Due to the diversity of sampling strategies and definitions employed, as well as a variety of methodological problems, accurate data regarding the extent of homelessness in American are absent. The numbers provided by various researchers and agencies that have investigated this question are as varied as the purposes and methodologies employed in their quests. Thus a point of embarkation for this discussion would be consideration of who is counting/estimating, how the counts/estimates are derived, and for what purposes will the numbers be used?

### General Population

Advocates of the homeless have a vested interest in portraying homelessness as a pervasive and growing problem; government may have an interest in reporting conservatively. A 1984 estimate by the U.S.

Department of Housing and Urban Development placed the number of homeless between 200,000 and 350,000. The National Alliance to End Homelessness (1988) estimated that on any given night, 736,000 individuals were homeless, with up to 2.3 million in the homeless ranks over the course of a year. The National Coalition for the Homeless (1990), using a slightly broader definition of homelessness, estimated that America has at least 3 million homeless people.

Homeless advocacy groups defend their numbers as realistic; others argue as vehemently for a more conservative estimate—an argument that has spilled over into the popular press. Reflecting the growing polarization between advocate/conservative viewpoints, Bidinotto claimed in the June 1991 *Reader's Digest* article "Myths About the Homeless" that the 3 million number was "picked out of the air" and "the numbers have often been inflated to attract government funding" (p. 99).

Wright (1988) characterized well the conflicting purposes and politicalization of the process of counting the homeless:

> Quite naturally the use that one will make of these numbers has a tremendous impact on how one goes about negotiating to receive the count and the amount of elasticity that one will employ in defining who is to be counted as homeless. If one is an advocate for the homeless and persuaded by the politics of social betterment, the more people one defines as being homeless, the greater the magnitude of the problem, and consequently the more that can be called for by way of advocacy. [If one is conservative] the more one is persuaded by the conservative political philosophies that hold people who are down and out are there because of their own inability or unwillingness to deal with social expectations. The focus of a . . . decision making process narrows the definition to those fully without resources, living on the streets, eating out of dumpsters, and generally occupying the very bottom positions within the social system. Researchers, on the other hand, often, but not always, attempt to be objective, refining their tools of measurement to the point where one can operationally define the homeless, identify this person in any location, and subsequently provide an enumeration. (p. 11)

In an effort to reflect more accurately the severity of the problem of homelessness, the U.S. Census Bureau, as part of the 1990 census count, assigned approximately 15,000 workers on the night of March 20-21 to make an actual count. In every city with 50,000 or more residents and in smaller communities and rural areas where local officials had reported a homeless population, the census workers were assigned to visit temporary housing locations, as well as to count people on the streets.

Preliminary figures from the Census Bureau's Shelter and Street Night (S-Night) revealed that approximately 180,000 people in emergency shelters and 50,000 in pre-identified street locations were counted. The results of the count, however, have provided more controversy than resolution to the numerical accuracy issue. As reported by the National Alliance to End Homelessness, a Census Bureau official stated that "S-Night was not intended to, and did not, produce a count of the homeless population of the country" (1991, p. 3). Moreover the National Law Center on Homelessness and Poverty threatened to sue the Census Bureau over the release of the numbers unless the bureau issued a disclaimer stating that the count is inaccurate (National Alliance to End Homelessness, 1991).

Most certainly, based on the confining procedures employed in the study, the final census figures will reflect an undercount of the number of homeless in America. Levitan and Schillmoeller (1991) noted that the count "cannot be regarded as an estimate of the total homeless population because it excludes the isolated and hidden homeless" (p. 8). How much the figures are deflated cannot be judged. Is it possible that the numbers generally confirm the previously cited HUD estimates? Is it possible that the census workers actually identified only approximately 10% of the real homeless population (as estimated by homeless advocacy groups)?

### School-Age Population

As with the general population, the extent of homelessness among the school-age population is unclear. The National Coalition for the Homeless estimated the 1990 annual school-age homeless population at 500,000 to 750,000. Of these, approximately 43% were thought to be not attending school on a regular basis. In a report to Congress by the U.S. Department of Education in which a compilation of statistical information from 1988 state final reports on homeless was summarized, an estimate was made of approximately 220,000 homeless school-age children throughout the United States. Of these, 157,000 were identified from actual counts made by the states, with the remaining numbers derived from estimates. Approximately 67,000 (30.8%) children were reported as not attending school (U.S. Department of Education, 1989). The 1989 estimate by the DOE increased to 273,000. As with other aspects of enumerating the extent of homelessness, the level of school enrollment of homeless children is disputed. Contradicting the U.S.

Department of Education figures, a study conducted by the Stanford University Center for the Study of Families, Children, and Youth found that nearly 90% of homeless children were enrolled in school. A plausible explanation for the discrepancy between these reported enrollment figures is that the Stanford study primarily surveyed children and families who were located in shelters, whereas the DOE study relied on a more broadly based population count.

**General Trends**

While there is considerable disagreement regarding the number of homeless in America, there is general accord that families with children are increasingly represented in the growing homeless population. Of these homeless families, research suggests that more than three fourths are single-parent families, typically headed by women (Bassuk & Rosenberg, 1988; Waxman & Reyes, 1990). In a statistical profile of children in poverty, the National Center for Children in Poverty (1990) found that more than half of all poor children in America lived with single mothers. A U.S. Conference of Mayors 30-city survey in 1990 found that requests for shelter by homeless families increased an average of 17% in 1 year. Every survey city except one anticipated that overall requests for emergency shelter, and requests by homeless families in particular, would continue to increase during 1991 (Waxman & Reyes, 1990).

## *Factors Related to Homelessness*

The nature of homelessness in contemporary society defies simple explanation. One of the primary problems with attempting to identify the causes is that such an effort would be an oversimplification of the complexities of homelessness. The causes are myriad; no single factor or even a combination of factors can reliably explain homelessness. The causes of homelessness for one individual or family may not be relevant to the next. Another problem with seeking to identify the causes of homelessness is the inability to determine causality accurately. For instance, is alcoholism the cause or the effect of homelessness? Or are both alcoholism and homelessness the outcomes of some yet unidentified variable (e.g., personal socioemotional problems)? Thus not only can the directionality of a cause-effect relationship not be established but also the claim of a cause-effect relationship can be elusive.

To claim specific causes of homelessness would be a gross generalization that is hit or miss—and more likely miss than hit for its explanatory value. Because we cannot identify in a reliable fashion the precise cause(s) of homelessness in every instance does not mean that we cannot identify factors that are associated with homelessness. Thus the following factors related to homelessness will be explored: housing problems, economic problems, personal problems, and family problems.

**Housing Problems**

Of particular concern for families with school-age children is the obvious factor of homelessness: insufficient affordable housing (Hombs, 1990). It has been estimated that as many as 40% of homeless families became homeless because of eviction (Homeless families, 1987). Kozol (1988), discussing families living at a shelter hotel in New York City, reported that of these families, 34% became homeless after eviction by a landlord, 47% after doubling up with other families, and 19% after living in substandard housing (p. 66). Hombs (1990), in describing the relationship between housing problems and homelessness, stated that "it is the critical shortage of low-cost housing that makes the difference between chronic hardship and outright homelessness" (p. 9).

Numerous factors have contributed to the lack of available low-cost housing. Of particular concern in large urban areas is the factor of gentrification, in which low-cost apartments and single room occupancy (SRO) residences have been demolished or renovated to attract higher rent clientele. For example, the SRO units available in Manhattan decreased from 110,000 in 1970 to 18,000 in 1982, largely due to gentrification and urban renewal, among other causes (Levitan & Schillmoeller, 1991). Overall, since the 1970s, almost half of all SRO housing has been eliminated. Even when housing is available, frequently it is not within the reach of poorer families. This fact is reflected in the disproportionate representation of female head-of-household families among the homeless ranks. The 30-city survey by the U.S. Conference of Mayors found that 77% of homeless families were headed by a single parent (Waxman & Reyes, 1990).

Vulnerability to homelessness is another factor closely related to the housing dilemma. Mihaly (1991) reported in a Children's Defense Fund position paper that "the fundamental cause of homelessness among children today is the rapidly growing gap between the incomes of poor, minority, and young families and the cost of available housing" (p. 10).

A study conducted by the National Low Income Housing Coalition (1991) found that rent burdens among young single-parent householders increased from an average of 38% of income in 1974 to 58% in 1987. Housed families who pay such a high proportion of their income for housing are especially vulnerable to homelessness. Moreover families who lose their affordable living accommodations because of layoffs, domestic upheaval, illness, and other reasons often have a difficult time reentering the housing market. Not only is it difficult for them to locate replacement housing, but they often are unable to amass the money required for first and last month's rent and utility deposits (National Alliance to End Homelessness, 1990).

McChesney (1990) analyzed the problem of family homelessness from the perspective of "the 'low-income housing ratio'—the number of households living below the poverty line divided by the number of affordable housing units available" (p. 191). When the number of poor households exceeds the number of low-income housing units, the families have three basic options: (a) those who can, pay more for housing; (b) those who cannot pay more, double up with family or friends; (c) those who cannot do either, become homeless. Thus "only those programs that reduce poverty or increase the supply of affordable housing will be effective in decreasing the total number of homeless families in the United States" (McChesney, 1990, p. 191).

For those individuals and families who are in need of temporary shelter, the facts are not encouraging. The U.S. Conference of Mayors 1990 survey estimated that 19% of requests for emergency shelter went unmet and that in 70% of the cities surveyed, shelters turned away homeless families due to insufficient resources. For those who do find temporary shelter, strict time limitations are frequently placed on the length of stay, with 30- to 90-day limits being typical.

**Economic Problems**

*Unemployment.*  A growing number of families and individuals become homeless due to unemployment. One reason for the devastating effects of unemployment is that the unemployed are frequently permanently separated from their last jobs rather than being temporarily laid off.

In a study of self-reported reasons for homelessness, Hagen (1987) found that both men and women listed "unemployment" as the number one reason for their homelessness. Unemployment is not a disinterest in working; rather it is more one of a lack of opportunity. Surveys of the homeless have found that the homeless in fact do seek employment. The longer they are unemployed, however, the less employable they become as they grow "more dishevelled, anxious, depressed and lack an address" (Stoner, 1984, p. 4). "Many people are unable to find a job if they cannot give a permanent address or a telephone number. Single parents who head their families and need to work cannot do so unless they have access to day care or their children are enrolled in school" (National Coalition for the Homeless, 1990, p. 3).

*Underemployment.* Even for those individuals who have jobs or who find work, underemployment may not bring housing within an affordable range. From 1960 to 1980, the United States lost approximately 20% of its middle-income manufacturing jobs. Most of these were replaced by lower paying and less secure service jobs (National Alliance to End Homelessness, 1989). The National Center for Children in Poverty (1990) found that many families have been unable to work their way out of poverty:

> Part-time or part-year employment offers little assurance of economic well-being. One full-time minimum wage job does not assure well-being either; it does not bring a family's income above the poverty line. In 1987 a minimum-wage job paid only 77 percent of the poverty line for a family of three, and 60 percent for a family of four. Between 1979 and 1989 the minimum wage constituted a progressively smaller fraction of the income needed to keep families out of poverty. (p. 46)

Further reflecting the dramatic growth in the homeless population of families with young children, the center reported that "the median income for young families is declining, particularly for black families and families headed by parents without high school diplomas" (p. 47). In addition, 53% of all poor children under 6 years of age had at least one parent either working or looking for work.

*Restrictions in social support programs.* Another economic problem related to homelessness is that of cuts and restrictions in social support programs, particularly at the federal level. Hombs (1990) stated, "the benefit programs that once would have constituted a final protection from the streets have been greatly eroded" (p. 8). Budget cuts and restricted eligibility in such programs as the Food Stamps Program, Aid to Families With Dependent Children, and Social Security Disability Benefits have increased the likelihood of homelessness. A 1990 study conducted by the House Ways and Means Committee estimated that almost half of the increase in poverty between the period 1979 to 1988 was the result of cuts in federal low-income and social support programs (cited in National Coalition for the Homeless, 1990). Moreover "the very fact of being homeless—having no fixed address . . . being unable to keep appointments—can make it impossible to establish benefits to which the homeless persons are legitimately entitled" (Hombs, 1990, p. 8).

*Cumulative effect.* Whether it be the effects of unemployment, underemployment, or cutbacks in support programs, the burden of economic deprivation falls inordinately on the shoulders of the most innocent, the most susceptible, and the least able to respond to the ill effects of poverty—the children. The National Center for Children in Poverty (1990) found that children under age 6 are our poorest citizens. For 1987, the poverty rates by age groups were as follows: children from birth to age 6, 23%; children ages 6 to 17, 19%; adults ages 18 to 64, 11%; adults ages 65 and older, 12%. Additionally the center provided a statistical profile of poor children under age 6 in 1987 that included the following highlights:

- Of the approximately 5 million poor children, 42% (2.1 million) were white, 32% (1.6 million) were black, 21% (1.0 million) were Hispanic, and 5% (0.3 million) were other minorities.
- Of all children, black and Hispanic children were disproportionately represented in the poverty rates (48% and 42%, respectively).
- Child poverty rates were highest in urban areas (urban, 31%; rural, 28%; suburban, 13%).

Relating family/child poverty directly to homelessness, the U.S. Conference of Mayors found that families with children comprised 34% of the homeless population (Waxman & Reyes, 1990). In the study, it was estimated that 20% of the total homeless population in the surveyed cities was composed of children. In light of a study of homeless people in more than 100 United States cities, Burt (1992) suggested that the primary cause of homelessness was the demise of the nation's economic infrastructure. She argued that a combination of insufficient low-cost housing, inflation that outpaced wages, unemployment, and the shrink-age of social programs resulted in a dramatic increase in homelessness.

**Personal Problems**

*Substance abuse.* Substance abuse is a major problem that is found among the homeless population. Stark (1987) noted that alcoholism is found in approximately 30% of the homeless population and has been at this level at least since the early 1900s. Wright and Lam (1987) indicated that substance abuse among the homeless population ranged between 10% and 30%. The U.S. Conference of Mayors reported in their survey that 38% of the homeless were substance abusers (alcohol-ism, drug abuse, or both) (Waxman & Reyes, 1990). While the figures may vary, one point is abundantly clear: Substance abuse is found in the homeless population at a significantly higher rate than in the total population. Additionally, whether substance abuse is the cause or the effect, it perpetuates homelessness.

*Physical and mental health problems.* Health-related problems con-stitute another major factor of homelessness. Rossi, Wright, Fisher, and Willis (1987) found in their study of Chicago's homeless that 36% of the sample indicated they experienced fair or poor health, and 28% were unable to work during the previous year due to health-related factors. The National Center for Children in Poverty (1990) suggested that "limited financial resources, lack of knowledge, low self-esteem, youthfulness, and other factors contribute to the sometimes risky lifestyles of people living in poverty" (p. 55). Moreover the center reported that poor children are at greater risk of poor health than are other children. Among the health threats noted in the study are delivery of low birth weight babies, prenatal drug exposure, AIDS, poor nutrition, lead poisoning, and accidental injury.

Mental health problems are another major factor reflected in the home-less population. The U.S. Conference of Mayors estimated that persons with mental illness account for 28% of the homeless population (Waxman & Reyes, 1990). One reason frequently cited for the high rate of mental health problems among the homeless is the policy of deinstitution-alization. The 1963 federal legislation that encouraged community care of patients through outpatient care rather than institutionalization led to the release of a large proportion of institutionalized patients with mental illnesses. In the mid 1950s, the number of mentally ill patients in mental hospitals in the United States was approximately 550,000; in 1990, the number was 70,000. Despite these striking numbers, the high incidence of mental illness among the current homeless population cannot be fully or even primarily explained by the deinstitutionalization policy. The vast majority of deinstitutionalized patients occurred in the 1960s and 1970s, and it was not until the early 1980s that the contemporary homeless population grew dramatically. As Magnet (1987) surmised, "today, however, the homeless mentally ill are more often not the deinstitutionalized but the younger never institutionalized" (p. 176).

## Family Problems

Family problems, such as spouse abuse, may cause a family to break up, creating a need for independent housing for both parties—a circumstance that leaves women and children especially vulnerable to homelessness. Bassuk and Rosenberg (1988) found in their study that "about two-thirds of the men with whom homeless women had their most recent relationships had poor work histories, substance abuse problems, battering tendencies, or other problems" and that 41% of the homeless mothers willing to respond detailed a relationship in which they had been battered (p. 785). Thus, when living conditions became intolerable, women and their children frequently were forced to move out of the house and into the ranks of the homeless. This unfortunate social ill has increased in recent years. The National Low Income Housing Coalition (1991) reported that shelters and programs for battered women experienced a 100% increase in service demands between 1983 and 1987. In 1987 alone, these shelters for domestic violence provided emergency housing for 375,000 women and their children, with approximately double that amount being turned away due to nonavailability of space.

In economic terms, domestic violence and family breakups have a devastating effect on children. The U.S. Census Bureau found in a recently completed 3-year study that children can expect to become 37% poorer almost immediately upon the breakup of their families. After their parents separate, fewer than half of the children included in the survey received child support, further impoverishing them (Bianchi & McArthur, 1991).

When homelessness occurs as a result of domestic violence, economic problems, or other root causes, these families frequently face the added difficulty of isolation. Many are unable to turn to immediate family members because their relatives are out of state, estranged, or deceased (Homeless families, 1987). Rossi et al. (1987) found in their study of urban homelessness that the social contacts of the homeless were limited: 33% were not in contact with any relatives, and 24% were not in contact with family or friends.

Adolescents are another segment of the population forced to flee home because of various family-related problems and unlikely to be in touch with family. Two identifiable groups are reflected in the population of independent youth: runaways and throwaways. While research indicates that independent homeless youth experience extensive parent-child conflict prior to leaving home, a distinction, based on the reason for leaving, can be drawn between the two groups. *Runaways* are youth who choose to leave home for various reasons, whereas *throwaways* are forced to leave and are told not to return (Adams, Gullotta, & Clancey, 1985). Types of abuse experienced prior to leaving home, as reported by both male and female youth, include physical abuse, neglect, emotional abuse, and sexual abuse (Powers, Eckenrode, & Jaklitsch, 1988). The Stanford Center for the Study of Families, Children, and Youth (1991) found that more than half of the homeless adolescents in the study reported being physically abused at home. In some cases, youth leave home simply because their families are no longer able to support them. Regardless of the cause, the net result is a population of independent school-age homeless youth who tend to become more troubled the longer they remain independent and who pose especially complex problems for educators wishing to deliver educational services to them.

## Problems Associated
## With Educating the Homeless

One of the significant problems facing the American educational system is that of translating the concepts of access and equity in educational opportunity into reality for children from at-risk situations. No population of students is more at-risk of school failure, if not outright school exclusion, than the homeless. Homelessness places the educational opportunity of these students in jeopardy by creating a myriad of problems associated with the provision of traditional schooling. Problems associated with homelessness (e.g., financial barriers, transiency) and problems associated with the organization of schools (e.g, residency requirements, transportation) combine to pose formidable barriers to their education. Of particular concern as inhibiting factors to educational opportunity for homeless children and youth are legal barriers, education and support service impediments, financial constraints, and social and psychological concerns.

## Legal Barriers

Compulsory school attendance is required for students of specified ages, and it places an obligation on parents or their substitutes. Public education provided by a state is primarily a duty imposed on students and their parents for the public good, as well as an individual right they possess. The difficulty with this policy as it applies to homeless students is the restriction that their education take place in the district in which they reside. Providing students who have no identifiable or permanent address a free appropriate public education, while acknowledging the tradition of educational provision within the district of residence, is a primary barrier of concern. When students do not have a permanent address, educational enrollment can be delayed due to lack of a central policy, or an outright denial of education can occur in schools that do not want the students enrolled. Even if a state assures access to free education, school districts may interpret state procedures in a manner favorable to their own purposes. In other situations, school districts may enact rules that effectively deny eduction to homeless children and youth by setting up requirements that are impossible for them to meet (Stronge & Helm, 1991). It should be noted, however, that the problem of access to education may have moderated in recent years as school officials have become more sensitive to the plight of homeless students and have modified enrollment procedures to better accommodate the students' educational needs (Stanford Center for the Study of Families, Children, and Youth, 1991).

## Educational and Support Service Impediments

Among the educational programs and support service impediments is the matter of availability of educational records. Ely (1987) reported that the lack of records resulted in difficulty in registering or actual denial in 25% of the school districts surveyed. Many states require immunization records and/or grade reports for school enrollment. Families who lose their home and belongings, as well as youth living on their own, are often unable to produce these records. Further complicating matters, parents of runaway or throwaway youth may refuse to furnish records if they are on poor terms with their children.

Appropriate placement in educational programs is another area of concern. For example, homeless students often need special education due to the developmental lags many of them experience. Due to the transient nature of homelessness, however, they may not stay in one school district long enough for their needs to be fully identified, to be evaluated, and to be placed in special education or other appropriate programs. Indeed some school districts may wait to find out whether the student is going to stay in the district before investing in the assessment and placement processes. Thus, when a homeless student is enrolled in school, he or she may be underserved or inappropriately served.

Regardless of the placement, available evidence on the educational performance of homeless children and youth tends to indicate that they experience developmental delays in their academic skills. Bassuk and Rosenberg (1988) found in their study of homeless families in Boston that 40% of the students were failing or producing below-average work, 25% were in special classes, and 43% had repeated one grade. In a review of educational performance among homeless students in San Diego, Stronge (1989) found that, on a standardized achievement test, students averaged approximately 1 year below their grade level in reading, spelling, and mathematics in grades four through six; students in grades seven and eight averaged 1 to 3 years below in the various academic areas.

### Financial Constraints

The issue of financial constraints affects both school children and school districts. Although from quite different perspectives, both homeless children and the schools they attend may experience a shortage of funds needed for their education. The shortage can lead to conflicts and problems for both sides.

### Social and Psychological Issues

The challenge of educating homeless children and youth invokes concerns for the socioemotional well-being of the students, as well as for the more traditional emphasis on academic progress. While academic success is fundamental to breaking the grip of poverty, educators may not be able to bring into focus academic goals for these students until pressing social and psychological needs have been addressed. Particularly, properly addressing concerns for stress, social acceptance,

SAINT PETER'S COLLEGE LIBRARY
JERSEY CITY, NEW JERSEY 07306

and self-esteem may be paramount to making education relevant (Stronge & Tenhouse, 1990).

### *Education and the Homeless: Implications for Policy and Practice*

Contemporary homelessness is complex and is rooted in the broader aspects of society. Clearly no simple solutions exist. Providing adequate housing is not enough to break the cycle of homelessness. Rather it must be addressed on multiple fronts, including the classroom (Stronge, 1991). As Notkin, Rosenthal, and Hopper (1990) stated, "without adequate support services, simply providing new apartments neither guarantees a family's stability nor prevents future homelessness" (p. 35).

Support services, including adequate attention to the unique educational needs of homeless children and youth, are vital for any comprehensive intervention strategy that holds a hope of success. The National Association of State Coordinators for the Education of Homeless Children and Youth captured this sentiment in their position statement:

> Beyond all else, homeless children need homes. However, to the extent that the nation can meet the educational needs of homeless children, we can help ensure that homeless children do not become homeless adults. Public education can play a significant role in meeting both the long- and short-term needs of homeless children and youth, providing an environment that supports their physical, social, and emotional growth. (Johnson & Wand, 1991, p.1)

"While providing appropriate educational opportunities to these students may not result in the disappearance of homelessness, ignoring education for the homeless will most certainly perpetuate it" (Stronge & Tenhouse, 1990, p. 31). The best solution would be to eliminate the causes of homelessness and thus eliminate the issue altogether. Unfortunately, solutions to the problem posed by homelessness will not come easily. Natriello, McDill, and Pallos (1990) noted that "the problems of disadvantaged students are the results of long-term conditions that are not susceptible to short-term solutions" (p. 1). It is precisely for their purpose that this text is dedicated: seeking to identify the problems related to educating homeless children and youth and offering meaningful long-term policy recommendations that are translatable into practice.

## References

Adams, G. R., Gullotta, T., & Clancey, M. A. (1985). Homeless adolescents: A descriptive study of similarities and differences between runaways and throwaways. *Adolescence, 20,* 713-724.

Bassuk, E., & Rosenberg, L. (1988). Why does family homelessness occur? A case-control study. *American Journal of Public Health, 78,* 783-788.

Bianchi, S., & McArthur, E. (1991). *Family disruption and economic hardship: The short-run picture for children.* (U.S. Department of Commerce, Bureau of the Census, Current Population Reports, Household Economic Studies Series P-70, No. 23). Washington, DC: Government Printing Office.

Bidinotto, R. J. (1991, June). Myths about the homeless. *Reader's Digest,* pp. 98-103.

Ely, L. (1987). *Broken lives: Denial of education to homeless children.* Washington, DC: National Coalition for the Homeless. (ERIC Document Reproduction Service No. ED 292 897)

Giamo, B. (1989). *On the Bowery: Confronting the homeless in American society.* Iowa City: University of Iowa Press.

Hagen, J. L. (1987). Gender and homelessness. *Social Work, 32,* 312-316.

Hoch, C. (1987). A brief history of the homeless problem in the United States. In R. D. Bingham, R. E. Green, & S. B. White (Eds.), *The homeless in contemporary society* (pp. 16-32). Newbury Park, CA: Sage.

Hombs, M. E. (1990). *American homelessness: A reference handbook.* Santa Barbara, CA: ABC-CLIO.

Homeless families: How they got that way. (1987, November/December). *Society,* p. 4.

Hope, M., & Young, J. (1986). *The faces of homelessness.* Lexington, MA: D. C. Heath.

Hopper, K., & Hamburg, J. (1984). *The making of America's homeless: From skid row to new poor.* New York: Community Service Society of New York.

Jackson, S. (1990). *State plans for the education of homeless children and youth: A selected survey of thirty-five states.* Cambridge, MA: Center for Law and Education.

Johnson, Jr., J. F., & Wand, B. (1991). *Homeless, not hopeless: Ensuring educational opportunity for America's homeless children and youth.* A position document of the National Association of State Coordinators for the Education of Homeless Children and Youth. (Available from P. Jackson-Jobe, Maryland Department of Education, 200 W. Baltimore St., 4th floor, Baltimore, MD 21201)

Kaufman, N. (1984). Homelessness: A comprehensive policy approach. *Urban and Social Change Review, 17*(1), 21-26.

Kozol, J. (1988, January 25). The homeless and their children (Part 1-A reporter at large). *New Yorker,* pp. 65-84.

Levitan, S. A., & Schillmoeller, S. (1991). *The paradox of homelessness in America.* Washington, DC: George Washington University, Center for Social Policy Studies.

Magnet, M. (1987, November 23). The homeless. *Fortune,* pp. 70-79.

McChesney, K. Y. (1990). Family homelessness: A systemic problem. *Journal of Social Issues, 46*(4), 191-206.

Mihaly, L. K. (1991). *Homeless families: Failed policies and young victims.* Washington, DC: Children's Defense Fund.

National Alliance to End Homelessness. (1988). *Housing and homelessness: A report of the National Alliance to End Homelessness.* Washington, DC: Author.

National Alliance to End Homelessness. (1989). *There's no place like home.* Washington, DC: Author.

National Alliance to End Homelessness. (1990). *Homeless fact sheet.* Washington, DC: Author.

National Alliance to End Homelessness. (1991). Census Bureau 1990 decennial counts for persons enumerated at S-night. *Alliance, 7*(5), 3.

National Center for Children in Poverty. (1990). *Five million children: A statistical profile of our poorest young citizens.* New York: Columbia University, School of Public Health, National Center for Children in Poverty.

National Coalition for the Homeless. (1990). *Homelessness in America: A summary.* Washington, DC: Author.

National Low Income Housing Coalition. (1991). *Unlocking the door: An action program for meeting the housing needs of women.* Washington, DC: Author.

Natriello, G., McDill, E. L., & Pallos, A. M. (1990). *Schooling disadvantaged children: Racing against catastrophe.* New York: Teachers College Press.

Notkin, S., Rosenthal, B., & Hopper, K. (1990). *Families on the move: Breaking the cycle of homelessness.* New York: Edna McConnell Clark Foundation.

Peroff, K. (1987). Who are the homeless and how many are there? In R. D. Bingham, R. E. Green, & S. B. White (Eds.), *The homeless in contemporary society* (pp. 33-45). Newbury Park, CA: Sage.

Powers, J. A., Eckenrode, J., & Jaklitsch, B. (1988). *Running away from home: A response to adolescent maltreatment.* Paper presented at the Biennial Meeting of the Society for Research on Adolescence, Alexandria, VA. (ERIC Document Reproduction Service No. ED182 465)

Rivilin, L. (1986). A new look at the homeless. *Social Policy, 16*(4), 3-10.

Ropers, R. (1988). *The invisible homeless.* New York: Human Sciences.

Rossi, P., Wright, J., Fisher, G., & Willis, G. (1987). The urban homeless: Estimating composition and size. *Science, 235,* 1336-1341.

Stanford Center for the Study of Families, Children, and Youth. (1991). *The Stanford studies of homeless families, children, and youth.* Palo Alto, CA: Author.

Stark, L. (1987). A century of alcohol and homelessness. *Alcohol Health and Research World, 4,* 8-14.

Steinbeck, J. (1939). *The grapes of wrath.* New York: Viking.

Stewart B. McKinney Homeless Assistance Act of 1987. P.L. 100-77, Codified at 42 U.S.C. 11301-11472. (1987, July 22).

Stoner, M. R. (1984). An analysis of public and private sector provisions for homeless people. *Urban and Social Change Review, 17*(1), 3-8.

Stronge, J. H. (1989). [Academic performance of homeless children]. Unpublished raw data.

Stronge, J. H. (1991, April). *Emerging service delivery models for educating homeless children and youth: A sociological perspective.* Paper presented at the Annual Meeting of the American Educational Research Association, Chicago, IL.

Stronge, J. H., & Helm, V. M. (1991). Residency and guardianship requirements as barriers to the education of homeless children and youth. *Journal of Law and Education, 20*(2), 201-218.

Stronge, J. H., & Tenhouse, C. (1990). *Educating homeless children: Issues and answers.* Bloomington, IN: Phi Delta Kappa Educational Foundation.

U.S. Department of Education. (1989, February). *Report to Congress: Education of homeless children and youth—state grants.* Washington, DC: Author.

Wallace, S. E. (1965). *Skid row as a way of life.* Totowa, NJ: Bedminster.

Waxman, L. D., & Reyes, L. M. (1990). *A status report on hunger and homelessness in America's cities: 1990.* Washington, DC: U.S. Conference of Mayors.

Wright, J. D., & Lam, J. A. (1987). Homelessness and the low-income housing supply. *Social Policy, 17*(4), 48-53.

Wright, R. D. (1988). *Research project pertaining to the problem of homeless children and children of homeless families in Iowa.* (Final report presented to the Iowa Department of Education). Des Moines, IA: Drake University.

*2*

# The Legal Context

## From Access to Success in Education for Homeless Children and Youth

VIRGINIA M. HELM

### Historical Background

The creation of legal rights of homeless children and youth to education closely parallels the development of legal rights of handicapped and at-risk children. This development has in each instance begun with the problem of initial access for young people previously excluded or ignored. Almost immediately, however, educators and advocates realized that mere access alone was insufficient for these variously disadvantaged children really to benefit from the school environment. For the hard-won access to be meaningful, support services and programs would be required. With these additional support structures, we could begin to think about success for children who might otherwise have gained little by mere access to programs and activities.

---

AUTHOR'S NOTE: All references to the original Stewart B. McKinney Homeless Assistance Act and to its subsequent amendments will cite the legislation by the commonly used citations: Stewart B. McKinney Homeless Assistance Act and 1988 and 1990 McKinney Amendments. The official bibliographical citations are listed in the References at the end of the chapter.

In the case of homeless children and youth, the initial problem of access stemmed from state residency requirements for admission to school. Specifically, nearly all state compulsory attendance laws require children to attend school in the district in which they and their parents/guardians live (demonstrating evidence of permanent residency). Homeless families moving from one temporary living arrangement to another by definition had no permanent residence. Unable to document a permanent residence when living in a homeless shelter, in an apartment with friends or relatives, or in a car, tent, or other temporary setting, homeless youth and the children of homeless families were denied admission to school by school authorities who were simply following state laws.

In their efforts to gain access to schools, the homeless turned to the branch of government that has a history of breaking new ground in the delineation of rights for disadvantaged victims of discrimination: the judicial branch. With the help of advocates, they appealed their denials. Two state commissioners of education and three state or federal courts upheld the appeals of homeless parents to enroll their children either in a nearby district where they had previously attended school or in the district where they were temporarily living. In a few short years, administrative law (in the form of decisions rendered by commissioners of education) and common law (court decisions) had clarified for the nation both the problem (residency requirements as a barrier to enrollment in school) and the remedy (addressing these residency requirements). As with minority, handicapped, and at-risk children before them, the path for homeless children and youth—with the help of strong advocates—turned from the courts to Congress.

Responding no doubt to a combination of organized advocacy and a media blitz focusing on the plight of the homeless, Congress enacted the Stewart B. McKinney Homeless Assistance Act in July, 1987. This comprehensive legislation contained a series of provisions relating to education for homeless children and youth. The policy focus of the educational provisions of the original McKinney Act was two-pronged. It specifically stated that (a) all homeless children and youth should "have access to a free, appropriate public education" (the guarantee for handicapped children) and that (b) any state having a residency requirement as a component of its compulsory school attendance laws should "review and undertake steps to revise such laws to assure that the children of homeless individuals and homeless youth are afforded a free and appropriate education" (Sec. 721). The entire focus at this point was on ensuring access by removing barriers caused by residency requirements.

Little more than 3 years later, the nation's consciousness was raised: We began to understand that access alone was an insufficient benefit. Again the growth of this awareness paralleled the evolution of concern and provision of rights for the handicapped, minority, and at-risk disadvantaged children whose problems had been confronted earlier. Reflecting this more informed awareness, the 1990 McKinney Amendments broadened the policy statement to require states to review and undertake a revision of any attendance laws "or other laws, regulations, practices, or policies that may act as a barrier to the enrollment, attendance, or *success* [italics added] in school of homeless children and homeless youth" (Sec. 612, amending Sec. 721). Not just theory or humane philosophy but legislation now stated the change in focus from access to success. And success for those whose ability to benefit from access is handicapped by environmental disadvantages requires additional support. That support was incorporated into the 1990 McKinney Amendments in a variety of provisions, discussed below.

In order to transform access into educational success, the federal government, unready to appropriate more than a little seed money, tried to shift the responsibility to the states. This was not totally inappropriate, because education is a state responsibility and state laws and programs contained both the problems and the potential remedies to access and success in education for the homeless. Both the original McKinney Act and the amendments that followed encouraged, where they could not mandate: (a) cooperation and coordination between school personnel and state and local social services agencies dealing with homeless families; (b) evaluation of homeless children and youth for eligibility in compensatory, special education, or gifted programs; and (c) participation of homeless children and youth, where eligible, in government-funded food programs, in after-school and before-school programs and summer programs, and, where necessary, transportation programs (1990 McKinney Amendments, Sec. 612 [b]).

While the intent of the McKinney Act clearly reflected a humane and caring attitude, the ability of Congress or the Department of Education to enforce these mandates seems limited. No "stick" has appeared, and the only "carrot" has been the meager appropriations (minimum of $50,000 per state in FY87 and FY88) to states that submitted a state plan for increasing their efforts to provide educational opportunities for homeless children and youth. Although Congress appropriated $7,200,000 for FY91, that was grossly inadequate to support the level of services by local and state education agencies that the legislation requires. Surveys of state compliance with the McKinney Act have revealed wide variances in compliance (Bowen, Purrington, & O'Brien, 1990; First & Cooper, 1989). Perhaps not surprisingly, those states with the greatest compliance (Connecticut, Massachusetts, New Jersey, New York, and Texas) have tended to be states where early litigation, preceding the McKinney Act, prompted political and education officials to develop policies and procedures to eliminate barriers and to provide support programs and services for homeless children and youth (First & Cooper, 1989).

After the courts, Congress, and to varying degrees the state legislatures and education agencies all issue their decrees, much of the real action in providing access and success in education rests with the local education agencies: the schools and school district officials. If it was at this level that the original problems were encountered, it is now at this level where changes will be implemented. Money has always been an effective motivator, but so far, little money has come from the federal government or the states to promote programs and services for educating homeless children and youth. Yet in many instances, local schools, knowing that "it is the law" and maybe caring about individual families and youth, may respond with greater concern and flexibility than a decade ago.

### What Are the Legal Barriers to Education for Homeless Children and Youth?

As indicated above, the initial focus was on state residency requirements until fuller awareness identified additional barriers. The most frequent and most problematic barriers to an education for homeless children and youth include residency requirements, guardianship requirements, immunization requirements, availability of records, and transportation (Stronge & Helm, 1991). The specific nature of each of these barriers and how they impede enrollment or attendance in school is explained below.

*Residency requirements.* Most if not all states include in their compulsory attendance laws a provision specifying that all children will be provided access to schools in the district in which they or their parents/guardians reside. Many states also prohibit enrollment of students who move without their parents into a district for the sole purpose of attending the school(s) in that district. Such prohibitions generally are designed to prevent a student from moving in with friends or distant relatives in order to play on a desirable athletic team in that district. When parents wish to enroll their children in a school district other than the one in which they reside, they usually are required to pay "tuition" comparable to the cost of per pupil expenditures in that district.

Residency requirements cause a two-pronged problem for homeless families with school-age children. First, a family moving—or moved by a social service agency—to what may be temporary quarters in a shelter, motel, or apartment with family or friends in another school district are not considered residents either of the district in which they previously attended school or in the district where they temporarily live, because they have not established permanent residency there. Both school districts, in denying admission to their schools, would (prior to the McKinney Act) have claimed accurately that they simply were implementing state laws.

Second, homeless families not infrequently are split up among two or more residences, with some children being sent to relatives, others perhaps to live with friends, and sometimes one or more becoming wards of the state. They may find themselves in several different school districts, and if the state law requires evidence of permanent residency in the district, it is easy to see that the children and their parents or guardians cannot meet that requirement.

*Guardianship requirements.* Similar to residency requirements, guardianship requirements are generally found in state mandates that require students to be registered by either parents or official guardians designated by parents or the state. Yet homelessness, as mentioned above, often forces families to separate in order to provide adequate care for all members. Children may stay with family friends or with relatives— who will not qualify as the guardians necessary to sign for school registration. At a shelter in Oregon, for example, it was reported that 10% of all school-age shelter youth were denied admission to school for lack of a legal guardian to register them (Ely, 1987).

Runaway youth are even more likely to have problems in registering for school (in those rare instances where they might choose to make the effort). In Houston and San Francisco, for example, personnel from Runaway Youth Shelters reported that their clients were denied admission to school when guardians could not sign for their enrollment or would not cooperate in obtaining school records (Ely, 1987). In some states, such as New Jersey, guardians must not only enroll students but also must document that they live in the school district in which they are enrolling the student. At one youth home alone, a New Jersey administrator reported that 25 students a year were denied access to education because of this residency/guardianship requirement (Ely, 1987).

In other states, however, guardianship requirements have not been as stringent or as stringently enforced as residency requirements; some districts and even some states define *parent* as "anyone serving in loco parentis, or in place of the parent, with whom the child lives and who is currently responsible for the child's day-to-day welfare." Thus children staying with relatives or friends for a semester or year after parents move to another town or state, or teenagers temporarily living with another family due to problems in their own family usually are regarded as continuing residents in the district and are allowed to continue attending the school where they have been enrolled. In most instances, however, guardianship laws, in tandem with the residency laws with which they are closely aligned, tended to be used against homeless families for no other reason than their homelessness.

*Immunization requirements.* Most if not all states mandate that students receive and present records of immunization against common communicable diseases before or very shortly after being admitted to school. Homeless children, depending on the length of time their families have been homeless, may have difficulty meeting this requirement in several ways: (a) The parents may not know about immunization requirements, (b) the parents may not be able to afford immunization or know about public health immunization programs, (c) the parents may have difficulty contacting the appropriate physician or public health office for copies of immunization records, and (d) the schools in which the children were previously enrolled may be slow in responding to requests for school records from the school in which the family is trying to enroll their children. Without proof of immunization, most schools are required by law to exclude children trying to enroll or already enrolled.

*Availability of records (birth certificates, school records, immunization records, other records).* Record availability can be a barrier to school attendance for homeless children. Nonetheless less evidence exists of this problem being an obstacle to the education of homeless children and youth, perhaps in part because denial of admission based on residency precluded families and schools from getting to the point of talking about children's records. Ely's 1987 survey, however, found that in 25% of the shelters surveyed, lack of records from a previous school district impeded or prevented their clients from registering in school.

The logistics of obtaining and keeping records of immunizations, birth certificates, and school grades can be daunting even for stable, organized families. For homeless families, the task may seem impossible. How easy is it for anyone, let alone someone without a home, to get a money order in order to get a notarized copy of a birth certificate in order to register a child in school? For runaway youth, the problems are even more insurmountable because these youth seldom have the necessary identification documents required to enroll in school.

The problems here are similar to those discussed in connection with immunization: parents or runaway youth having difficulty in locating their own records or in obtaining records from schools the children previously attended. In large cities, bureaucratic responses to requests for documentation can be distressingly slow, and homeless families may move with considerable frequency for a period of time ranging from a month or two to several years. When they do, the delays in transfer of records may result in children being excluded from one school after another. In short, the difficulty of transferring and sometimes even of identifying or locating documentation required for admission to schools can seriously delay and occasionally perhaps prevent homeless children and youth from enrolling in school.

*Transportation.* Like several of the immediately preceding issues, transportation was not addressed in the original McKinney Act as an education-related problem. The 1990 Amendments, however, reflected the new awareness that transportation can be a major component of access to schools. In Ely's 1987 survey of shelter providers, 15% reported attendance problems related to difficulties in obtaining transportation to school. By 1991, the Center for Law and Education asserted that "lack of transportation poses one of the greatest barriers—if not the greatest barrier—to enrollment, attendance and success in school for homeless children" (Center for Law and Education, 1991).

Lack of transportation in some cases causes parents to keep their children home for weeks because of delays in obtaining city-funded transit passes and because they cannot afford the $2.00 per day cost of public transportation while waiting for the transit pass to be processed (Ely, 1987). In other cases, when shelter children must be bused long distances, they are forced to leave the shelter before breakfast is served. When a parent does have a car, he or she is unlikely to have money for gasoline to drive the child(ren) to school. Or the family may have difficulty learning about the school bus routes and where they might access those routes.

## What Are the Sources of These Legal Barriers?

The barriers of residency, guardianship, and immunization requirements arise from state legislation, sometimes reinforced by state administrative law or state education agency regulations. The barriers of availability of records and transportation are more local in origin. Problems in these latter two areas may originate with either the school (district) or the parents or, more likely, both school and parents. As indicated, parents may be unaware of the procedures for locating and obtaining copies of records or for getting access to school-provided transportation—if it is even available. When school districts do not have records of homeless children and youth living within the district boundaries, it is not easy to provide such families with information about transportation routes and opportunities. School offices can be slow in responding to requests from other schools, within or outside the district, for student records. When homeless families move around frequently, as sometimes happens, they may begin to despair of ever having school records catch up with them, and if they have received impatient responses from school personnel about the failure of a previously attended school to produce their children's school records, they may choose to keep their children out of the next school rather than face condescending or impatient treatment from a school official.

### Surmounting the Barriers Prior to the McKinney Act

Prior to the passage of the McKinney Homeless Assistance Act in 1987, the only recourse of homeless families whose children were denied admission to school for failure to meet residency or guardianship requirements was to appeal to the courts or to the state commissioner/superintendent of education. At least four such legal actions were brought prior to the McKinney legislation.

The first reported case pertaining to residency requirements applied to homeless children was *Richards v. Board of Education of Union Free School District Number 4* (1985). In this administrative ruling by New York Commissioner of Education Ambach, the plaintiff mother, Mary Richards, was successful in persuading state authorities that her children were entitled to receive an education in the Port Chester-Rye school district where they had previously lived and attended school. The commissioner's reasoning may be more important than the decision itself: "It is well settled that a residence is not lost until another residence is established through both intent and action expressing such intent" (see *Matter of Callahan*, 1970; *Matter of Lundburg*, 1973; *Matter of Wadas*, 1982). Commissioner Ambach found that Mrs. Richards's intent to remain in Port Chester was clear: She reported weekly to the Department of Social Services office in that community, requesting housing there; she kept a post office address there; she went to church there; and she had extensive family there. Ambach ruled that she still technically resided in Port Chester because she neither established nor gave evidence that she intended to establish permanent residence elsewhere. She was understood simply to be temporarily absent from her previous permanent residence. The commissioner refused, however, to generalize this ruling to all homeless children in the future. Rather he explicitly held that until the legislature enacted legislation "specifically addressing the education of homeless children, the residence of such children must be determined on a case-by-case basis."

Six months later, a New York federal district court ruled against Iraida Delgado who, like Mrs. Richards, sought to enroll her children in the school district where they had attended school prior to becoming "homeless." Neither Freeport, where the family had lived for several years, nor the Roosevelt district, in which they were temporarily housed, would admit the Delgado children because they could not demonstrate permanent residency in either community. The court issued a ruling (*Delgado v. Freeport Public School District*, 1986) different from the commissioner's, based on a different line of reasoning. The Freeport schools' refusal to admit the Delgado children was held to be not arbitrary, capricious, or unreasonable, and therefore it did not deserve to be overturned. Mrs. Delgado had not established the clear and strong ties to her family's previous community as had Mrs. Richards. The court held, however, that the children were entitled to attend school in the Roosevelt district where they then lived, regardless of how temporarily.

Freeport's role as a defendant in the courts did not end with the Delgado decision. Shortly after that decision, the district expelled (for no longer meeting residency requirements) the five children of a family who had lived in Freeport for 10 years prior to eviction from their apartment. During the 4 months following eviction, the family was placed by the social services agency in eight shelter locations. In this case, *Mason v. Board of Education, Freeport Union School District* (1987), the Supreme Court of Nassau County in New York ruled that bodily presence established children's residence for attendance purposes. As in Delgado, then, the temporary residence rather than prior residence determined school placement of children even though the parent requested placement in the district where the children had previously attended school.

In Hingham, Massachusetts, the school superintendent refused to enroll the four children of a family who lived in a tent in a state park within the town. He reasoned that they were living on state property and therefore were not legally residents of the local community. The Massachusetts Commissioner of Education disagreed, ordering the school district to educate children living within the district boundaries "irrespective of their living situation" (Jennings, 1989).

A fifth court case, brought and decided shortly after passage of the McKinney Act, is mentioned here because no claims or decisions were made or based on that legislation. In this instance, the New Jersey town of Wrightstown ordered a motel owner to evict several homeless families placed there for temporary shelter by the welfare board. The order was based on a city ordinance that limits motel residence to 30 days. To protect the homeless families and the school-age children, the public advocate charged that "by enforcing the 30 day limit against plaintiffs, defendant [city] is attempting, through exclusionary zoning, to expel homeless children from its borders and thereby protect its educational budget from any increased costs" (Letter brief by plaintiffs and Pub. Adv. of New Jersey at 14, *Vingara v. Wrightstown*). Two months after the order to evict, the city repealed this discriminatory provision and the complaint was dismissed (*Vingara et al. v. Borough of Wrightstown,* 1987).

Prior to the enactment of the McKinney legislation, then, homeless families whose children were denied access to schools turned to the legal system when the educational system responded with what appeared to be bureaucratic insensitivity. Without knowing the motivation or the thinking behind the school officials' decisions, we can choose to give them the benefit of the doubt by viewing their responses as another attempt to comply with the numerous state laws and regulations that now govern the operation of our schools.

**Surmounting the Barriers**
**After the McKinney Act (1987)**

The original McKinney Act, reflecting legal actions in several states by homeless families denied admission to any school district or to the district of their choice, mandated that states review and revise residency requirements to ensure access of homeless children and youth to school. Specifically in Section 721 of Subtitle B—Education for Homeless Children and Youth the law reads:

> It is the policy of the Congress that—
> (1) each State educational agency shall assure that each child of a homeless individual and each homeless youth have access to a free, appropriate public education which would be provided to the children of a resident of a State and is consistent with the State school attendance laws; and
> (2) in any State that has a residency requirement as a component of its compulsory school attendance laws, the State will review and undertake steps to revise such law to assure that the children of homeless individuals and homeless youth are afforded a free and appropriate public education.

Small appropriations were made available for each state to establish an office for a Coordinator of Education of Homeless Children and Youth. These coordinators were expected to gather data about the number and location of homeless children and youth and about the kinds of problems they experienced in enrolling and attending school. Each state was also to develop and submit a state plan to provide for the education of homeless children and youth. Major components of this plan were to include (a) procedures for resolving disputes regarding the educational placement of homeless children and youth and (b) placement of homeless children either in the "district of origin for the remainder of the school year;" or "in the school district where the child or youth is actually living; whichever is in the child's best interest or the youth's best interest" (Sec. 722, [e][3]). In addition, local education agencies (schools and school districts) were to provide "services comparable to services offered to other students in the school . . . including [where eligible] compensatory educational programs for the disadvantaged, and educational programs for the handicapped and for students with limited English proficiency; programs in vocational education; programs for the gifted and talented; and school meal programs" (Sec. 722, [e][5]). Finally mention was made of the need to make school records available for transfer "in a timely fashion."

In addition to the state plan to be developed and submitted in order to qualify for continued funding, the McKinney Act contained a major provision authorizing the Secretary of Education to "make grants for exemplary programs that successfully address the needs of homeless students." The catch here was that these grants were to come from "funds appropriated pursuant to subsection (f)" and, unfortunately, adequate funds were never appropriated to enable the Secretary of Education to make such grants. (In the 1990 Amendments, Congress totally eliminated the exemplary program grants.)

After the McKinney Act became law, several other lawsuits were filed in New York. Patti Tynan first petitioned the new Commissioner of Education, Thomas Sobol, to require the Spackenkill Union Free School District to admit her two children. They had been refused admission because they failed to meet the residency requirement: They and their mother were housed temporarily in a motel while seeking low-income housing. In *Tynan v. Wooley* (1988), Commissioner Sobol held that even though the Tynans lived temporarily in a motel, that was their official residence for purposes of school district attendance.

Several months later, Diane Harrison brought action against the Peekskill school district for refusing to allow her children to continue attending school there after they were forced to leave their father's residence in Peekskill. The children returned to live with their mother in the Mahopac motel (which was not in the Peekskill district), where she was living after a fire destroyed their apartment in another town. When Westchester Legal Services filed suit for Ms. Harrison, they not only sought declaratory and injunctive relief but also brought charges against both the school district and the commissioner for denial of due process in failing to provide written notice of the reasons for excluding the Harrison children and for failing to inform her of her right to a hearing and to a decision by the commissioner. By the time the judge issued his ruling (*Harrison v. Sobol,* 1988), the petitions for access were rendered moot by state legislation allowing homeless parents to determine whether their children would attend school in the district where they were previously enrolled or in the district where they were temporarily living. The judge did, however, find Commissioner Sobol and the school district guilty of denial of due process, though only nominal compensatory damages of $1.00 were awarded, with no punitive damages in the absence of evidence of willfulness or motivation by education officials in their neglect of informing Ms. Harrison of her rights to due process.

Little more than a month later, in January 1989, the same court issued yet another decision in *Orozco by Arroyo v. Sobol* (1989). Ms. Arroyo, mother of Sixta Orozco, had tried to enroll her daughter in the Mt. Vernon (NY) public schools, although as public aid recipients, they were temporarily housed in an emergency shelter at the Trade Winds Motel in Yonkers. Mt. Vernon had been their home for 4 years when Sixta was of preschool age. Both the Mt. Vernon and the Yonkers school districts refused admission based on residency requirements, holding that Ms. Arroyo and her daughter were not legally residents of either district. A preliminary injunction from the federal district court required the Yonkers schools to admit Sixta because her current residence, however temporary, was in that district. Westchester Legal Services again brought charges of denial of due process against the school district and the Commissioner of Education for failing to provide Ms. Arroyo with an opportunity for a hearing about the decision. More detailed discussion of this case is not necessary at this point because the lengthy proceedings focused almost entirely on procedural due process issues having little bearing on any discussion of substantive (e.g., residency requirements) due process issues as barriers to education for homeless children and youth.

In addition to legal actions brought by individual parents on behalf of their children, a number of advocacy groups and individuals began bringing legal action against the government for failure to implement the McKinney Act. The National Coalition for the Homeless filed actions against Education Secretary Bennett, HUD Secretary Pierce, the Veterans Administration, and others, trying to force compliance with the McKinney mandates (National Coalition for the Homeless, 1989). In each instance, the defendants either settled at the last minute or were ordered by the courts to comply by making funds or properties available that had previously not been made accessible.

### Surmounting the Barriers
### After the McKinney Amendments (1990)

The 1990 McKinney Amendments expanded some components of the original McKinney Act and eliminated others. Specifically Section 723, "Exemplary Programs and Dissemination of Information Activities," was replaced by Section 723, "Local Educational Agency Grants for the Education of Homeless Children and Youth." The activities to be funded— "from amounts made available to such [State education] agency under section 722"—reflect the expansion of policy from concern about residency barriers, to access, to concern about attendance and success once homeless children are enrolled. Section 612 (Title VI, Subtitle A) adds that the policy of Congress is that any state having a residency requirement as a component of its compulsory attendance laws "or other laws, regulations, practices, or policies that may act as a barrier to the enrollment, attendance, or success in school of homeless children and homeless youth" must review and undertake steps to revise such legal and administrative barriers. With these additions, Congress made it clear that everyone at state or local levels was expected to provide every possible support for homeless children and youth attempting to pursue their education.

While the original 1987 McKinney Act specified only residency requirements as obstacles to be removed by the states, the 1990 Amendments listed four additional barriers to access and enrollment. Now each state is required to "address problems with respect to the education of homeless children and homeless youth, including problems caused by

(i) transportation issues; and
(ii) enrollment delays which are caused by—
    (I) immunization requirements;
    (II) residency requirements;
    (III) lack of birth certificates, school records, or other documentation; or
    (IV) guardianship issues

Of these barriers, four involve issues of documentation or family status that can be remedied by more flexible responses on the part of schools; little or no money is required to comply with the attempt to "address" these issues. The one area that could require additional funds is transportation. On this issue, the 1990 Amendments require any local education agency receiving a state grant not only to address transportation issues but to provide services "including transportation services" along with other educational services, such as compensatory, gifted and talented, and special education. The amendments also allow "provision of assistance to defray the excess cost of transportation for students not provided under . . . and not otherwise provided through Federal, State, or local funding, where necessary to enable students to attend the school" (Sec. 723, [b][2]D).

Again paralleling the protections afforded handicapped children, Congress added a third policy statement that "homelessness alone should not be sufficient reason to separate students from the mainstream school environment" (Sec. 721, par. 3). Every reasonable effort should be made to involve (or mainstream) homeless children in their schools' programs and services without undue separation from their classmates.

## Summary

Several studies have been conducted to assess the level of activity (compliance and beyond) by the states in implementing the McKinney Act (Bowen et al., 1990; First & Cooper, 1989). As might be expected, widely varying levels of programs and services are being provided. Except for the original mandate to review and undertake to revise any state laws impeding access to education for homeless children and youth, it is difficult to know how much state activity directly results from the McKinney Act. It seems unlikely that the minimal level of funding deriving from the act has been a major factor, in light of the fact that the appropriations have averaged from $50,000 per state in FY87 to $130,000 per state in FY91. Advocacy groups may claim considerable influence. Litigation or the threat of it, along with general consciousness raising during the last 4 years, may also contribute to whatever progress is slowly being made. Whether the 1990 McKinney Amendments' emphasis on interagency cooperation will help or hinder that progress remains to be seen. Bureaucracies are often slow enough without having to coordinate with other equally slow bureaucracies. Nevertheless homeless families and their advocates can remain hopeful that the McKinney Amendments, with their broadened concerns and mandates—though little more than suggestions until adequately funded—will reduce the bureaucratic barriers and encourage cooperation between social service agencies and educators to provide the services and programs so essential for the success of homeless children and youth.

## References

Bowen, J. M., Purrington, G. S., & O'Brien, K. (1990, February). *State educational plans and policies pertaining to homeless children.* Paper presented at American Association of School Administrators, San Francisco, CA. (ERIC Document Reproduction Service No. ED 307 033)

Center for Law and Education. (1991). Comments on transportation provisions of Massachusetts draft revised state plan. Cambridge, MA: Author.

Delgado v. Freeport Public School District, 499 N.Y.S. 2d 606 (1986).

Ely, L. (1987). *Broken lives: Denial of education to homeless children.* Washington, DC: National Coalition for the Homeless. (ERIC Document Reproduction Service No. ED 292 897)

First, P. F., & Cooper, G. R. (1989, November). *The Stewart B. McKinney Homeless Assistance Act: Evaluating the response of the states.* Paper presented at the National Organization for Legal Problems of Education, San Francisco, CA.

Harrison v. Sobol, 705 F. Supp. 870 (S.D.N.Y. 1988).

Jennings, L. (1989, February 8). Report expected to sharpen policy debate of homeless. *Education Week,* pp. 1, 19.

Mason v. Board of Education, Freeport Union School District, No. 2865/87, N.Y.Sup.Ct. Mem. Op. (1987, April 22).

Matter of Callahan, 10 Ed Dept Rep 66 (1970); Matter of Lundburg, 12 Ed Dept Rep 268 (1973); Matter of Wadas, 21 Ed Dept Rep 577 (1982).

National Coalition for the Homeless. (1989). *Federal lawsuits involving the National Coalition for the Homeless.* Washington, DC: Author.

Orozco by Arroyo v. Sobol, 703 F.Supp. 1113 (S.D.N.Y. 1989).

Richards v. Board of Education of Union Free School District Number 4, No. 11490, N.Y. Dept. of Education (1985).

Stewart B. McKinney Homeless Assistance Act, Pub. L. 100-77, codified at 42 U.S.C. 11301-11472.

Stewart B. McKinney Homeless Assistance Amendments Act of 1988, Pub. L. 100-628, 102 Stat. 3224-3285.

Stewart B. McKinney Homeless Assistance Amendments Act of 1990, Pub. L. 100-645, 1990 U.S. Code Cong. & Ad. News (104 Stat.) 4673.

Stronge, J. H., & Helm, V. M. (1991). Residency and guardianship requirements as barriers to the education of homeless children and youth. *Journal of Law and Education, 20,* 201-218.

Stronge, J. H., & Tenhouse, C. D. (1990). *Educating homeless children: Issues and answers.* Bloomington, IN: Phi Delta Kappa Educational Foundation.

Tynan v. Wooley, No. 12010, N.Y. Dept. of Education (1988).

Vingara et al. v. Borough of Wrightstown, Civil Action No. 87-7545 (S.Ct. N.J. filed September 29, 1987).

*3*

# The Psychosocial Context

## Supporting Education
## for Homeless Children and Youth

CYNTHIA CROSSON TOWER

Wherever 6-year-old Nan went, she carried with her a small, tattered, and very dirty pillow. In time of real stress, she clutched it feverishly to her and popped her thumb into her mouth. Her first-grade teacher, feeling that the pillow was indeed an encumbrance, tried to coax it away from her.

"No! No!" screamed Nan with more determination than the gentle request necessitated. "My Gramma gave it to me!"

The teacher knew a bit of the child's history—raised on a farm with her now dead grandparents. After the death of her grandfather, Nan and her mother bounced from shelter to welfare hotel.

Calming her, the teacher said, "It's a beautiful pillow. May I see it?"

Tentatively the child held out the beloved possession, and there, amidst the dirt, was evidence that someone had lovingly stitched the words: "Home Sweet Home."

### Introduction

For a child, there is more to being homeless than not having a specific place to call home. The further implications of being homeless can affect every aspect of a child's life. Homelessness permeates the thinking and influences the behavior of each and every member of the family, including the child.

Eddowes and Hranitz (1989) suggested the use of Maslow's (1970) hierarchy of needs to analyze the impact of homelessness on children. Homeless families experience a cycle of homelessness (see Figure 3.1), and in looking at this cycle one can see how the needs Maslow outlined in his hierarchy are not being met. Maslow stated that the most basic concern for the individual is his or her bodily needs, such as food, water, and shelter. While children who are well cared for may give little thought to these necessities, the homeless child is often painfully aware of the fact that these vital needs, if being met at all, are in jeopardy. The availability of food and shelter may not be totally lacking, but concern over the future is certainly uppermost in their minds. The stresses the parent(s) feels in this area are frequently transmitted to the children.

Even when children are assured of food and at least temporary housing by residence in a homeless shelter or welfare hotel, they are usually aware of the lack of permanence in their situation, and the resulting predicament results in feelings of insecurity. In addition, children are at risk in a number of ways.

In shelters, they are subject to the stresses, problems, and behaviors of the other residents. Families describe fights, both verbal and physical, between shelter residents, which the children observe. Children who reside in shelters, welfare hotels, on the streets, or even with friends or relatives may be subjected to a variety of abuses. Sometimes these abuses may be at the hands of the overwrought parents, but often the abuses result from the inadequate living conditions of their stressed parents' inability to protect them. Homeless children who miraculously escape concerns over their physical needs being met or who are somehow protected from harm often suffer from what Maslow referred to as the need for belonging and the need for affection. Parents, who may have had the ability to nurture their children adequately, are placed under incredible stress as a result of their homelessness. Bassuk and Gallagher (1990) reported homeless mothers as having limited relationships and feeling overwhelmed by the tasks of providing for their families when they are preoccupied with issues of survival. These anxious, depressed parents have little energy left to give affection to their children. In fact, they often vent their frustrations on their offspring; such ventings may result in the children feeling rejected and isolated from the only potential source of affection available in their itinerant life-style.

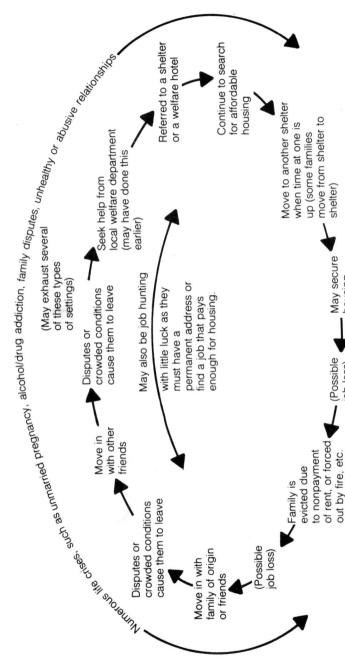

**Figure 3.1.** Typical Cycle of Homelessness

SOURCE: *Homeless Students*, copyright 1989, National Education Association. Reprinted with permission.

44

While shelter life might provide some element of community, welfare hotels rarely do. Families in welfare hotels are often isolated from one another "behind closed doors" and are subject to devaluation and further isolation by hotel managers (Bassuk & Gallagher, 1990).

Certainly children who do not fare well on Maslow's first three levels are unlikely to achieve adequate self-esteem and self-actualization. Their inability to have even their most basic needs satisfied translates into a variety of problems, most of which have significant impacts on the children's performance in school.

## Psychosocial Effects of Homelessness on School-Age Children

Perhaps the most pervasive result of homelessness on school-age children is the confusion under which they are forced to labor. Developmental experts attest to the fact that consistency is vital for a child's healthy development. Instead of consistency, homeless children's lives are characterized by constant change. The result is a profound sense of confusion, which may impair the children's ability to trust in the future or even to commit themselves to relationships. The confusion and lack of stability are also manifest in issues related to control. Homeless children may feel so out of control that they become depressed and unable to organize their responses to the simplest stimuli. The converse may also be true.

Those dealing with homeless children may not give them credit for the survival patterns they have developed. Instead seemingly antisocial behavior may be interpreted as dysfunctional. It is important for helpers to recognize what necessitates the way in which children relate to others. Often this ability to find creative adaptations to their unstable lives is a strength rather than a weakness.

Larry, an adolescent living literally on the streets, serves as a good example of a homeless youth who has developed a complex set of survival techniques:

Larry attended high school regularly. His clothes, however, began to puzzle his homeroom teacher. Although they appeared clean, they were often too small or too large and were always a different outfit. The teacher eventually heard from another student that Larry lived on the street. The clothes he wore were stolen from laundromats where he would abandon his old clothes. He ate either at shelters or soup kitchens or by stealing bits of food from markets. Unlike many of his counterparts, however, Larry stayed free of drugs, allowing himself an occasional smoke of marijuana or a beer when these could be obtained. He loved school and was determined to finish despite the life-style that he worked to keep secret. (Tower & White, 1989, p. 22)

Homeless children develop their own individual manner or affect in response to their situation. Some adopt an aggressive or even hostile style when dealing with their environment. While for some this hostility is a method of voicing their anger, for others an added element of control is involved.

A teacher who found 8-year-old Roy vandalizing the school corridor with a can of spray paint and a knife enlisted the help of the school counselor to talk with him. "I hate it here," Roy blurted out, "If I trash it, I can move."

The story eventually emerged that Roy's family had lived in numerous housing projects. Roy's older brother, an extremely disturbed adolescent, had done much damage to their various residences. Because the rent was paid by welfare, the family was never charged for damages but was evicted on numerous occasions. Roy's mother, overwhelmed by her oldest son's behavior, felt powerless to stop it. Now the family moved from apartment to apartment. Currently they resided in a shelter, having exhausted the good graces of local landlords. Thus Roy had learned the usefulness of vandalizing and found such acts an outlet for his own anger. (Tower & White, 1989, p. 20)

Some homeless children, however, may react to their dilemma by becoming withdrawn and listless or depressed. Bassuk and Rubin (1987) found that depression was especially prominent among the 156 homeless children they studied.

Withdrawn, depressed children can be difficult for teachers or other helpers to reach. Subject to the stresses of instability and intent primarily on survival, homeless children often lack the ability to organize their own thinking and to concentrate. Concentration necessitates not only the ability to formulate a systematic approach to conceptualizing but also the opportunity—the time and space—to think. Shelter life, punctuated by chaos, full of stimuli, and lacking in privacy, provides little or no opportunity for children to concentrate. Robbed of this opportunity, children often lose the ability to concentrate. This loss creates problems for them in school. Survival seems to them more important than the mundane mental tasks that promote scholastic learning.

These general problems experienced by homeless children often distort their attitudes about themselves and influence their interaction with others. It is important for teachers and other helpers to consider the effects of homelessness not only on the child's perception of him- or herself but also on the way he or she relates to others.

### Problems Related to the Child's Perception of Self

*Shame.* The homeless child's feelings about being unable to control life have further implications and manifestations. Children often demonstrate a great deal of shame over the plight in which their family has found itself. Television—a significant influence on children of recent decades—tells them that people live in families and that families have homes. Yet this is not their experience—at least at the moment. Children sometimes perceive that they have somehow caused this predicament.

> Eight-year-old Howie was convinced that he was the cause of his mother and siblings being homeless. At their old apartment, he was constantly running up the halls. His mother told him that he had "better stop it or they'd get kicked out." When the family was evicted for nonpayment of rent, Howie was sure he was the cause. The family then went to live with the mother's boyfriend and his sister. Howie disliked the boyfriend and made no secret of the fact. When the sister decided that the extra people in the apartment were "just too much," Howie assumed that he had once again engineered their move by his feelings. He felt ashamed and responsible. His mother, caught up in her own problems, failed to notice that her son had become extremely withdrawn, depressed, and secretive.

Children in school would often prefer that no one knew that they lived in a shelter or welfare hotel. One child went to great lengths to have the bus driver drop him off two blocks away rather than in front of the hotel in which his family was now living. Children who feel this shame become secretive, distort facts, and may become isolated from their families and/or their friends. For example, while Sabrina spent as much time as possible at her friends' homes, denying to herself that her own family was housed in a shelter, her brother John returned to the shelter immediately after school. He had no friends and refused any overtures made by his peers.

*Parentified children.* Some homeless children, in addition to feeling shame over their circumstances, direct their feelings of distress toward their parents. Older children especially may perceive that their parents are not doing all they can to remedy the situation of being without a permanent place to live.

> "Every time we got a place to live," recounted 16-year-old Margot, "my Mom messed it up. If we got an apartment, she wouldn't pay the rent; if we were staying with someone, she'd have a big fight. She complained a lot, and finally I couldn't take it. We fought all the time, and I wanted to leave, but I was afraid for my little brother."

Margot, in her shame over what she perceived as her parents' irresponsibility, chose to become the caretaker—the parentified child—in her family. Many homeless children cope with their situation by becoming caretakers for their younger siblings or even for their parents.

This identification and then seeming replacement of the nurturing figure may be functional for the family's stability initially. Children who think for their overburdened parents are often quite creative in their methods of coping. But according to Bassuk and Gallagher (1990), this identification can also be pathological. These authors cited, for example, a girl whose mother was a cocaine user, while the daughter worked and functioned as caretaker, supporting her mother's habit by the money she made. Boxhill and Beatty (1990) suggest that shelter living "unravels responsibility" on the part of adults who then begin—due to their inability to cope—to adopt childlike behavior. This coping mechanism places their children in positions in which they may overcompensate and therefore become more responsible than their developmental ages would indicate. This overly responsible behavior is also generated by the children's need to have some control in an environment that seems to them so unpredictable and out of control.

*Self-esteem.* Paradoxically, while some homeless children become overly competent in the area of caretaking, they feel less competent in other areas. These children's self-esteem is extremely low. They perceive that they have no skills, and this assumption translates into their lack of ability to achieve, especially in the scholastic arena. As one teacher put it:

> Charlene, age 14, is a very bright, talented girl. I know that her brains have kept her family intact. She mothers her sisters, and it is Charlene who negotiates with shelter staff and landlords. But she sure does not think she

has it in school. She just stares at her books as if they were Greek. I think I have explained something to her and she seems to understand, but then she will totally fail her tests. I really think that it is because she does not believe she can do the work.

Children learn positive self-esteem in a combination of ways. When adults and peers react positively to children's accomplishments, these children perceive themselves as capable. For the parentified children, their most significant accomplishment often is that they have cared for their family. Yet because this is not a role in which we would like to see children, we often do not give them sufficient credit. Peers are also often unkind to the homeless child. Sometimes other children cannot get beyond the homeless child's unkempt appearance or seemingly strange behavior.

Children also learn positive self-esteem by modeling their parents. But homeless parents often see themselves as failures. These parents have little to give their children in the way of models for healthy self-esteem.

*Reliance on fantasy and phobia.*  When children do not see the world as a nurturing place, or when they perceive that they cannot measure up, some escape in fantasy. Fantasy lives can be extremely important. Some children dream of the homes they will have someday, often conjuring up an idealized picture.

While these fantasies may be relatively benign, the fantasies of other homeless children are more problematic. Fantasies are not only the children's attempt to cope with their dysfunctional life-styles but also may be metaphoric indicators of a variety of problems. For example, Frank's fantasies were punctuated with images of coffins, skeletons, and executions. A perceptive art therapist uncovered not only Frank's real fear of his family's homeless state but also his conviction that losses that were too overwhelming provoked death. Frank's mother, suffering from an undetected brain tumor, had died soon after the family had been burned out of their apartment. The much-loved family dog had been killed in the fire. Frank's father, unable to deal with the multiple losses, as well as being homeless, had attempted suicide. Now Frank and his siblings lived in separate foster homes while his father worked through his issues and sought adequate housing in order to reunite his family.

Sometimes rather than dealing with their situations through fantasy, children internalize their fears, manifesting them through psychosomatic illnesses or phobias.

Roger, age 10, lives in a welfare hotel with his alcoholic mother. His father, separated from the family for several months, visits them weekly. After each visit, Roger's mother goes to a local bar and becomes quite .runk. Roger finds her and takes her home. He then calls his father and bec nes hysterical that they will once again be asked to leave their living ar. gements because of his mother's alcoholism. Father rushes to his son's . ., but once his wife is sober, leaves with his usual admonitions. Predictab y Roger will awake the next day with a migraine headache. For the duration of his pain, his mother will cater to him and promise that she will never again drink. The next week, the cycle repeats itself with no apparent awareness on the part of the participants that there is any type of pattern.

Homeless children also develop phobias, or irrational fears. Although all children have fears, phobias are more acute. *Fears* are normal reactions to perceived or actual threats. *Phobias,* however, have four components: They are (a) out of proportion to the demands of the situation, (b) cannot be explained or reasoned away, (c) are beyond voluntary control, and (d) lead to avoidance of the feared situation (Marks, 1969, p. 3).

Particularly problematic for school-age children is school phobia— the fear of going to school. School phobia is manifested by a child's refusal or extreme reluctance to go to school. This refusal may be punctuated by such somatic symptoms as nausea, dizziness, and headaches. Homeless children may indeed be afraid to go to school because of their shame over their situation or because something unpleasant has occurred at school.

Gewirtzman and Fodor (1987) suggest that children may be particularly reluctant or even afraid to attend school because they have been teased about their below-standard clothing or because their families cannot afford the necessary school supplies. A child may fear going to school for yet another reason: When parents move frequently, as homeless parents often do, children may fear abandonment. Will my mother/father be there when I come home from school? is the question that runs through their minds, either consciously or subconsciously. Generally the older the child, the more problematic the phobia.

Wayne, age 12, developed nausea and cramps every morning when the school bus was due to arrive. After several mornings of allowing him to remain at the shelter, the staff insisted that he go off to school. An hour later, a caller from the school requested that someone pick up Wayne. He was again nauseous. When we got to the shelter, he hugged his mother as though he had not seen her for weeks. An exploration of family history disclosed that Wayne and his mother had been homeless before. They had bounced from shelter to shelter. Wayne's fear—though somewhat irrational, based on history—was that when he returned to the shelter, his mother would no longer be there.

## Problems Related to the Child's Relationships With Others

*General issues.* Homelessness for children affects not only their perception of self but also their relationships. Homeless children are usually emotionally needy. This neediness may or may not be obvious in the classroom but should be assumed. Emotionally needy children express their needs in different ways. As previously mentioned, some are withdrawn and some are hostile. What becomes problematic for teachers, however, are two specific issues. First, extreme neediness can be very draining. In a classroom of 30 children, 1 or 2 particularly needy children represent more of a time commitment than some overworked teachers are able to make. In addition, children with numerous unmet needs place emotional stressors on teachers. One teacher described her feelings:

> Our school is in the district where the city's homeless shelter is located. Although some kids are bused back to their original schools, many come here. One year, I had four shelter kids in my class of 30. That was an experience! I really tried to give time to these kids, but they needed so much emotionally. One little girl would be at my elbow constantly. All four needed constant praise. One little boy would sabotage any success he made. He'd rip up his pictures and scribble on his papers. I kept trying to remember how tough life had been for them, but at night I'd go home really drained.

Second, homeless children often have an impaired ability to trust. Even if their early years were relatively stable, their new life-styles may have left them feeling betrayed and suspicious of any adults. Adults are supposed to nurture and protect children, and yet this has not necessarily been their experience. For children, adults represent faith in an ordered, consistent world. The destruction of this faith leaves them not only unable to trust others but also unable to trust their own perceptions of reality. Thus homeless children may be difficult to reach. Rebuilding trust takes time and consistency. Time is not always a resource available in abundance. By the time a teacher has developed a rapport with a homeless child, which has the potential of becoming a trusting relationship, the child moves on. The understandable inclination for frustrated teachers in this position is to give up trying to establish trust with these children. It is easy to assume that the effort has no point when all will be lost when the child moves again. The more consistent, responsible, caring individuals that children have around them, however, the better is the chance for them to learn to trust to some degree.

*Perception of and relationship with peers.* Homeless children also have difficulty with their peers. Some children have poor hygiene—a result of crowded shelter life or their overwhelmed parents' inability to care for them (Bassuk & Gallagher, 1990; Gewirtzman & Fodor, 1987; Russell & Williams, 1988). Often their peers complain about these unkempt children and may ostracize them as a result. Other children tease their homeless classmates about inadequate or out-of-style clothing or even about living in a shelter. Some homeless children would prefer to avoid school altogether rather than chance feeling different or being teased. Children who live in shelters often go to great lengths to hide this fact from peers.

This attempt to keep the secret of their residence isolates them and robs them of normal peer relationships. While some children withdraw into their own shells, others strike out against peers, causing arguments and fights and further perpetuating their classmates' rejection.

*Perception of and relationship to authority figures.* For homeless children, the adults in their lives have been a disappointment. Children from healthy families are nurtured and cared for. For children, the media abound with messages that adults will take care of them, yet homeless parents are not able to care for their children as they should. Some homeless children become disillusioned by the fact that their parents are as much victims as they are. These children, feeling betrayed, assume that all adults will disappoint them. Thus teachers may find that homeless children will constantly test limits with the message, "How much can I trust you? How far can I go before you too will cease to be there for me?" Older children may have given up on adults altogether. These are the rebellious, acting-out children who are saying by their actions that they cannot trust adults.

Homeless children often perceive authority figures as being punitive. For these children, authority is synonymous with the landlord who evicted them, the police officer who told the family to move on, or the busy, overburdened shelter personnel who were there to enforce the rules. Teachers are thrown into this category by the child who is too scared or travel-worn to see the individual.

An occasional homeless child—especially a young one—sees authority figures as omnipotent "gods" who can help them. One homeless mother told her daughter, "If we can only get you into school, things will be okay." While the mother, who had had to interrupt her own education very early, saw finishing school as a way to ensure her daughter's future, the child believed that somehow the school would wave a magic wand and find them a home. The misunderstanding made for a great deal of pain for the child when enrollment in school did not materialize the home she expected. Thus teachers and other school personnel will need to assess intuitively the child's perception of authority figures in order to really reach the child.

### Psychosocial Problems Related to the School Setting

*Problems related to interpersonal issues.* The shame and low self-esteem felt by a homeless child transfers itself to the classroom. The need to isolate him- or herself from peers or from authority figures who are seen by the child as untrustworthy leads to further feelings of rejection and depression. The resulting conflicts are manifested in a variety of ways.

One way to structure a supportive environment for homeless children is to educate their peers about the issues of homelessness. Coles (1970) recounted how one teacher turned the experiences of a migrant child into a learning experience for all. As the child explained:

> There was one teacher who said that as long as we were there in the class, she was going to ask everyone to join us; that's what she said, and we could teach other kids what we know and they could do the same with us. She showed the class where we traveled on the map and I told my daddy that I never knew before how far we went each year. . . . But when you look on the map and hear other kids say they'd never been that far and they wished someday they could, then you think you've done something good too, and they'll tell you in recess that they've only seen where they live and we've been all over. (p. 52)

Older students too can be helped to recognize the social and economic causes of homelessness to remove some of the stigma associated with being homeless. In particular, students should be acquainted with facts about the decrease in available housing perpetrated by the industrialization of areas formerly occupied by housing and by the number of apartment houses converted to condominiums. This may help them understand the plight of those forced out of the housing market. Even efforts to help students understand homelessness and participate in helping the victims may not always protect homeless children from being hurt. For example:

> One school sent home a note with the students asking for donated clothing for the "homeless shelter." Nine-year-old Sally said nothing when she came home to the shelter that day, but her letter was later found crumpled behind the couch. Fortunately communication between the shelter and the school transformed this unfortunate incident into a positive experience. In the end, shelter children worked side by side with their peers sorting out clothing that had been donated.
>
> "Isn't this a neat skirt?" the shelter director overheard as a friend helped Sally sort clothes. "It was mine, but now it's too small for me; you'd look great in it!" Giggles of admiration followed as Sally tried on the skirt. (Tower & White, 1989, p. 30)

Not all incidents are handled as well as this one. Teachers must be constantly vigilant to what can help their students understand homelessness and also the impact this knowledge can have on the homeless child.

*Problems with scholastic achievement.* Scholastic achievement presents special problems for homeless children. Bassuk & Rubin (1987) found that in their sample of 156 shelter children, (according to their parents) 43% had already repeated one grade, 25% were in special classes, and 50% were currently failing or doing below average work (p. 28). Kozol (1988), in his study of homeless children housed in welfare hotels, described children who were two or three grade levels behind their peers scholastically. They had sporadic school attendance, suffered from withdrawal or hyperactivity, or fell asleep in school because they had difficulty sleeping in their temporary homes. A report from the National Coalition for the Homeless (1987) stated that 43% of all homeless children do not even attend school.

Children who do attend school find that the developmental delays, inability to concentrate, and fears and anxieties that are part of their lives make school a difficult experience. The experience of homelessness also adds its own punctuation to the child's ability to do school work. Teachers find that these children frequently do not finish their work. Homeless children's experiences have taught them to live for today. Thus, while the immediate task may be important, if something else comes up they turn to the new stimulus. Furthermore many of these children lack the organizational skills to complete school assignments.

Coles (1970) described these characteristics in migrant children, a group frequently compared with the homeless:

Migrant boys and girls are quite willing to interrupt their particular tasks . . . for any number of reasons. It is not that they are agitated or anxious or unable to concentrate and finish what they start. . . one has to see the habits of their parents. If parents take in their stride (because they have learned they must) the necessity for constantly moving from one field to another, from one responsibility to another, each of which can be partially filled by any given person and indeed requires a whole field of people, then it is only natural that the children of migrants will experience no great need to stay with things to work at them endlessly and stubbornly or indeed consistently. Always the child has learned there is the next place, the next journey, the next occasion. (pp. 94-95)

Children who move from school to school find that they often miss basic information. For example, while one school is teaching multiplication tables in the spring term of third grade, another school has already taught them in the fall. With increased emphasis on competency-based exams at the completion of high school, children who have not mastered these basic skills are destined to suffer.

Teachers find that when it is probable that they will not have access to previous records, it is vital to make their own initial assessment of what children have learned. Remedial work may be necessary to bring the homeless child up to the level of his or her classmates. Remediation does not always necessitate an abundance of time on the part of the teacher. One teacher explained her technique:

Every few years our school gets rid of old textbooks. I usually keep a few copies—especially workbooks. When a child comes into the class who needs remedial work, I give him or her one of these old books. We go over a few assignments until the child feels he or she understands. I let the children keep the old books, and for kids who don't have much, this really makes them feel good.

Granted, some schools do have teacher aides or programs for remedial help, but with the increasing scarcity of funds, these services are becoming less and less available. As this happens, creativity on the part of the teacher is crucial.

One of the biggest concerns for teachers is that the homework given to homeless children is often not completed. This may be attributed to the child's lack of comprehension, but more often it is a result of the homeless life-style. Shelter life provides little or none of the quiet time or the privacy necessary for concentration. Often the only space a child can find to do homework is in the common room where the noise level can be overwhelming and the distractions myriad.

Teachers and schools have worked out solutions in a variety of ways. Children who have no space in which to do homework can benefit from in-school or after-school study halls. One teacher recounts what her school provides:

> About a year ago, we started offering an after-school "Homework Session." For an hour or two, we teachers volunteered to sit with kids who wanted to get their homework done. We had planned the session because we had a number of shelter children who we felt needed it. We soon found that other kids were asking to stay too. They knew they'd have quiet—and if needed— help to finish their homework.

City or town libraries also provide a place where children can go after school to have quiet and to complete their work. If shelters have the space, many directors are amenable to designating space where children can work. Some even include a "homework" or quiet time in the evening schedule. Schools are wise to work with shelters to suggest solutions to homework problems. As one shelter director put it:

> I was glad when the school contacted me about the need for homework time. Trying to run a busy shelter with all the scheduling, meal planning, purchasing and so on isn't easy. I was tuned into the infants' needs, but it hadn't even occurred to me that the school-age children had scholastic needs beyond just getting them to school.

*Additional psychosocial implications for school-age children.* Learning requires not only a sequence in acquiring skills and the time and place to practice those skills, it also requires energy. Energy is sapped by depression, anxiety, and conflict. Thus homeless children often have difficulty learning while they are trying to make sense of their disordered lives. Counseling to help them sort out their feelings might be helpful, but such a luxury is not always possible. Instead teachers must be open to reaching out to their homeless students. Referrals to guidance counselors, school adjustment counselors, and special education programs are vital. Children who are allowed or even encouraged to voice their concerns and who do not have to expend energy on keeping their feelings secret have more energy to expend on learning.

Other factors that sap the energy of homeless children are hunger, malnutrition, and lack of sleep. Schools often provide free breakfast or lunch programs for children in need of them. Some teachers report keeping available such quick energy snacks as raisins or granola bars and giving them to children who are in need of a pickup.

It is also not uncommon for children of the homeless to have been subjected to physical abuse, neglect, or even sexual abuse. When it becomes obvious that a child is being victimized, the picture becomes more complex. In every state, teachers (and other school personnel) are mandated reporters of child abuse and neglect; that is, within their professional capacity, they are required to report their suspicions to the designated agency (usually the Department of Social Services, Department of Family and Children's Services, or Protective Services Division). The fear is that if one reports itinerant parents, they will just move again. This may be true, but it is also quite possible that they will receive help. Any advocating and intervention that the teacher can provide for the child will be of help (see Tower, 1987, for more information).

The goal with homeless students should be to remove as many barriers as possible to their learning. This necessitates not only creativity but teamwork on the part of the entire school.

### Remedies for the Classroom: Meeting the Homeless Child's Psychosocial Needs

*Prior planning—Anticipation of student needs.* Every teacher should anticipate the possibility of a homeless child appearing in his her classroom. Being prepared for that eventuality is important. The number of books, lectures, training seminars, and courses on the subject are increasing. Schools in areas where homelessness is prevalent are conducting in-service training for their teachers. The more prepared the teacher is, the more comfortable he or she will be in dealing with homeless children and their families. In learning about homeless children, the teacher will want to be especially aware of the psychosocial issues discussed in this chapter and how he or she can anticipate dealing with those in the classroom. Because homelessness sometimes goes hand in hand with child abuse and neglect, the prepared teacher will want to become knowledgeable in this area too.

One of the most important aspects of the anticipation of the enrollment of homeless children is knowing how the school will respond once a child arrives. The following are some issues to consider:

- Does this school have an easy and uncomplicated enrollment process?
- How will we respond if the following are not immediately available?
    previous school records
    aptitude tests
    immunization records
    proof of residence
- Does this school have facilities to provide
    remedial help?
    transportation?
    free meals?
    school supplies?
    time/space for homework sessions?
    counseling for students?
    time for teachers to give extra help (e.g., teacher's aide to free up teachers' time)?
- Are any extra supplies and books available immediately?
- Do our school policies having to do with acting out behavior take into consideration the causes rather than just the behavior?

The last point necessitates some explanation. So often schools respond to disruptive behavior by punishing, suspending, or expelling a student before the cause of the behavior is known. Certainly school rules must be upheld, but if a careful consideration of what caused the behavior is taken into account, it may help in deciding on a form of punishment that allows for the continuation of school attendance.

Once the questions above have been answered, teachers might want to consider unique ways to make new children feel comfortable. A box of extra clothing kept at school might provide little extras for children who come without mittens, hats, or other needed articles of clothing. Careful consideration and anticipation of the needs of a new and homeless child might suggest other preparations.

*Assessment of student needs.* The needs of a new child often require that teachers with minimal data available from previous records make quick informal judgments on what skills the child possesses. Some teachers devise their own assessment tools based on where they are in the curriculum and what the child will need to know to keep up with the class. This assessment can be accomplished best in an informal and nonthreatening way. Children often have test anxieties (compounded for homeless children by the pervasiveness of anxiety experienced in their daily lives), and being faced with a lengthy placement test could increase their anxiety. One teacher suggested:

> I make my assessment in the form of an interview. I have notes about what I need to know, but the child and I just chat. I might present him or her with a problem or two that demonstrate knowledge, but I don't sit them down to a test. I also watch their reactions as we talk. Their affect often tells me a lot about what they feel comfortable with and how they'll feel about being in my class. Some kids need a lot of TLC and support—others need just a little coaching and an opportunity to succeed.

Most schools have formal procedures (e.g., psychological and scholastic testing), but these pose several disadvantages for homeless children. First, a time lag may exist between the referral and the actual testing. For homeless children, time is a luxury. Before the tests are scheduled, the family could move on, taking the child with them. Second, a great many formalized procedures might create additional trauma for an already confused child. It is always useful to have a complete and thorough evaluation (e.g., special education assessment), but until this can be arranged, teacher assessments are vital.

Sometimes a child will become homeless while already enrolled in a classroom. At this point, the need for assessment is not as much scholastic as it is emotional. How is the child reacting to this trauma? What can be done to support him or her? What must be done to ensure that this child can remain in this classroom and thus experience continuity? These are just a few questions to be considered.

*Individualized strategies.* Each homeless child's needs will be different. Individualized plans can be as formal as special education contracts or as informal as teachers' responses to their own observations. A child may demonstrate some skill or talent (e.g., drawing) that the teacher observes and can help develop. Providing opportunities for children to be successful in something they are good at will greatly enhance their self-esteem.

Teachers must also be aware of other needs peculiar to homeless children. For example, Rothman (1991), in his discussion of runaway and homeless youth, mentions the need for physical fitness activities. Children who go from school to the confinement of a shelter or welfare hotel may have little opportunity for physical activities. It may be up to the school to provide this.

*Classroom integration strategies.* Strategies to integrate homeless children into the classroom have already been discussed to some extent. The need for the education of fellow classmates cannot be overemphasized, however. As human beings, we tend to reject and stigmatize what we do not understand. If other children understand the issues faced by homeless children, they might be better able to help them integrate.

Some teachers prefer to teach lessons of empathy metaphorically. For example, one elementary teacher reported using the story of baby rabbits who had lost their nest to consider the issues of homelessness:

> I made up this story of the rabbit family whose burrow was plowed up by a farmer. We talked about how the rabbits felt and what they could do. The children could really empathize. I believe it helped them understand their homeless classmates.

A high school social studies teacher used a devastating hurricane in the Caribbean to discuss the plight of the homeless. He then talked about homelessness in this country. He initiated an exercise that encouraged students to explore how they would feel if they were placed in this situation. A student who was in fact homeless was able to speak openly about his feelings with the complete support and empathy of his classmates.

## Conclusion

The increase in the numbers of homeless families with children has necessitated that educators take a hard look at what they can do. It can be one concerned teacher, guidance counselor, nurse, or other school personnel who makes the difference for the homeless child. Perhaps one day, programs will be established to meet the needs of homeless children in schools. For today, the answers lie in the awareness, sensitivity, and creativity of individual teachers and schools.

# References

Bassuk, E. L., & Gallagher, E. M. (1990). The impact of homelessness on children. *Child and Youth Services, 14*(1), 19-33.

Bassuk, E. L., & Rubin, L. (1987). Homeless children: A neglected population. *American Journal of Orthopsychiatry, 57*(2), 279-286.

Boxhill, N., & Beatty, A. (1990). Mother-child interaction among homeless women and their children in a public night shelter in Atlanta, Georgia. *Child and Youth Services, 14*(1), 49-64.

Coles, R. (1970). *Uprooted children: The early life of migrant farm workers.* Pittsburgh: University of Pittsburgh Press.

Eddowes, E. A., & Hranitz, J. R. (1989). Educating children of the homeless. *Childhood Education, 65*(4), 197-200.

Gewirtzman, R., & Fodor, I. (1987). The homeless child at school: From welfare hotel to classroom. *Child Welfare, 66,* 237-245.

Kozol, J. (1988). *Rachel and her children: Homeless families in America.* New York: Crown.

Marks, I. M. (1969). *Fears and phobias.* New York: Academic Press.

Maslow, A. (1970). *Motivation and personality* (2nd ed.). New York: Harper & Row.

National Coalition for the Homeless. (1987). *Broken lives: Denial of education to homeless children.* Washington, DC: Author.

Rothman, J. (1991). *Runaway and homeless youth.* New York: Longman.

Russell, S., & Williams, E. (1988). Homeless handicapped children: A special education prospective. *Children's Environment Quarterly, 5*(1), 3-7.

Tower, C. C. (1987). *How schools can combat child abuse and neglect.* Washington, DC: National Education Association.

Tower, C. C., & White, D. J. (1989). *Homeless students.* Washington, DC: National Education Association.

## 4

# The Context of Family

## Implications for Educating Homeless Children

### MEREDITH VAN RY

"Becoming homeless—no longer having a place to rest in privacy, prepare one's food, care for one's children, and store one's goods—is perhaps the most profound privation imaginable in our society" (McGerigle & Lauriat, 1983, p. xix). It is also extremely dangerous to body, mind, and spirit (Bassuk, 1986; Brickner, 1985; Institute of Medicine, 1988; Wright, 1990).

Because most homeless children live in a family unit, the events that result in a family becoming homeless have a strong impact on the children. The condition of being homeless, the reactions of the parents, and the mirroring behavior of the children (Hall & Maza, 1990) in turn influence the children's attendance at school, their behavior in and out of school, and their ability to concentrate and to learn. This chapter seeks to convey an awareness of difficulties homeless families face and some challenges homeless children present for education.

### Homeless Families With Children

By the late 1980s, families with children became recognized as the fastest growing segment of the homeless population (Institute of Medicine, 1988). Reports claimed that homeless families comprised from 33% to 40% of the general homeless population (National Coalition for the Homeless, 1987, 1988b; U.S Conference of Mayors, 1987). In individual cities like Seattle, Philadelphia, Portland, New York, Yonkers, and Roanoke, families made up 50% to 80% of the total number of homeless persons (U.S. Conference of Mayors, 1987; U.S. House of Representatives, 1986). In 1988, the Institute of Medicine estimated the number of homeless children in the United States to be 100,000 per night. The National Coalition for the Homeless reported that homelessness continued to escalate in 1989, and the most dramatic increases (ranging to over 100%) were among families (National Coalition for the Homeless, 1989).

To find out how homeless families were affected, early studies focused on living conditions in New York welfare hotels (Coalition for the Homeless, 1984; Kozol, 1988; Simpson, Kilduff, & Blewett, 1984; Wackstein, 1983, 1984) or in shelters. Bassuk, Rubin, and Lauriat (1986) studied the mental health of women and children in Boston shelters, and Miller and Lin (1988) reported on physical health of children in West Coast shelters. As destructive as homelessness was to the adult, it was found to be even more serious for children (Bassuk, 1986; Gewirtzman & Fodor, 1987; Institute of Medicine, 1988).

To increase the information about longitudinal homelessness for families, Johnson (1988) reported on the demographics of families staying in Salvation Army shelters in St. Louis over a 6-year period. Maza and Hall (1988) undertook a study of homeless families not staying in shelters. Across the country, homeless children were observed to be suffering physically, mentally, and socially (Boxill & Beaty, 1990; Hayes, 1984; League of Women Voters of Seattle, 1985; Miller & Lin, 1988; Wackstein, 1983, 1984; Wright, Weber-Burden, Knight, & Lam, 1987).

Frequently school-age children were not enrolled in or attending school, and those attending were often discriminated against (Gewirtzman & Fodor, 1987; Maza & Hall, 1988; National Coalition for the Homeless, 1988a). The Department of Education estimated that more than 65,000 homeless school-age children do not attend school regularly. The National Coalition for the Homeless claimed these numbers were based on an undercount of the number of homeless children and that the problem was actually much larger.

## *Family Interviews*

To gain a different perspective, an investigation was undertaken on the etiology of homelessness for families and its effects on family members, as described by the families (van Ry, 1990). Most of this chapter is based on those findings. Some of the issues explored were

1. the sequence of events that leads families with young children to become homeless,
2. the measures taken by families to prevent or ward off homelessness,
3. the gender- and age-related effects of homelessness on families,
4. the difficulties reported by family caregivers while homeless, and
5. the intervention services needed to address and ameliorate the stresses and suffering experienced by homeless families.

Interviews were conducted with 68 families that included 190 children and who were staying in shelters in Seattle during December 1987 and February 1988.

*Family demographics.* In the study, 50% of the families were headed by single females, 4% were headed by single males, and 46% were two-parent households. The number of children in the homeless families ranged from one to seven, with three the average. Exactly 12% of the families were split up, with some of the children staying with relatives or friends and others in foster care. Nearly half the children (48%) were school-age, between 6 and 18 years old. The adults in the families reported having an education not unlike that of the general population for that age group. Indeed 69% had high school diplomas, GEDs, vocational training, or some college; 6% were university graduates, with 2% of those having master's degrees; and 24% had completed junior high school or some high school before abandoning their formal education.

*Geographic origin.* In many cities, it is believed that the homeless in the area are primarily migrants from other parts of the country. In this Seattle shelter study, it was found that the majority of families (57%) were long-term residents of the state before becoming homeless. The other 43% lived in another state prior to becoming homeless. When the latter group of families could not solve their problems locally, they decided to seek a solution elsewhere. The problems they were trying to work out or to get away from fell into three primary categories: unemployment, domestic violence, and crime in their neighborhoods. The move precipitated their homelessness when, after arriving, they could not find jobs or affordable housing. Some of the families became homeless in the process of traveling from state to state, following job leads.

*Time in shelter.* Many families doubled up with relatives or friends after losing their housing, which delayed their need for emergency shelter. Other families stayed in motels, camped out, or lived in their cars until that no longer worked for them. In fact, 32% of the families waited from 1 month to more than a year after becoming homeless before they used emergency shelters. For 40% of the families, the shelter where they were interviewed was the first emergency shelter they used. Some families stayed in a shelter for a month and then moved in with relatives or friends until the crowding could no longer be tolerated; they then sought other shelters. Just 3% of the families had been homeless for 2½ to 3 years.

## Factors Contributing to Family Homelessness

### Primary Problems

Families experienced a series of problems or circumstances that resulted in their becoming homeless, but the ordering and importance of similar problems varied by the family. Lack of employment or not having enough money was reported by 47% of the families as the most pivotal problem contributing to their loss of housing. For some, lack of employment was due to such medical conditions as a back injury, stomach ulcer, leg problems, cancer, and pregnancy. For others, lack of money was due to becoming unemployed or some other unanticipated event or expense.

Another 22% of families reported problems of domestic violence, divorce, separation, problems with boyfriends, or problems with relatives or friends, caused or exacerbated by the conditions of doubling up. For most families, doubling up was not seen as a consequence of homelessness but as a way of dealing with a temporary difficulty. For some, relatives were considered morally responsible to take in family members and to help them until they got past the problem. Friends were often considered quasi-family with similar quasi-obligations. In some cases, overcrowding resulted in up to six children having to stay in one bedroom. Substance abuse was reported by 9% of homeless families as the primary problem that led to their homelessness.

When the problems of homeless, single-parent families were compared with those of homeless families in general, the position and importance of each of the above problems changed. No money, domestic violence, and substance abuse all tied for first place as the primary factor contributing to homelessness.

### Domestic or Personal Problems

*Health problems.* Physical health problems prior to becoming homeless were reported by 44% of families as having directly or indirectly affected their housing stability. Although mental illness was not found to be an issue, most homeless families reported such emotional problems as stress or depression prior to becoming homeless. Experiencing one or more extremely stressful life events prior to losing their housing was reported by 82% of the families. In some cases, stress and depression resulted from the death of a family member, baby, or young child. Families reported strain at having to split up their families—sending some of the children away to live with relatives. Other families reported tension at the involvement of Child Protective Services, a state agency with responsibility to protect children, taking them out of the home if necessary. Domestic violence or not getting along with other family members was reported as causing emotional problems for 19% of the families who later became homeless. Depression and stress, complicated by their own or another's alcohol or drug use, was reported by 7%.

*Domestic violence/abuse.* Domestic violence or abuse was reported by 32% of families as a problem in their families; it was identified as a problem for 51% of single-parent families. For 17% of homeless families, domestic violence or abuse lasted less than 6 months; for 9%, from 6 months to 1 year; for another 9%, from 1 to 2 years; for 13%, from 2 to 3 years; for 30%, from 3 to 5 years; and for 17%, from 5 to 12 years.

For 20% of families, substance abuse, predominately by the perpetrator of the domestic violence, was reported as contributing to their becoming homeless. Divorce contributed to or preceded homelessness for 37% of the families.

### Effects of Homelessness on Family Members

*Health-related effects.* New health problems after becoming homeless were reported by 50% of homeless families. Colds, tiredness, and generally not feeling well were frequent and common problems, similar to the Health Care for the Homeless statistics cited by Wright (1990). Families with existing health problems reported that they worsened after becoming homeless.

Homelessness increasingly affected the families' mental or emotional health. Depression in one or all of the family members was reported by 62% of homeless families. Families revealed that since becoming homeless they worried more, were angrier, had problems with stress, and fought more with their children. They reported being overwhelmed by having to cope with so much. They were confused and did not know what to expect from day to day. Families described the emotional effects of being homeless and in a shelter as "mental anguish." An increase in alcohol or drug use since becoming homeless was admitted by 12% and was attributed to the additional stress incurred by being homeless. Some families reported that their first exposure to seeing drug dealing was in the vicinity of the emergency shelter.

*Effects of the move to shelter on children.*  Although 75% of parents tried to explain their family's circumstances to their children, 48% of the children were upset, shocked, or angry at becoming homeless; 16% accepted the move to a shelter either with resignation or a willingness to do what was necessary; and 28% of the homeless children were reportedly glad to leave their previous living situation.

*Effects on school-age children.*  Sixty-nine percent of the families in shelters had school-age children. Of those families, 72% had their children enrolled in school, with the majority also attending school. Because many of the families were living in the area before becoming homeless, children of 66% of the families attended the same school as they did before becoming homeless. Forty-one percent of the families reported that the children's school-related behavior was negatively affected by becoming homeless: School work suffered, grades were lower, some children were required to repeat a grade, and others were in jeopardy of being put back a year. More of the school-related problems were suffered by children who had missed school, had changed schools, or were from out of state. Sixty-four percent of the families claimed the behavior of their school-age children outside of school had also been affected.

The changes seen in the 11- to 16-year-old children were described as moodiness, showing resentment, trying to get away with things, becoming wild, picking up negative attitudes, and being more scatterbrained. Some adolescents were reported as spending increasingly more time with downtown street youth. The behavior of some 5- to 9-year-old children was described as rebellious, more daring, more disruptive, and antisocial. For others in that age group, the opposite behaviors were noticed: They became shy and insecure, without many friends; in addition, they expressed a need to be with their mothers often.

Parents reported that while at the shelter, the school-age children's activities were more restricted because they could not be involved in extracurricular activities. They did not live near their friends, could not visit their friends, and did not have access to a telephone. Older children were required to take on more responsibility for younger siblings. Occasionally changes in behavior were seen as positive. The behavior of some children reportedly changed "from wild to stable" after moving from a situation with even more insecurity and turmoil.

*Effects on preschool-age children.* Seventy percent of families reported changes in the behavior of their small children since becoming homeless. Young children were described as restless, hyperactive, not listening, rebellious, cranky, aggressive, and harder to handle. Some young children were reported to be more withdrawn, insecure, losing sleep and appetite, going back to diapers, and exhibiting a lot of finger-sucking behavior, a regressive behavior like that reported by Bassuk and Gallagher (1990). Other children were troubled because they missed absent family members.

The daily activities of young children also changed after moving into the shelter. They usually had to be taken everywhere the mother went, which precluded naps and a regular routine. Mothers reported that they did not have toys for their children and would not let their babies "crawl on the floor with roaches." Some who left abusive situations were found to be exhibiting the positive response of "not hitting other kids as much."

*Effects on caregiving.* Fifty-six percent of families stated that the difficulties of taking care of the family had increased since becoming homeless. Acquiring food, food storage, and getting adequate food was a problem. Transportation, both to get food or supplies and to keep appointments, was also a problem and made caregiving more difficult. Families claimed that because they were out in the cold a lot, not having enough clothing was a problem; they needed shoes and warm clothes. Caregivers reported that it was difficult to stay clean.

Many homeless families had no income; every time they needed soap, shampoo, toilet paper, diapers, cleaning supplies, or to wash clothes, they first had to find money. Family caregivers reported it took a lot of "running around" to get things done. They reported that they had more responsibility, more to do, and it was more difficult keeping things together; for example, job interviews interfered with picking up children from school. Often they did not know where they would stay from night to night.

Parents found it more difficult to take care of their children in the shelter because of no toys and no TV, but with alcohol and drugs prevalent in the neighborhood, they felt strongly that they could not let their children go outside to play. Family house rules instituted before becoming homeless either had to be changed or dropped.

To the contrary, families who had been living in a car felt relieved that they were in a shelter and reported their caregiving responsibilities had been made easier. While in the shelter, they had a place to stay and usually some food to eat.

### Typology of Homeless Families

When families, both single- and two-parent, were asked how they became homeless and what they did to avoid losing their housing, a kaleidoscopic picture appeared. No typical homeless family was detected, nor did a common sequence of problems, actions, or inactions appear that resulted in a family becoming homeless. No single story predominated. The image of what a homeless family looked like continually changed, influenced by the variety of ways families reported becoming homeless. Not all homeless families were forced out of their housing; over half said they left intentionally. Analyzing their stories, a complex typology of homeless families began to appear. It contained two main categories: those who were evicted or forced out, and those who left with purpose or ambition (see Figure 4.1).

*Maintainers.* The first category of families became homeless as the result of events that seemed to befall them, as they just were trying to hang on to what housing and resources they had. The three typical events that resulted in such families becoming homeless were (a) eviction by landlords or apartment managers, (b) rejection by relatives or friends with whom they had been doubled up, and (c) abandonment by spouse, relatives, or friends with whom they had been living. The families' reactions varied from accepting to resisting. In the typology, these families are referred to as *Maintainers* because they are seen as trying to keep things together, to maintain the status quo.

Forty-three percent of homeless families struggled to retain housing by a variety of means, depending on their situation. Some sought legal

**MAINTAINERS**
**(Left when events they could not control took over)**

**Evicted** (evicted by landlord or relatives)
   [Acquiescers (accepted move with resignation)]
   [Fighters (tried to get help or reprieve)]
**Rejected** (told by relatives or friends to leave)
   [Acquiescers (accepted move with resignation)]
   [Fighters (tried to negotiate, get reprieve)]
**Abandoned** (relatives or friends left, moved away)
   [Acquiescers (accepted move with resignation)]
   [Fighters (tried to get help or reprieve)]

**IMPROVERS**
**(Instigated a move to better their lives)**

**Workers** (moved geographically to find work)
   [Planners (researched and prepared for move)]
   [Reactors (left in a hurry without planning)]
**Defenders** (moved to safeguard children)
   [Planners (researched and prepared for move)]
   [Reactors (left in a hurry without planning)]
**Escapers** (fled from domestic violence)
   [Planners (researched and prepared for move)]
   [Reactors (left in a hurry without planning)]

**Figure 4.1.** Definitional Outline of Typology

help to avoid eviction, but to no avail; they then attempted to find less expensive housing. Others tried to negotiate longer stays with their landlords or relatives. Some families reported trying to find jobs or additional jobs to avoid losing their housing. Other families tried to get welfare for help or borrowed money. All families gave up, sold, or lost belongings in the process of becoming homeless. Fifty percent of families sold things to raise money to stay in housing longer, to pay bills, or to be able to move for a new start.

*Improvers.* The second category of families left their homes intentionally. The three major reasons that such families abandoned housing were (a) to escape from domestic violence, which is well documented (Hagen

& Ivanoff, 1988; Stefl, 1987; Stoner, 1983); (b) to safeguard their children, because some families found situations to be so threatening or dangerous that just getting away, removing their family, was seen as the only viable alternative; and (c) the most common reason families gave for voluntarily leaving their home and familiar surroundings, to find better employment opportunities.

The families were described as *Improvers* because bettering their lives was their stated purpose for choosing to leave their homes. Some families reported that they prepared for the move by doing research on various states and their laws, making job contacts, selling belongings to get money for the move, and locating places to stay on the way or when they got to their destination. Others who fell into the Improver classification seemed to move from their housing as a reaction to aversive situations, seemingly without a great deal of forethought or planning.

## Comparisons

The number of both single- and two-parent families in each major category was found to be approximately the same (see Table 4.1). In the sample from which this typology was derived, Improver families had an average of two children per family. Maintainer families had an average of three children. More children in Maintainer families may be interpreted as negatively influencing their ability or willingness to initiate a move.

With a high school education the common denominator, the groups were judged similar in formal education. Parents in both groups had some college education.

*Residence.* As might be expected, more families from the Improver group than the Maintainer group were from out of state. The families' decision to move to the area was not made randomly. Families from both groups picked a particular area for the same reasons (e.g., they had family nearby, were looking for or had been promised a job, or were former residents). It was reasoned that when moving for a job or to get away from domestic violence, picking an area where one had relatives or had lived previously would make the transition easier and would increase the likelihood of success. The majority were not homeless before they left their previous area but became so when resources proved insufficient either for travel costs or when they got to their destination.

**Table 4.1**  Demographics of Improver and Maintainer Families

| | *N = 68 families (34 Maintainer, 34 Improver)* | |
| | *Maintainer* | *Improver* |
|---|---|---|
| No. of adults | 51 | 50 |
| Ages of females | 20-37 mn28 | 18-49 mn29 |
| Ages of males | 25-47 mn33 | 19-45 mn29 |
| Children | 113 | 77 |
| Average no. children | 3 (1-7) | 2 (1-4) |
| Single-parent families | 19 | 18 |
| Two-parent families | 15 | 16 |
| Average income per month | | |
| Before homeless | $864.00 | $1255.00 |
| After homeless | $501.00 | $215.00 |
| Education | | |
| JH or some HS | 10 | 13 |
| HS Diploma, GED | 23 | 21 |
| Voc. Ed. | 4 | 4 |
| Some college | 8 | 7 |
| College graduate | 2 | 4 |
| Where lived before homeless | | |
| Seattle | 19 | 5 |
| Other WA city or county | 10 | 5 |
| Other state | 5 | 24 |

In the Maintainer group, 85% of the families were state residents when they became homeless, and 15% came from out of state. Maintainer families, after losing housing, spent more time doubled up with relatives or friends and had been homeless for the most protracted length of time. Six percent of Maintainer families had been homeless for 2½ to 3 years.

More Maintainer families used government programs, food banks, and utility assistance than Improver families prior to homelessness. Improver families had higher average earned income before becoming homeless and consequently had greater expectations at the time they left their housing. They intended and expected to find jobs to obtain needed income. Because they did not have the backup of government grants in place to assist them, they reported the most drastic change in income.

*Problems.* Differences already pointed out in determining typological categories give clues to the problems the families cited as contributing to their homelessness. Sixty percent of families citing divorce as a factor contributing to homelessness were in the Improver group. Physical health problems were not a significant factor separating the Improver group families from the Maintainers. Stress and depression before becoming homeless were also found to be roughly equivalent in each group. Financial concerns and threatened eviction were more prevalent as causes of Maintainer stress before becoming homeless. Domestic violence was more commonly given as a cause of stress for families in the Improver group. Although fewer Maintainer families reported domestic violence or abuse, no Maintainer family reporting abuse described it as lasting for less than 2 years. Both Improver and Maintainer families said alcohol or drug use by the perpetrator resulted in an increase in violence. Nine percent of Maintainer families reported job loss as a key factor in increased violence. In 9% of Improver families, a perceived loss of control over the female resulted in violent behavior by the male.

*Children.* Moving from their homes to a shelter was disruptive for all the children, but their reactions varied. More Maintainer children were upset about moving, and more Improver children were glad to leave their previous housing, but the differences were small. A difference was also noted in the effects of homelessness on the school behavior of children in the two major typological categories. The percentages of families with children enrolled and attending school were approximately the same for each group, but more Maintainer children attended the same school as they did before becoming homeless. The school behavior of more Improver children (53%) than Maintainer children (29%) was affected negatively by homelessness. This might be explained by the fact that more children from Improver families had to change schools and were out of school while traveling.

## Implications for Educating Children
## in Homeless Families

Homeless children encounter many obstacles to receiving an education. Physical access, or just getting to the school, is but one problem and, for those attending school, perhaps the minor one. Research on homeless families indicates that in some shelters the majority, up to

75%, of school-age children are enrolled in school. Enrollment was required in the emergency shelters where the interviewed families stayed, albeit only temporarily.

These shelters allowed families to stay for 1 month and then required them to move on. Unless they found some way of acquiring permanent housing or a relative or friend willing to take them in, another emergency shelter would be their next destination. In each of the above scenarios, a change of schools would necessitate reenrolling and reconnecting to the educational system, sometimes in a new school district.

Even when required by the shelter, school enrollment and attendance do not happen for all children, and transportation problems are but one of the reasons. Other obstacles are the ill health of the child, a parent, sibling, or other family member, requiring either the parent's time or the school-age child's time to care for the sick family member. Some children are so upset by the many changes they are facing that they are afraid to leave their parents even for the day. Some parents, experiencing the same upsetting circumstances and changes, draw their only comfort from having their children close by and do not want them out of sight. Single parents who have left an abusive relationship are often afraid to send their children to school, terrified by the thought that their abusers may find and take or harm them. Other parents feel that the time they are in the shelter will be too short to make school worth the effort. The reality is that educating the homeless child will be difficult for both the child and the teacher.

*Teacher challenges.* The child enters the classroom, often mid-quarter, sometimes with a lengthy gap in schooling, other times from another school where the subject matter was paced differently. The child may be behind or even ahead of the class he or she is entering and thus either disrupts the routine and sequence of learning already established with others students or remains quiet and feels confused or ignored. A month later, after being integrated into the classroom, the child may leave abruptly when the family is forced to move out of the shelter. This sequence then is repeated by that child in another school in another district, and in the first school by a child whose family took the previous family's place at the shelter. If the child is fortunate, she or he may move to a shelter within a school district where designated schools cater to homeless children. Such designated schools allow homeless children to continue at the same school when they move to another shelter or living arrangement in the district.

*Student challenges.* The "lucky" homeless child, who does not have to change schools, only has to deal with the normal demands of school and homework plus the trauma of having to move all of her or his remaining belongings to a new shelter. The child will also have to get used to new rooms, new arrangements for eating, new arrangements for bathing, new arrangements for sleeping, new beds, new times to get up, and new transportation systems and routes to get to and from school. Underneath all the immediate concerns are new worries about how long before the family has to move again and where that might be. Homeless children are distressed that they might be forced to live in the family car, if they have one, and fret about whether they will have food and will ever have a home again.

The emotional distraction and distress caused by being homeless and the problems that led up to a family losing or leaving their housing are enormous for both the adults and the children. The constant changes and adjustments required after becoming homeless result in having little energy or attention available to spend on academic subjects.

For a few homeless children, school is their only haven, and weekends are dreaded and depressing. For others, school is a place of shame, where other children make fun of them, call them names, and push and shove them. They are new and unfamiliar in the classroom, often wearing the same shabby clothes and appearing stupid, not knowing the answers to questions learned weeks ago by the "regular" students. Older children try not to let other students know they are homeless because they are embarrassed and have been shunned when found out. High school students are often not able to keep up with classes and lose credits because of missing school, making it impossible for them to graduate in a regular program.

### Building on Strengths and Characteristics of the Families

It is suggested that knowledge of the very characteristics that differentiate the families may be helpful in assisting teachers and social service providers working with these families. Although Maintainer and Improver families are initially seen as having different behaviors and coping styles in dealing with adversity, children are regarded as equally important for both Maintainer and Improver families. Parents from both groups gave evidence of a willingness to sacrifice and to do what they considered best for their children, often going without food so that their children would not have to suffer. Extrapolating from behaviors reported by the families, the following recommendations are suggested:

1. Improver families are initiators, determined to improve their living situations and the lives and well-being of their children. Bettering their lives is so important to them that they are willing to sacrifice the security of the familiar for that of the unknown. Many Improver mothers extend themselves to provide the extras for their children, often arranging to take advantage of free recreational and cultural activities for their children. These parents would try to make themselves available for parent-teacher conferences and would encourage their children to participate in any opportunities for tutoring.

2. Maintainer families try to avoid disruptions in their lives and are less likely to take chances and to venture into the unknown. To minimize change, they will try to stay close to family and will try to keep their children in the same school. The focus most acceptable to this family is one that prevents disruption. Because Maintainer families are more familiar with utilizing grants and services, they will probably show little reluctance or resistance to the children using such services as free tutoring, if made available at school or in or near the shelter.

## Conclusions

The initial characteristics seen in risk-taking Improver families and risk-avoiding Maintainer families may be blurred after they lose their housing. If the families remain homeless for any length of time, those differences will seem to all but disappear. Homelessness wears down the whole family and acts as a great leveler of physical and emotional energy and of ambition. An understanding of some of the difficulties homeless families face, providing special services (e.g., transportation, tutoring, and counseling), along with encouraging and recognizing positive steps, will go far in helping both the children and parents in homeless families. Special programs for homeless children that recognize the unique situations that they present can prove successful in keeping children in school and can provide some stability in a very stressful time in their lives.

# References

Bassuk, E. L. (1986). Homeless families: Single mothers and their children in Boston shelters. In E. L. Bassuk (Ed.), *The mental health needs of homeless persons* (pp. 45-54). New directions for mental health series, no. 30. San Francisco: Jossey-Bass.

Bassuk, E. L., & Gallagher, E. (1990). No fixed address: The effects of homelessness on families and children. *Child & Youth Services, 14,* 35-47.

Bassuk, E. L., Rubin, L., & Lauriat, A. (1986). Characteristics of sheltered homeless families. *American Journal of Public Health, 76*(9), 1097-1101.

Boxill, N., & Beaty, N. (1990). Mother/child interactions among homeless women and their children in a public night shelter in Atlanta, Georgia. *Child & Youth Services, 14,* 49-64.

Brickner, P. W. (1985). *Health care of homeless people.* New York: Springer.

Coalition for the Homeless. (1984). *Perchance to sleep: Homeless children without shelter in New York City.* New York: Author.

Gewirtzman, R., & Fodor, I. (1987). The homeless child at school: From welfare hotel to classroom. *Child Welfare, 66,* 237-245.

Hagen, J. L., & Ivanoff, A. M. (1988). Homeless women: A high-risk population. *Affilia, 3*(1), 19-33.

Hall, J., & Maza, P. (1990). No fixed address: The effects of homelessness on families and children. *Child & Youth Services, 14,* 35-47.

Hayes, R. M. (1984). Testimony before the House Intergovernmental Relations and Human Resources Subcommittee of the Committee on Government Operations from *Perchance to sleep: Homeless children without shelter in New York City.* New York: Coalition for the Homeless.

Institute of Medicine. (1988). *Homelessness, health, and human needs.* Washington, DC: Author.

Johnson, A. K. (1988, August). *A survey of the St. Louis area emergency shelters for the homeless.* St. Louis: Homeless Services Network Board.

Kozol, J. (1988). *Rachel and her children: Homeless families in America.* New York: Crown.

League of Women Voters of Seattle. (1985). *Children in our city: Children at risk: Street youth.* Seattle: Author.

Maza, P. L., & Hall, J. A. (1988). *Homeless children and their families: A preliminary study.* Washington, DC: Child Welfare League of America.

McGerigle, P., & Lauriat, A. (1983). *More than a shelter: A community response to homelessness. Report and recommendations.* Boston: Massachusetts Association for Mental Health.

Miller, D. S., & Lin, E. H. (1988). Children in sheltered homeless families: Reported health status and use of health services. *Pediatrics, 81,* 668-673.

National Coalition for the Homeless. (1987). Homeless increase 25%, major factor: No housing. *Safety Network, 5*(3), 1.

National Coalition for the Homeless. (1988a). Homeless children denied access to education, lawsuit charges. *Safety Network, 6*(4), 1.

National Coalition for the Homeless. (1988b). Oklahoma's homeless face crisis: Advocates battle current myths. *Safety Network, 6*(4), 4.

National Coalition for the Homeless. (1989). Homeless population increasing dramatically nationwide. *Safety Network, 8*(10), 1.

Simpson, J. H., Kilduff, M., & Blewett, C. D. (1984). *Struggling to survive in a welfare hotel.* New York: Community Service Society.

Stefl, M. E. (1987). The new homeless: A national perspective. In R. D. Bingham, R. E. Green, & S. B. White (Eds.), *The homeless in contemporary society* (pp. 46-63). Newbury Park, CA: Sage.

Stoner, M. R. (1983). The plight of homeless women. *Social Science Review, 57,* 291-301.

U.S. Conference of Mayors. (1987). *The continuing growth of hunger, homelessness, and poverty in America's cities: 1987.* Washington, DC: Author.

U.S. House of Representatives, Committee on Government Operations. (1986). *Homeless families: A neglected crisis.* Washington, DC: Government Printing Office.

van Ry, M. (1990). Homeless families: Causes, effects, and recommendations (Doctoral dissertation, University of Washington, 1990). *Dissertation Abstracts International,* Abstract number 01118966 (Order number AAD90-26030)

Wackstein, N. (1983). *No one's in charge: Homeless families with children in temporary shelter.* New York: Citizens Committee for Children of New York.

Wackstein, N. (1984). *7000 homeless children: The crisis continues.* New York: Citizens Committee for Children of New York.

Wright, J. D. (1990). Homelessness is not healthy for children and other living things. *Child & Youth Services, 14,* 65-87.

Wright, J. D., Weber-Burden, E., Knight, J. W., & Lam, J. A. (1987). *The national health care for the homeless program: The first year.* Amherst: University of Massachusetts, Social and Demographic Research Institute.

# 5

# The Reality

## The Status of Education
## for Homeless Children and Youth

PATRICIA F. FIRST

The reality is that large numbers of homeless children are growing up uneducated. The reality is that the Stewart B. McKinney Homeless Assistance Act (1987) created an entitlement program administered by a clumsy intergovernmental bureaucratic structure that is repeating the implementation mistakes of the Great Society programs. The reality is that we have not learned from the past. The reality is that little children are homeless on our streets, their life chances drastically curtailed.

The structural contributors to this unsatisfactory reality are examined in this chapter. Federalism and the implementation of the redistributive programs are examined. A research study of the McKinney state plans and the response of the states to the implementation of the Mckinney Act are described. In the concluding section, implications of and policy recommendations for the pace of change and stages of social program implementation are discussed.

### Federalism and the Redistributive Programs

Our federalist system respects the balance of power among the federal, state, and local layers of government, but in the actual operation of the system the balance of power is often perceived to be leaning in favor of one of the three participatory layers. After the steady stream of educational and civil rights legislation and court decisions coming from the federal level after the Brown decision (*Brown v. Board of Education,* 1954), many people familiar with United States educational institutions believed the federal role to have become excessive. In response to this view, the 1980s became a decade of scaling back the federal presence in education, as well as in other social programs.

The 1981 Education Consolidation and Improvement Act reduced federal education spending, streamlined the program for socioeconomically disadvantaged children (which was the largest federal categorical program in education), and consolidated 28 categorical grants into a single block grant. The U.S. Office of Management and Budget (1981) plainly stated that these changes were intended to "shift control over education policy away from the Federal Government and back to state and local authorities—where it constitutionally and historically belongs" (p. 136). The Stewart B. McKinney Act was a federal initiative needed but unfortunately enacted at an inopportune time. Coming as it did in the mid-1980s, implementation was begun when the balance of power and the supporting public sentiment were clearly with state and local governments.

Ours is an intergovernmental system, and in education we can see clear powers at the federal, state, and local levels, with shifting influences and overlapping responsibilities clouding the scene. This shifting and overlapping causes problems in policy implementation. Who is really making what decisions where and when is always a question. The term *federalism* refers to the balance of power between the national and state governments. Campbell, Cunningham, Nystrand, and Usdan (1985) wrote that we have moved from dual federalism, which has a separation of power between the state and national governments, to a shift of power more and more to the national government. We now have national federalism, though they wrote that some recent slowing of this trend had occurred.

Some feel, particularly because of the omission of a direct reference to education in the Constitution, that the state level of government has a claim to being closer to the people and thus by "rights" should be more influential in education. Elmore (1986) wrote that "the federal and state governments are in fact but different agents and trustees of the people" and that "neither federal nor state government has a claim to being 'closer' to the people, since both take their authority directly from the people" (p. 171).

Power related to educational governance shifted among the layers of government during the period 1950 to 1987. Both the federal and state levels of governance were winners of power during this time period despite the shifts in power between the two. Wirt and Kirst (1989) wrote that the local level of educational governance clearly lost influence during this time period. Though this is true as one looks at trends over decades, the McKinney Act arrived at precisely the time that public favor was with the local and state levels of governance.

At its best, federalism is a cooperative venture. The ideal is to establish grant-in-aid programs that incorporate state and local governments into the administration of federal policy—that is, a role for Washington in social programs that reinforces rather than usurps state and local responsibilities. This *cooperative federalism,* as Grodzins (1966) labeled it, was the model for the design of a number of federal categorical programs, including vocational, compensatory, special education, and later, education for homeless children and youth. Criticism and adverse characterization of this idealized model have come from both capture theorists and implementation theorists.

*Capture theorists* (Grubb & Lazerson, 1982; McConnell, 1966; Selznick, 1949; Stigler, 1975) wrote of the ease with which narrow, organized interest (especially "producer") groups whose economic livelihood is affected by the question at hand are able to "capture" complex administrative processes. Today's criticism of political action groups would be one example of criticism in the vein of the capture theorists. Using this viewpoint, one could view the creation of the national organization for state coordinators for services to the homeless as "producers" organizing to perpetuate their services.

*Implementation theorists* would view the creation of this national organization quite differently, perhaps as the creation of a needed lobbying group. Implementation theorists (Levin & Ferman, 1985; Pressman & Wildavsky, 1973) condemn federal programs as having imposed excessive controls on the producer groups who will ultimately deliver the federally funded services. Examples of the excessive burden include regulations and guidelines imposed on state and local governments, overly ambitious federal goals, and complex administrative structures.

A third, more moderate, view is that the federal government has in the long run followed a pragmatic path located somewhere between the extreme views of the capture and implementation theorists (Rabe & Peterson, 1988). In their research on the two largest federal education programs—compensatory education for the poorest and lowest achieving students, and educational services for the handicapped—Rabe and Peterson found that accommodation had been reached among the three levels of government and that relations had been established on the premise that each participant needed the other. "The 'feds' had crucial legal and fiscal resources; the states played an intermediary role; and the locals had the operational capacity without which nothing could be achieved" (p. 470). Significantly it was also noted that these cooperative arrangements were facilitated by the fact that these programs belonged to broader social movements that had both national and local adherents. Thus acquiescence to federal policy in these areas occurred at the state and local levels.

The implementation structure for the McKinney Act was modeled after these earlier social and educational programs. (See Chapter 2 for detail regarding this point.) This framework was designed in the time of widespread confidence in the capacity of the federal government to promote more effective and more equitably delivered educational services. In other words, the Stewart B. McKinney Homeless Assistance Act of 1987 was designed for a pre-1980 social reality, for the time of belief in cooperative federalism. And while evidence exists that the implementors are playing the games of capture and implementation, as yet no sign has been found of good faith accommodation by the three levels of government so that services can get smoothly and quickly to those who need them. Beginning with the original state plans in response to the McKinney Act, states and localities have demonstrated more recalcitrance than responsiveness. And day by day, homeless children grow older, missing their chances for an education.

### Implementation of the McKinney Educational Provisions

#### An Evaluation of the State Plans

One of the provisions of the McKinney Act was that each Office of the Coordinator of Education of Homeless Children and Youth would gather data on homeless children in the state and develop a plan providing for their education. The plans that the states then developed were evaluated and analyzed (First & Cooper, 1990a). In this study, elements of the plans were subjected to criteria of quality versus mere compliance, as opposed to the review done by the U.S. Department of

Education, which was for compliance to the terms of the act, not for indicators of quality or excellence. (Enforcement of the act has been limited to minimum compliance, and even state participation to that level has been deemed voluntary.)

An impact evaluation using the orientation of naturalistic inquiry was conducted. The techniques of naturalistic inquiry were particularly suited to this project because naturalistic inquiry lends itself to understanding and portraying the complexities of an educational innovation about which little is known. Multiple realities can be reflected without compromising the integrity of the outcome, and it is suited to "illuminating problems, issues and features" (Worthen & Sanders, 1987, p. 132). Attention to academic rigor consisted of addressing the criteria for rigor in naturalistic inquiry (Lincoln & Guba, 1985). These criteria are truth/credibility, applicability or "fit" of the findings, consistency/auditability, and neutrality.

The response of the states to the McKinney Act was analyzed via the content of the state plans that were required in order for states to access the second round of money authorized under the act. The plans of 49 states plus Puerto Rico and the District of Columbia were analyzed in terms of quality criteria—that is, efforts at excellence beyond the minimum criteria in the act. Hawaii chose not to submit a plan.

All of the state plans were received by the reviewing unit in the Department of Education by July 1989. After review for strict compliance with the law, 20 of the plans were returned to the states for adjustment. The analysis reported here was done with the plans in the form in which they were approved by the Department of Education by December 1989.

The provisions of the act applicable to the access to education were analyzed in *West's Education Law Reporter* (First & Cooper, 1989). They are summarized below.

1. Each state educational agency shall assure that each child of a homeless person, and homeless youth, shall have access to a free appropriate public education that would be provided to the children of a resident of the state.
2. Each state that has a residency requirement for school attendance purposes shall review and revise such laws to assure that such children are afforded a free and appropriate public education.
3. Each state shall establish or designate an Office of Coordinator of Education of Homeless Children and Youth. This office shall gather data on homeless children in the state and develop a plan providing for their children.

4. The plan developed shall contain provisions designed to authorize the state educational agency, the local education agency, the parent organization of the homeless child, or the homeless youth of the applicable determinations required. The plan shall also provide procedures for the resolution of disputes regarding the educational placement of these children.

5. Under the plan, the local education agency of each homeless child shall either continue the child's enrollment in the school district of origin for the remainder of the year or enroll the child in the school district where he or she is living, whichever is in the child's best interests.

6. Each homeless child shall be provided services comparable to the services provided to other students in the school being attended.

7. The educational records of each homeless child or youth shall be maintained so that records are available in a timely fashion.

Determining the categories for measurement of these provisions was accomplished by reviewing the basic requirements to which states were to respond, the nonregulatory guidance issued by the U.S. Department of Education, and the law itself. Regarding the requirements to establish a state Office for Homeless Children and Youth, all states did this. Because it does not address policy issues in itself, the establishment of a state office was not measured and was assumed adequate for all states.

The following categories were chosen for analysis:

    I.  Data Gathering and Problem Analysis

        States were to collect data and analyze them for determining barriers to education for homeless children and youth and to assess needs the state should address. Points were assigned according to a 4-point evaluative scale from a high of 4, where the plan reflected thoughtful data gathering and thorough analysis, to a low of zero, where the category was not addressed in the original plan.

   II.  State Goals Relative to Federal Mandates

        A higher ranking in this category indicated that definite action was taken and that active plans were in progress.

  III.  State Goals Relative to Needs Identified in Data

        This category was ranked high if definite action was taken and active plans were in progress.

  IV.  Issue Sensitization—In-Service Education

        This category was ranked high if full plans were indicated for public and in-house issue sensitization and a strong in-service component was included.

V. Interagency Cooperation

This category was ranked high if evidence was seen of strong interagency coordination of action and resources from the beginning through all stages of the plans.

VI. Role of the State Education Agency (SEA) in Relation to the Local Education Agency (LEA)

This category was ranked high if the SEA was dominant and issued directives, set plans in motion immediately, and included a strong compliance component.

Using the categories and criteria described above, the 49 state plans plus those of Puerto Rico and the District of Columbia were analyzed. As can be seen in Table 5.1, the states varied widely in evidence of these quality indicators in their plans. At the high end, composite quality scores of 24 were earned by Connecticut, Massachusetts, New Jersey, New York, Pennsylvania, and Texas. Rhode Island scored the lowest at 2, followed at the low end by several states with a composite score of 6. It should be noted that Connecticut, Massachusetts, New Jersey, and New York were the states in which the earliest court cases on behalf of homeless children's access to education were filed. And Texas is the home state of the cases most closely paralleling cases on behalf of homeless children (First & Cooper, 1989). Additional planning time might therefore account for the completeness and quality of these plans.

In Table 5.1, scores for all six categories, a composite score, and a mean score are reported. In Table 5.2, the states are arranged by composite scores from highest to lowest. No geographic pattern was found in the distribution of scores other than the northeastern cluster of high-scoring states where the previous litigation on behalf of the homeless occurred.

The aspect of the state plans most consistently addressed at a quality level was the review of state laws regarding residence and attendance. Action on these items varied from (a) immediate action via policy-making and recommendations for statutory action to the legislatures to (b) providing for intermediate procedures to ease access for homeless children and youth to an education to (c) justifying current state laws as adequate even though ease of access involved complicated procedures for the homeless to handle.

*Text continues on page 89.*

**Table 5.1** Analysis of Initial State Plans in Response to the McKinney Act.

| State | Data gathering and problem analysis | State goals relative to federal mandates | State goals relative to needs identified | Issue sensitization and in-service education | Interagency cooperation | Role of SEA in relation to the LEA | Composite score | Mean score |
|---|---|---|---|---|---|---|---|---|
| Alabama | 1 | 1 | 1 | 0 | 1 | 3 | 6 | 1.0 |
| Alaska | 2 | 2 | 2 | 2 | 2 | 2 | 12 | 2.0 |
| Arizona | 3 | 2 | 2 | 3 | 2 | 3 | 15 | 2.5 |
| Arkansas | 4 | 3 | 2 | 2 | 3 | 2 | 16 | 2.7 |
| California | 2 | 2 | 2 | 2 | 2 | 2 | 12 | 2.0 |
| Colorado | 2 | 2 | 2 | 2 | 1 | 2 | 11 | 1.8 |
| Connecticut | 4 | 4 | 4 | 4 | 4 | 4 | 24 | 4.0 |
| Delaware | 1 | 1 | 1 | 1 | 1 | 1 | 6 | 1.0 |
| Dist. of Col. | 0 | 1 | 2 | 1 | 2 | N/A | 6 | 1.2 |
| Florida | 3 | 3 | 3 | 3 | 3 | 3 | 18 | 6.0 |
| Georgia | 2 | 1 | 2 | 0 | 1 | 0 | 6 | 1.0 |
| Hawaii | did | not | submit | plan | | | | |
| Idaho | 2 | 2 | 2 | 1 | 2 | 2 | 11 | 1.8 |
| Illinois | 2 | 3 | 2 | 2 | 2 | 2 | 13 | 2.2 |
| Indiana | 1 | 2 | 1 | 2 | 1 | 1 | 8 | 1.3 |
| Iowa | 3 | 3 | 3 | 3 | 3 | 3 | 18 | 3.0 |
| Kansas | 2 | 2 | 2 | 1 | 1 | 2 | 10 | 1.6 |
| Kentucky | 3 | 2 | 4 | 3 | 2 | 4 | 18 | 3.0 |
| Louisiana | 2 | 2 | 2 | 2 | 2 | 2 | 12 | 2.0 |
| Maine | 2 | 2 | 2 | 2 | 2 | 1 | 11 | 1.8 |
| Maryland | 2 | 2 | 3 | 2 | 3 | 3 | 15 | 2.5 |
| Massachusetts | 4 | 4 | 4 | 4 | 4 | 4 | 24 | 4.0 |

|  | | | | | | |
|---|---|---|---|---|---|---|
| Michigan | 2 | 2 | 2 | 2 | 12 | 2.0 |
| Minnesota | 1 | 1 | 1 | 1 | 6 | 1.0 |
| Mississippi | 1 | 1 | 1 | 1 | 6 | 1.0 |
| Missouri | 1 | 1 | 1 | 1 | 6 | 1.0 |
| Montana | 2 | 1 | 1 | 1 | 8 | 1.3 |
| Nebraska | 1 | 1 | 1 | 1 | 6 | 1.0 |
| Nevada | 2 | 4 | 3 | 4 | 18 | 3.0 |
| N. Hampshire | 2 | 2 | 2 | 2 | 12 | 2.0 |
| N. Jersey | 4 | 4 | 4 | 4 | 24 | 2.0 |
| N. Mexico | 1 | 1 | 1 | 1 | 6 | 4.0 |
| N. York | 4 | 4 | 4 | 4 | 14 | 1.0 |
| N. Carolina | 1 | 1 | 1 | 1 | 6 | 4.0 |
| N. Dakota | 2 | 1 | 2 | 1 | 9 | 1.0 |
| Ohio | 1 | 1 | 1 | 1 | 6 | 1.5 |
| Oklahoma | 2 | 3 | 2 | 3 | 16 | 1.0 |
| Oregon | 3 | 3 | 3 | 3 | 18 | 2.7 |
| Pennsylvania | 4 | 4 | 4 | 4 | 24 | 3.0 |
| Rhode Island | 0 | 1 | 0 | 1 | 2 | 4.0 |
| S. Carolina | 2 | 2 | 2 | 1 | 11 | 3.3 |
| S. Dakota | 1 | 1 | 1 | 1 | 6 | 1.8 |
| Tennessee | 1 | 1 | 1 | 1 | 6 | 1.0 |
| Texas | 4 | 4 | 4 | 4 | 24 | 1.0 |
| Utah | 2 | 2 | 2 | 2 | 12 | 4.0 |

**Table 5.1** Continued

| State | Data gathering and problem analysis | State goals relative to federal mandates | State goals relative to needs identified | Issue sensitization and in-service education | Interagency cooperation | Role of SEA in relation to the LEA | Composite score | Mean score |
|---|---|---|---|---|---|---|---|---|
| Vermont | 2 | 2 | 3 | 2 | 1 | 2 | 12 | 2.0 |
| Virginia | 1 | 1 | 1 | 1 | 1 | 1 | 6 | 1.0 |
| Washington | 3 | 2 | 2 | 3 | 3 | 2 | 15 | 2.5 |
| W. Virginia | 2 | 2 | 2 | 2 | 2 | 2 | 12 | 2.0 |
| Wisconsin | 1 | 1 | 2 | 1 | 1 | 2 | 8 | 1.3 |
| Wyoming | 2 | 2 | 3 | 2 | 2 | 2 | 13 | 2.1 |
| Puerto Rico | 1 | 1 | 1 | 1 | 1 | 1 | 6 | 1.0 |

SOURCE: First, P. E., & Cooper, G. K. (1990) The McKinney Homeless Assistance Act: Evaluating the Response of the States. *Education Law Reporter, 60*, 1047-1060, (August 16, 1990).

**Table 5.2** Composite Scores of the States.

| | | | |
|---|---|---|---|
| Connecticut | 24 | West Virginia | 12 |
| Massachusetts | 24 | Colorado | 11 |
| New Jersey | 24 | Idaho | 11 |
| New York | 24 | Maine | 11 |
| Pennsylvania | 24 | South Carolina | 11 |
| Texas | 24 | Kansas | 10 |
| Florida | 18 | North Dakota | 9 |
| Iowa | 18 | Indiana | 8 |
| Kentucky | 18 | Montana | 8 |
| Nevada | 18 | Wisconsin | 8 |
| Oregon | 18 | Alabama | 6 |
| Arkansas | 16 | Delaware | 6 |
| Oklahoma | 16 | District of Columbia | 6 |
| Arizona | 15 | Georgia | 6 |
| Maryland | 15 | Minnesota | 6 |
| Washington | 15 | Missouri | 6 |
| Illinois | 13 | Nebraska | 6 |
| Wyoming | 13 | New Mexico | 6 |
| Alaska | 12 | North Carolina | 6 |
| California | 12 | Ohio | 6 |
| Louisiana | 12 | South Dakota | 6 |
| Michigan | 12 | Tennessee | 6 |
| New Hampshire | 12 | Virginia | 6 |
| Utah | 12 | Puerto Rico | 6 |
| Vermont | 12 | Rhode Island | 2 |

SOURCE: First, P. E., & Cooper, G. K. (1990). The McKinney Homeless Assistance Act: Evaluating the Response of the States. *Education Law Reporter*, 60, 1047-1060. (August 16, 1990).

## Problems in the Implementation
## of the State Plans

A problem with these state plans arises from the requirement that each education agency shall assure that each child of a homeless person and each homeless youth shall have access to a free, appropriate public education that would be provided to children of a resident of the state. It is open to question whether grouping homeless children in a "shelter" school or a "transition" school is appropriate under the act. It is not unlikely that advocacy groups will litigate to determine whether anything other than traditional schooling in a traditional setting is appropriate. Setting up separate schools could be seen as perpetuating another entitlement group. Capture theorists would see it as perpetuating the need for services provided by the service producer.

Another problem arises out of the requirement that each state that has a residency requirement must review and revise such laws to assure that homeless children are provided a free and appropriate education. Historically school districts have been required to provide free and appropriate public education for students who are residents of the district, and payments for educational services have been provided by local funds with some assistance by the state. Because of the economic pressures created by requiring school districts to provide education for nonresident students, it is important that state revision of residency requirements include financial assistance for the full cost of educating the homeless child. Implementation theorists might see this review and/or loosening of requirements as freeing the local level to provide the needed services.

Yet another problem seen in these state plans concerns the act's requirement that the plan allow the child to continue enrollment in the district of origin for the remainder of the year or allow the child to enroll in the district where he or she is living, whichever is in the child's best interest. Besides the financial concerns discussed above, it is an open issue who will determine the best interests of the child and the criteria to be used. It should be expected that litigation will be initiated by advocacy groups when it is their opinion that the criteria for enrollment placement is inappropriate or when the decision regarding the child's best placement is contested for other reasons.

This is not, of course, an exhaustive list of problems and potential problems that may arise from these state plans. Other potentially problematic issues raised in these plans arise from proposed computerized tracking systems. If all homeless children are placed in state or school or data tracking systems, protecting the anonymity of children escaping from abuse becomes a problem. A conflict arises between the need to provide services and the need to protect identity.

Conflict also arises with other social problems. Most states still will have to review residency requirements and attendance laws. Changes in these laws for the benefit of homeless children may weaken laws that were designed to promote racial integration.

Conflict resolution mechanisms that depend on homeless parents struggling through complicated appeals processes may fail. Homeless parents are not in the position to be advocates for their children's welfare. Plans with provision for designated advocates have more promise of success. Absence of the required parental figure in trying to enroll runaways and throwaways (children who have been sent away from home by their families) may also call for the provision of designated advocates. (The use of advocates is no panacea, however. As experience with advocates for handicapped children shows, this avenue can also raise problems.)

Evidence still exists in these plans of fees for essential services integral to public schooling—for example, book fees. Homeless families cannot pay these fees, and the problem raises the larger question of the real meaning of a "free" public education.

Labeling and stereotyping within the school setting seem especially problematic with homeless children. The labeling relates to the larger problem of confidentiality for the families, as well as for the school children. Potential areas for breaches of confidentiality appear throughout these state plans.

These problems were articulated by numerous voices over the past few years (First & Cooper, 1989, 1990a; Kozol, 1988; National Academy of Science, 1988; National Coalition for the Homeless, 1987). Nevertheless the weakest of the plans submitted showed procedures perpetuating these problems.

These state plans, even the best of them, do not fulfill a reformer's dream of the public school becoming an advocate for children, particularly poor and homeless children. Instead these plans illustrate responsive instrumentalities. The responses vary from excellent to poor or even nonexistent. Even in excellence, the advocacy and coordinating role that some dream of is not there for children, and the school may be the only agency positioned to fill that societal need. The poor scores of so many of the states indicate that the cooperative momentum reported by Rabe and Peterson (1988) in the compensatory and handicapped programs has not begun. Further, though the plight of the homeless has continually been brought to the nation's attention, some observers think Americans are in "disaster overload" and have become hardened to the needs of even these most visible needy. The broad social movements that engendered both national and local adherents for the compensatory and special education programs are not in evidence for homeless children.

## *Glimpses of More Mature Social Programming*

### The Pace of Change

Change is necessarily gradual, as multiple actors assimilate a new policy into their field of relationships. The implementation of the McKinney Act has not demonstrated that the process of change is easily accelerated even when the need is seemingly visible to the public eye. Even though many thoughtful people think the balance of federalism is lost when the federal government initiates social change "from above," our history offers many examples of changes that state and local governments would not have made without insistence from the federal level.

Such examples include the desegregation of the schools, the mainstreaming of the handicapped, and equal opportunity for women. Decades into those federal initiatives, resistance still lingers in some local areas, and signs are evident nationally of retreat from further progress. Perhaps it was totally unrealistic to expect quicker relief for the needs of the homeless. Their needs are so great, so diverse, and so intertwined with the other major social problems that the nation is now facing, such as health care, affordable housing, and the curtailment of crime and illegal drug use, that solving their problems calls for a major turn in values.

Having homeless children in the classroom confronts one daily with the painful consideration of those values. And so we still have board members, superintendents, principals, and teachers who have not heard of the McKinney Act or who think it does not affect their schools or who cannot believe that these people really have no place to go at night. One said to me recently about a supply fee: "But it's only $2.00 per child." As the old saying goes, many of us would benefit from a walk in the other person's shoes.

The implementation of the McKinney Act is clearly repeating the three classic stages of the operation of federal redistributive programs. In *stage one,* delegation to the local level, the federal level provides the plan and some incentives and trusts to the good intentions of the other governmental levels to tackle this problem. The voluntary nature of state participation in the development of state plans under the McKinney Act signaled this opening stage. Via their state plans, many states passed this signal on to the local level by making local participation and compliance voluntary. In discussing the implementation of compensatory education, Murphy (1971) noted what may be a fundamental flaw of federalism:

> The federal system—with its dispersion of power and control—not only permits but encourages the evasion and dilution of federal reform, making it nearly impossible for the federal administrator to impose program priorities; those not diluted by Congressional intervention can be ignored during the state and local implementation. (p. 60)

In *stage two,* the federal government toughens up and intensifies oversight, and the states respond with the same treatment for the local level. With regard to McKinney implementation, we have yet to see signs that the federal government is moving into stage two, although it is documented that McKinney programs have had no impact on reducing the size of the homeless population in any state. Because of large increases in the homeless population, the few that are housed through McKinney programs are replaced immediately by newly homeless individuals and families (National Coalition for the Homeless, 1989). These families have children who are unable to obtain schooling at all or who are grossly underserved in their educational placement. According to Freedman (1990), it is estimated that of the approximately 600,000 homeless children of school age nationally, 200,000 do not attend school.

### The Better Way?

The better way of program operation that we might realistically hope for in implementation of the McKinney Act is *stage three,* or more mature program operation, described by Rabe and Peterson (1988). Consistent with change theory, stage three comes partly with the passage of time. As state and local agencies become increasingly staffed with professionals knowledgeable about and gaining experience with the problem, these people seek accommodations and understandings with the federal regulators that allow for more targeted and successful operations at the local level. Stage three comes with the acceptance that as a society we choose to address this problem. Examples of local districts trying hard to serve the special needs of homeless children are scattered, and individual heroes in the cause include dedicated teachers who are making a difference in the lives of some homeless children

(First & Cooper, 1990b). But as yet, no national movement exists to force the federal government to move into stage two and on to the cooperative implementation of stage three.

While we wait for the change processes to stumble slowly through the stages of implementation, 200,000 children do not attend school. In *Plyler v. Doe* (1982), the Supreme Court decision dealing with education for the children of illegal aliens (the group with the closest legal parallel to homeless children), Justice Brennan wrote the following about not educating these children:

> [It] imposes a lifetime of hardship on a discreet class of children not account- able for their disabling status. The stigma of illiteracy will mark them for the rest of their lives. By denying these children a basic education, we deny them the ability to live within the structure of our civic institutions, and foreclose any realistic possibility that they will contribute in even the smallest way to the progress of our Nation. (p. 2398)

This is the reality. This is the status of education for homeless children and youth.

## References

Brown v. Board of Education, 347 U.S. 483 (1954).

Campbell, R. G., Cunningham, L. L., Nystrand, R. O., & Usdan, M. D. (1985). *The organizational & control of American schools* (5th ed.). Columbus, OH: Charles E. Merrill.

Elmore, R. F. (1986). Education and federalism: Doctrinal, functional, and strategic views. In D. L. Kirp & D. N. Jensen (Eds.), *School days, rule days* (pp. 166-186). Philadelphia: Falmer.

First, P. F. (1992). *Educational policy for school administrators*. Boston: Allyn & Bacon.

First, P. F., & Cooper, G. R. (1989). Access to education by homeless children. *Education Law Reporter, 53,* 757-765.

First, P. F., & Cooper, G. R. (1990a). The McKinney Homeless Assistance Act: Evaluating the response of the states. *Education Law Reporter, 60,* 1047-1060.

First, P. F., & Cooper, G. R. (1990b, December). Homeless doesn't have to mean hopeless. *The School Administrator, 47,* 17-22.

Freedman, S. G. (1990). *Small victories.* New York: Harper & Row.

Grodzins, M. (1966). In D. E. Elazar (Ed.), *The American system.* Chicago: Rand-McNally.

Grubb, W. N., & Lazerson, M. (1982). *Broken promises: How Americans fail their children.* New York: Basic Books.

Kozol, J. (1988). *Rachel and her children: Homeless families in America.* New York: Crown.

Levin, M. A., & Ferman, B. (1985). *The political hand: Policy implementation and youth employment programs.* New York: Pergamon.

Lincoln, Y. S., & Guba, E. G. (1985). *Naturalistic inquiry.* Beverly Hills, CA: Sage.

McConnell, G. (1966). *Private power and American democracy.* New York: Knopf.

Murphy, J. (1971, February). Title I of ESEA: The politics of implementing federal education reform. *Harvard Educational Review, 41,* 36-63.

National Academy of Science. (1988). *Homeless, health, and human needs.* Washington, DC: Author.

National Coalition for the Homeless. (1987). *Broken lives.* Washington, DC: Author.

National Coalition for the Homeless. (1989). *Unfinished business.* Washington, DC: Author.

Plyler v. Doe, 102 S. Ct. 2382 (1982).

Pressman, J. L., & Wildavsky, A. (1973). *Implementation.* Berkeley: University of California Press.

Rabe, B. G., & Peterson, P. E. (1988). The evolution of a new cooperative federalism. In N. J. Boyan (Ed.), *Handbook of research on educational administration* (pp. 467-485). New York: Longman.

Selznick, P. (1949). *TVA and the grass roots: A study in the sociology of formal organization.* Berkeley: University of California Press.

Stewart B. McKinney Homeless Assistance Act, Pub. L. No. 100-77, 101 Stat. 482-538 (1987).

Stigler, J. (1975). *The citizen and the state.* Chicago: University of Chicago Press.

U.S. Office of Management and Budget. (1981). *Fiscal year 1982 budget revisions.* Washington, DC: Government Printing Office.

Wirt, F. M., & Kirst, M. W. (1989). *Schools in conflict.* Berkeley, CA: McCutchan.

Worthen, B., & Sanders, J. (1987). *Educational evaluation: Alternative approaches and practical guidelines.* New York: Longman.

# PART II

# *Education for the Homeless*

Overcoming the Barriers

*6*

# Children and Homelessness

## Early Childhood and Elementary Education

### E. ANNE EDDOWES

Most children have a home of one sort or another. It is the environment in which they spend much of their time. It forms the base from which new activity evolves and then extends into the wider world of community, school, and beyond. Children of all backgrounds have a variety of needs related to their development and learning—needs that may be satisfied by the parents, extended family members, child-care personnel, and/or school teachers. The home, however, plays a large part in meeting children's needs.

When children are homeless, many of the requisites necessary for normal child development and learning are missing. That is the time for child-care and school programs to provide additional support for homeless families to help the children develop and learn despite the turbulence in their lives.

### *Relationship of Homeless Children's Needs to Educational Programs*

#### Young Children

*Physical needs.* Comfort in terms of bodily needs being met is of prime importance for infants and toddlers. Nutritious food is necessary for growth and health. Consistency, continuity, and sameness contribute to the child's sense of well-being. Frequent interaction between infant and parent helps each to know the other. Through this reciprocity, the bond begins that leads to the infant's basic trust in the world (Erikson, 1963).

Many homeless infants do not get the nutritional balance necessary for healthy growth. The daily schedule has little predictability. Although parents may spend time with their young children, it is usually very stressful (Children's Defense Fund, 1991). Child-care programs can provide alternative care that may supplement, not substitute for, care the parents provide. Good nutrition, appropriate routines, and consistent, personalized adult-child interaction are all-important (Brazelton, 1987).

*Need for stability and security.* When watching a mobile infant or toddler explore a new situation, the child will first display interest in some new person or event. Then the child will invariably pull back and check to be sure that the secure base in the form of the parent or caregiver is nearby. Sometimes the child will move close and touch that person. Only then will the original activity be resumed. Stability of environment gives a young child the security necessary to try new things and to begin to gain a sense of autonomy (Erikson, 1963). When young children have the opportunity, they will explore and learn for the sheer joy of it.

Little stability is available in the lives of homeless children. Any shelter the family has is usually temporary. In many instances, it may be dangerous for a curious child seeking some measure of freedom (Kozol, 1988). The place may be dirty with peeling paint that contains lead (Children's Defense Fund, 1991). Child-care settings can include healthy spaces in which young children can venture forth, satisfy their curiosity, and be supported in their quest for independence (Weiser, 1991).

*Motor development needs.* When young children become mobile, they need ample, safe space and equipment to allow for vigorous physical play (Gordon, Khokha, Schrag, & Weeks, 1988). Gross motor movement, along with sensory experiences, are the base from which eye-hand coordination develops and fine motor skills are refined (Weiser, 1991). Toddlers can be seen running and jumping with great exuberance when the environment permits. Young children need opportunities to practice newly acquired skills in order to experience feelings of autonomy and success (Bredekamp, 1987).

Homeless children have few opportunities for movement. They spend much of their time in the cramped space of a shelter, or sometimes they live in a car. They have little opportunity to engage in activities that might enhance their physical development (Bassuk & Rubin, 1987). Gross and fine motor skills are an integral part of most child-care programs. A variety of equipment, materials, and surfaces should be available for young children to develop motor and sensory capabilities (Seefeldt & Barbour, 1990).

*Language development needs.* The greatest achievements in language learning occur in the first few years of life (Lamb & Bornstein, 1987). From the time the infant begins babbling and playing with sounds, until the young child is speaking in sentences, a need exists for adults to interact, using appropriate language (Bredekamp, 1987). Language development is closely related to cognitive development. Language gives children labels for them to use in thinking and talking. Young children need to be read to often. They should hear poetry and rhymes and learn to sing songs (Weiser, 1991).

Despite the importance of early language development, homeless children have little opportunity to engage in relaxed, appropriate language experiences. Children talk together, but the parents and other adults may be either too busy or too tired to talk with them. There are usually no children's books and little joy to motivate any singing. In addition, crowded conditions may not be conducive to children's verbal spontaneity (Kozol, 1988). While well-planned early childhood educational programs are advantageous for all children, such programs take on a dimension of necessity in the absence of home/parental language stimulation. Child-care personnel can provide the opportunities for young homeless children to engage in rich receptive and expressive language experiences (Seefeldt & Barbour, 1990).

*Opportunities for creative experience.* During the preschool years, children aged 3 to 5 typically have abundant energy. They need time and space to undertake activities in which they can use their initiative and experience success (Erikson, 1963). Young children should have choices. They need an environment that provides stimulating and challenging activities for problem solving and creative expression (Bredekamp, 1987).

Homeless children usually have no safe place to play. By virtue of their transient existence, they can have few personal belongings or educational materials, such as books, games, and crayons (Eddowes & Hranitz, 1989). Moreover their need for creative and intellectual expression may lead to dangerous situations for them in the shelters and streets in which they live (Kozol, 1988). As with the provision of age-appropriate language development opportunities, child-care programs are designed to give young children meaningful, developmentally appropriate experiences in which to engage. Each child has a place to keep belongings. They learn to follow simple rules, begin to learn to make choices, and express themselves through creative activities (Bredekamp, 1987).

### Elementary School Children

*Security needs.* Children old enough to attend elementary school continue to need a sense of security and predictability in their lives. They are venturing into a new world. Even when coming from a stable home, some children may have difficulty adjusting to the expectations of the school setting (Seefeldt & Barbour, 1990).

Because homeless children are denied the security a home can provide, they may have little confidence that the world can be trusted. In a world of disequilibrium, the school takes on the character of a safe haven; it may be the only place a child can feel safe. Thus it is understandable that research has shown that children living in hotel shelters are likely to want to attend school (Horowitz, Springer, & Kose, 1988).

*Need for familial support.* School children need support from their families throughout the elementary grades. Parents should express interest in school activities and provide assistance to their children when appropriate. In addition, the teachers in a school should communicate regularly with parents, respect their opinions, and welcome them into the classroom (Hollingsworth & Hoover, 1991).

Children who are not getting positive feedback from their family life situations may perceive themselves as less capable than peers with homes. Teachers can fill the gap and provide the support necessary to meet both the academic and psychosocial needs. For homeless students, schools must "establish a climate of sharing, caring, and learning" (González, 1990, p. 787).

*Self-expression needs.* When children come to elementary school with a positive self-image, they are more likely to take responsibility for their own learning. Self-esteem is influenced by others and is formed by interpretations of the match between one's aspirations and actual performance. Parents can contribute to positive self-esteem when they show concern for their children, provide rules and consequences, but have respect for their children's choices within the limits set (Coopersmith, 1967).

Children who live in temporary shelters may have difficulty being considered worthwhile by the adults in charge. They get no positive feelings of self-worth from the environment. Parents may try to be supportivę but usually are constrained by shelter rules or by their own energy levels (Kozol, 1988). Schools can enhance self-esteem by including experiences that support validation of both the physical and psychological self (Seefeldt & Barbour, 1990). Acceptance by teachers and experiences of living in a classroom society with rules and choices can be helpful. Provision of activities for children to experience success, however, can be the most beneficial of all (González, 1990).

*Need for age-appropriate friendships.* Children of elementary school age are very interested in making friends. Working and relating effectively with other children is an important dimension contributing to healthy social-emotional growth. The establishment of positive relationships with peers provides a foundation for social competence. Children who fail to do this are likely to suffer the consequences of rejection. They may become delinquent and subsequently drop out of school (Bredekamp, 1987).

Homeless children face many problems regarding this need. Because they move so much, it may be difficult for them to develop friends even in the best of circumstances. Because they may come to school hungry, unkept, and with the stigma of having no permanent home, many peers may not be interested in becoming their friends or allowing them to join a group (Eddowes & Hranitz, 1989). Teachers can assist with the integration of homeless children into school programs by providing facilities for their personal hygiene. Activities promoting cooperative learning would be helpful. Cooperative learning groups can include children with different backgrounds and talents. These groups positively affect intergroup relations and the ability to relate with others (Hollingsworth & Hoover, 1991). They can be a valuable asset in assisting homeless children to develop friendships in school.

*Competence needs.* Possibly the most important need of the elementary school child is that of developing a sense of competence. As children of this age struggle to develop a sense of industry (Erikson, 1963), they need to develop the skills that the greater society believes are important to become successful. Most children can accomplish this in school.

When homeless children arrive in the classroom with feelings of inferiority and inadequacy, it is difficult for them to succeed. Attempts at developing a sense of mastery may be met with failure. School programs should emphasize the basic skills of reading, writing, and math first, so that children can succeed in other school subjects (González,

1990). Elementary school children are ready to apply themselves to given skills and tasks. They have a need for success as they work with the tools of the society (Erikson, 1963).

## When Homeless Children's Needs Are Not Met

### Young Children

*Lethargy.* When young children's bodily needs for health and nutrition are not met, they become listless, have little energy, and are not interested in activities in which healthier children usually engage. Homeless mothers all too frequently have not had good prenatal care. Many babies born to homeless mothers die within the first year of life. The infant mortality rate in New York City for these babies was found to be 30% higher than for babies born into homes (Children's Defense Fund, 1991).

All infants develop expectations that they will be fed, changed, and comforted with some measure of consistency. They become frustrated when there is little or no predictability of their caregiver's actions over time. Thus a general state of mistrust of the world develops. This has been found to result in withdrawal and depression (Erikson, 1963). Young homeless children are particularly prone to suffer from depression (Bassuk & Rubin, 1987).

*Regression.* Toddlers are moving between independence and dependence. They need a secure base to move out from as they explore their world. When the gradual and well-guided experience of free choice is missing, the child loses dignity, and a sense of doubt prevails (Erikson, 1963). All children experience regression at times. Homeless children who have few acceptable ways of expressing their independence are likely to try to exert autonomy through regressive actions. They may suck their thumbs, wet the bed, or cling to a parent.

*Aggressiveness.* Developmental delays are common in homeless children. They can occur in gross and fine motor skills, language development, and personal-social growth. Homeless preschool children have been found to have problems with sleep, shyness, withdrawal, and aggression (Bassuk & Rubin, 1987).

Children who are stifled in their desire to undertake the completion of acceptable tasks will turn their quest for suitable action into a more aggressive mode of behavior (Erikson, 1963). The preschool child wants to feel capable. When those feelings are not forthcoming, the child may translate that need into behaviors that give some measure of control over the environment, such as biting, hitting, or destroying property (Seefeldt & Barbour, 1990).

## Elementary School Children

*Anxiety.* Many homeless children have suffered the stress of suddenly being evicted from their homes and losing their furniture, clothes, toys, and books. They then move from shelter to shelter or from one area of the country to another. Some may be placed in foster care. Usually they must change schools. While attending school, they live with the fear and anxiety that the parent will be gone when they return to the shelter and/or that they will be moving again soon (Children's Defense Fund, 1991).

All elementary school children have a need to succeed. When homeless students were asked what made them feel proud, they responded the same as other students by listing good grades, parental pride, and teacher's compliments (Horowitz et al., 1988). When children's sense of industry is disrupted by continually changing schools, feelings of inadequacy will arise. The academic skills of society are difficult for some children to learn even in the best of circumstances. When homeless children are continually moving, they can have difficulty learning basic skills, and they develop feelings of inferiority (Erikson, 1963).

*Depression.* Homeless students who are failing in school or performing below average work can be very depressed. Many of the homeless children have no privacy, structure, or routine in their lives in the shelter. Add to that the acute stress of the parent and the shame they feel because they have no home. Then the inability to compete in school becomes difficult to bear (Bassuk & Rubin, 1987). Few humans desire to stay in a situation in which they experience continual failure. When this happens to homeless students in a nonsupportive school environment, the tendency of many is to want to miss school or to drop out of school altogether (Gewirtzman & Fodor, 1987).

## *Characteristics of the More Resilient Homeless Children*

Some homeless children are able to cope with their adversity better than others. They are the "invulnerable" children, those whose potential for competence is not destroyed by the problems faced by the family

(Garmezy, 1971). The invulnerable or *resilient child* is defined as "the rare child who endures hardship and emerges as a competent and effectively functioning individual" (Neiman, 1988, p. 18). What are the characteristics of the resilient child?

## Individual Differences

*Early background.* Most resilient infants have few or no handicapping defects. Those infants probably had mothers with better diets, less exposure to teratogens, and few or no infections or diseases during the infants' prenatal development (Shaffer, 1989). Although many had birth weights considered low, they survived the stress of birth and also life with limited health care in the following year. Because a number of homeless infants die before the end of their first year, those that survive may be more resilient (Neiman, 1988).

*Gender.* Girls usually manage better than boys when there are adverse conditions in the early childhood years. Boys are less well developed neurologically. They seem less able to cope with stress related to home situation and family. Boys have more problems controlling aggression. They seem to need somewhat more structure with less crowding than girls (Garmezy, Masten, & Tellegen, 1984; Werner & Smith, 1982). A male presence is an important factor in resilience in young boys. Although resilient girls have been found to be more drawn to role models who are relatively independent, resilient boys are more attracted to nurturant role models (Werner & Smith, 1982). Thus homeless boys who have an adult male presence in their lives and nurturant mothers could exhibit resilient characteristics.

*Temperament.* The term *temperament* refers to a person's modes of response to the environment. Thomas and Chess (1980) described three temperamental constellations that have been found in children. The *easy* child has a positive approach to new situations, high adaptability to change, and a moderately positive mood. The *slow to warm up* temperament comprises a combination of mildly negative responses and slow adaptability to new situations. The *difficult* child exhibits negative withdrawal to new situations, nonadaptability, and intense, frequent negative expressions of mood. Easy children are likely to be the most resilient in a homeless family situation. They are pleasant to be around and are able to develop good coping abilities. Children who tend to withdraw from new situations would not adapt well in a continuously changing environment.

**Environmental Factors**

*Family interaction.* Characteristics that children bring into the world help determine their capacity for resiliency. Each child interacts differently with the people and events in the environment. The reciprocal exchange between mother and child in the development of attachment is of critical importance in relationship to resiliency. Early bonding, which leads to secure attachment, is promoted by the consistency and availability of an adult's presence during the first 6 months of life (Lamb & Bornstein, 1987). Early bonding leads to the perception of security in the infant, builds trust, and provides support during brief separations. Thus the child is provided the basis for developing coping strategies in stressful situations (Murphy & Moriarty, 1976).

Siblings can also be a source of support for children in developing resiliency. They sometimes substitute for the emotionally stressed homeless parent (Neiman, 1988). Stress is not always bad. Children with a past history of coping successfully in moderately stressful situations are likely to be more resilient than others (Murphy & Moriarty, 1976).

*Other supportive influences.* Relationships outside the family circle may provide emotional support for homeless children. Day-care personnel, teachers, clergy, and other supportive adults can help children during the disruption in their lives. Experiences providing for the development of autonomy, competence, and success are necessary (Erikson, 1963). Day-care centers and schools can provide support to assist children in the development of resiliency.

## Problems in Providing Successful Educational Programs

**Child-Care Programs**

*Availability and accessibility.* Some problems in providing child care to homeless children are similar to those of providing child care generally. It must be available when and where it is needed. For homeless families, availability means that child care for preschool children must be close to their shelter or other temporary home.

Even though child-care centers or family day-care homes may be available, they may not be accessible to a homeless parent. *Accessibility* means the programs have openings for children. Most child-care programs are licensed by the state for a certain number of children. The number is based on such considerations as space and adult-child ratios. Far more children are in need of care than spaces are available for them (Hofferth, 1989). Because homeless families usually need child care for an indeterminant length of time, space may not be available when it is needed.

*Cost and quality.* If space is available in a good location, is it affordable? And what is the quality of the program? Homeless families can afford little or no payment for child care. Yet direct assistance of the states in providing low-cost child care varies. The demand usually exceeds the supply (Children's Defense Fund, 1991).

Of even more concern is the quality of a program. State-licensed centers ensure only a minimum standard of quality. Child-care personnel usually are undertrained and underpaid. The field has a high turnover rate (Whitebook & Granger, 1989). A standard of quality that exceeds "minimum" has been determined by the accreditation system of the National Academy of Early Childhood Programs (National Association for the Education of Young Children, 1984) to ensure the following:

positive interactions among staff and children
developmentally appropriate curriculum
staff-parent interaction
trained personnel
effective administration
sufficient staff for number and ages of children
physical environment to foster optimum development
health and safety
good nutrition and food service
systematic evaluation of program

To meet the needs of young homeless children as outlined earlier in the chapter, some measure of quality must be available in the child-care programs accessible to them.

**Elementary School Programs**

*Accessibility.* Access to public school programs for homeless children can be difficult. Because homeless families move quite often, they may not bother enrolling the children in public schools (Eddowes & Hranitz, 1989). Some children are caught between the old school or district and the one where they are temporarily housed. In some instances, a child must continue to attend the previous school until the residency is resolved. Although attendance at the school is free, it may require the use of public transportation, which the parents cannot afford (Kozol, 1988; Stronge & Tenhouse, 1990).

The Stewart B. McKinney Homeless Assistance Act of 1987 (P. L. 100-77) requires that homeless children be guaranteed access to education. Many schools, however, are not complying with the law. In addition to residency requirements, schools still may also require birth certificates, immunization records, and records from the previous school attended (Children's Defense Fund, 1991).

*Health concerns.* When homeless children are accepted in school, a number of health and related concerns may impede their learning. They may be malnourished, have unattended medical and dental needs, poor hygiene, poor health, or have been neglected or abused (Tower & White, 1989). The stresses of living in unstable, crowded, and unhealthy conditions are compounded by little or no trust, little parental support, low self-esteem, few friends, and difficulty with learning (Bassuk & Rubin, 1987; Gewirtzman & Fodor, 1987).

*Inappropriate class placements.* Because homeless children may move unexpectedly, transfer records may not be available. A child arrives at a new school with no recorded information concerning age, grade level, or scholastic ability. This can result in an inappropriate grade placement. Homeless children coming from other districts or from other schools within a district may have been using different curricula and/or textbooks. It is important for teachers in the new school to recognize and validate the work the child has already completed (Tower & White, 1989).

*Homework.* Homeless children have great difficulty completing homework. Usually lacking where they live are a place to do it, a table and chair, and privacy or quiet space. Reference materials may not be available, and the parents may be unable to provide any assistance. Teachers should have an understanding of this problem and find ways to provide supplementary materials and/or a supervised place in which children can complete the homework at school (Kozol, 1988).

## Considerations in Developing Solutions

### Child-Care Programs

Homeless families with preschool children need accessible, affordable child-care programs. These may be child-care centers or family day-care homes. The spaces for the children must be there when the need arises and for as long as necessary if homeless parents are to get real assistance.

*Child-care personnel.* Personnel working in such programs should provide consistent, sensitive, individualized relationships with the children. A relatively stable schedule is necessary, with the same staff members caring for the same children daily. Staff members should have an understanding of children at risk from varied stresses in the environment and should know accepted methods of providing appropriate stimulation (Bromwich, 1988). At least one staff member should be male to support the development of resiliency in boys (Neiman, 1988). Some staff training is necessary, and wages must be high enough to curb potential staff turnover (Whitebook, Howes, Phillips, & Pemberton, 1989). Workshops for personnel caring for homeless children might be provided through local agencies, colleges, or professional organizations.

*Meeting varied needs.* The child-care programs serving homeless families should provide for both basic and personal needs of the children. Of prime importance is food in enough quantity to meet most of the daily nutritional needs of the children. Many homeless children are malnourished both before and after birth. Good nutrition can reduce growth retardation and disability in later life (Children's Defense Fund, 1991). Staff should model safe health practices and encourage the children in hand washing, tooth brushing, and other types of personal hygiene (National Association for the Education of Young Children, 1984). Provision should be available for washing and drying children's clothes. A place should be provided for each child's personal belongings.

*Developmentally appropriate practice.* Ample space must be available for activities that promote gross and fine motor development. A variety of equipment should provide for problem solving and creative expression. Children need to make choices and should have support in completion of tasks. Simple rules for behavior and care of the physical environment are important. Staff members should model standard English and provide a variety of daily language activities, including stories, finger plays, puppets, and songs (Bredekamp, 1987).

*Links with parents and community agencies.* Program personnel must reach out to the parents of the homeless children and be supportive in any way possible. The biggest problem in providing child care for homeless families is the cost. In most instances, *affordable care* means "no cost." To provide such care with the quality necessary to make a real difference for homeless children, social, health, and educational agencies must work together. One center might be accessible to several homeless shelters (Gordon, 1991). Perhaps space could be found in an elementary school. Although public school funds probably would not be available to cover the expenses, Title XX of the Social Security Act of 1975 provides funds for child care which might be used. When little or no tax support is available, creative solutions must be found if homeless children are to survive the early years and have the experiences necessary to be successful in elementary school programs.

## Elementary School Programs

*Administrative concerns.* Elementary school programs must be accessible to homeless children. Even though the McKinney Act of 1987 (P.L. 100-77) guarantees homeless children access to public education, three fifths of the states were not in compliance with the law by the end of 1989 (Children's Defense fund, 1991).

Texas provides an example of what can be done. The Texas Office of Assistance to Homeless Children has developed a statewide data base that enables school districts to get immunization records and other data from a centralized source within the state (Children's Defense Fund, 1991). Where requirements preclude admission to a public school, policies must be reviewed and revised to enable homeless children to attend school.

Sometimes it is in the child's best interest to remain in the school attended before moving (near the end of the school year). If a school district cannot provide transportation for children attending schools outside their temporary home attendance zone, then perhaps shelters can provide transportation by van, or a community agency can provide passes for public transportation. Children should not be deprived of an education because of problems with transportation (National Coalition for the Homeless, 1987).

*Teacher sensitivity.* School teachers and other personnel usually have had little training for working with the problems of homeless children. It is important that teachers know what is appropriate for these individuals in their classrooms. School personnel should have training workshops available that sensitize them to the problems of homelessness, as well as provide ways to teach the children. A tour of homeless shelters might promote a better understanding (Gewirtzman & Fodor, 1987).

As a homeless child begins attendance at an elementary school, it is important that someone in the school observe the child to discover what assistance is required to meet specific basic and personal needs. Facilities for personal hygiene, clothes, breakfast and lunch, books, school supplies, and/or individual counseling may be needed (Zeldin & Bogart, 1990).

*School programs.* Several approaches have been used to provide education for homeless elementary school students. Sometimes a school program is organized on the premises of a homeless shelter or near several temporary homeless facilities. These schools provide transitional programs. Students usually attend them for a relatively short period of time (Stronge & Tenhouse, 1990). Many transitional schools provide programs based on the "one-room school" model, with children of all grade levels taught at the same time (National Coalition for the Homeless, 1987).

Within a school, students are more likely to be mainstreamed into appropriate grade placements. They are screened as they enter the school. Sometimes a team approach is used. They may stay in a temporary classroom for a short time within a school until they become accustomed to the routines (Zeldin & Bogart, 1990). To integrate a homeless child into a classroom, a fellow student may be assigned as the new student's "special friend." In this way, the newcomer is made to feel welcome (González, 1990).

*Individualization and support.* Sensitive teachers can do much to make the homeless students' school experiences successful. They can provide a stable, structured, and nonthreatening environment in the classroom (Gewirtzman & Fodor, 1987). Space can be provided for personal possessions. Lessons can be tailored to individual needs in order to prevent failure. Cooperative group projects can allow for support from other students in the class, as well as for friendship. The teacher can listen to problems and concerns and seek professional help if necessary (Tower & White, 1989).

Parents of homeless children should be involved in the educational program whenever possible. They are not, however, usually able to help their children with homework. Because homeless children are usually behind in their studies and have no place to do homework, tutoring assistance can be helpful. A homework assistance program can be offered within a school, through a community agency, or on the premises of a homeless shelter (Zeldin & Bogart, 1990).

## Summary

Both the young homeless children and those of elementary school age have needs that must be met. When parents cannot provide the necessary support, community educational, social, and health agencies must work together in providing viable programs. If the cycle of homelessness is to be broken, homeless families must believe that education is a valuable resource. Their children should have an opportunity for success in their educational experiences.

## References

Bassuk, E., & Rubin, L. (1987). Homeless children: A neglected population. *American Journal of Orthopsychiatry, 57,* 279-286.

Brazelton, T. B. (1987). *Working and caring.* Reading, MA: Addison-Wesley.

Bredekamp, S. (Ed.). (1987). *Developmentally appropriate practice in early childhood programs serving children from birth through age 8* (rev. ed.). Washington, DC: National Association for the Education of Young Children.

Bromwich, R. (1988). High-risk or handicapped infants. In A. Godwin & L. Schrag (Eds.), *Setting up for infant care: Guidelines for centers and family day care homes* (pp. 28-29). Washington, DC: National Association for the Education of Young Children.

Children's Defense Fund. (1991). *The state of America's children 1991.* Washington, DC: Author.

Coopersmith, S. (1967). *The antecedents of self-esteem.* San Francisco: Freeman.

Eddowes, E. A., & Hranitz, J. R. (1989). Educating children of the homeless. *Childhood Education, 65,* 197-200.

Erikson, E. H. (1963). *Childhood and society* (2nd ed.). New York: Norton.

Garmezy, N. (1971). Vulnerability research and the issue of primary prevention. *American Journal of Orthopsychiatry, 41*(1), 101-116.

Garmezy, N., Masten, A. S., & Tellegen, A. (1984). The study of stress and competence in children: A building block for developmental psychopathology. *Child Development, 55,* 97-111.

Gewirtzman, R., & Fodor, I. (1987). The homeless child at school: From welfare hotel to classroom. *Child Welfare, 66,* 237-245.

González, M. (1990). School + home = a program for educating homeless students. *Phi Delta Kappan, 71*(10), 785-787.

Gordon, L., Khokha, E., Schrag, L., & Weeks, E. (1988). Elements to consider in establishing environments for infants. In A. Godwin & L. Schrag (Eds.), *Setting up for infant care: Guidelines for centers and family day care homes* (pp. 33-44). Washington, DC: National Association for the Education of Young Children.

Gordon, T. (1991, May 7). "No one is exempt": Day care for homeless proves lifesaver for many. *The Birmingham News,* pp. 1B-2B.

Hofferth, S. L. (1989). What is the demand for and supply of child care in the United States? *Young Children, 44*(5), 28-33.

Hollingsworth, P. M., & Hoover, K. H. (1991). *Elementary teaching methods.* Boston: Allyn & Bacon.

Horowitz, S. V., Springer, C. M., & Kose, G. (1988). Stress in hotel children: The effects of homelessness on attitudes toward school. *Children's Environments Quarterly, 5*(1), 34-36.

Kozol, J. (1988). *Rachel and her children: Homeless families in America.* New York: Crown.

Lamb, M. E., & Bornstein, M. H. (1987). *Development in infancy: An introduction* (2nd ed.). New York: Random House.

Murphy, L. B., & Moriarty, A. E. (1976). *Vulnerability, coping, & growth: From infancy to adolescence.* New Haven, CT: Yale University Press.

National Association for the Education of Young Children. (1984). *Accreditation criteria and procedures of the National Academy of Early Childhood programs.* Washington, DC: Author.

National Coalition for the Homeless. (1987). *Broken lives: Denial of education to homeless children.* Washington, DC: Author.

Neiman, L. (1988). A critical review of resiliency literature and its relevance to homeless children. *Children's Environments Quarterly, 5*(1), 17-25.

Seefeldt, C., & Barbour, N. (1990). *Early childhood education: An introduction* (2nd ed.). Columbus, OH: Charles E. Merrill.

Shaffer, D. R. (1989). *Developmental psychology: Childhood and adolescence* (2nd ed.). Belmont, CA: Brooks/Cole.

Stewart B. McKinney Homeless Assistance Act of 1987, 722 (e), 7 U.S.C. (1987).

Stronge, J. H., & Tenhouse, C. (1990). *Educating homeless children: Issues and answers.* Bloomington, IN: Phi Delta Kappa Educational Foundation.

Thomas, A., & Chess, S. (1980). *The dynamics of psychological development.* New York: Brunner/Mazel.

Tower, C. C., & White, D. J. (1989). *Homeless students.* Washington, DC: National Education Association.

Weiser, M. G. (1991). *Infant/toddler care and education.* New York: Macmillan.

Werner, E. E., & Smith, T. S. (1982). *Vulnerable, but invincible: A longitudinal study of resilient children and youth.* New York: McGraw-Hill.

Whitebook, M., & Granger, R. C. (1989). "Mommy, who's going to be my teacher today?" Assessing teacher turnover. *Young Children, 44*(4), 11-14.

Whitebook, M., Howes, C., Phillips, D., & Pemberton, D. (1989). Who cares? Child care teachers and the quality of care in America. *Young Children, 45*(1), 41-45.

Zeldin, S., & Bogart, J. (1990). *Education and community support for homeless children and youth: Profiles of 15 innovative and promising approaches.* Washington, DC: Policy Studies Associates. (ERIC Document Reproduction Service No. ED 322 249)

# 7

# *Adolescence and Homelessness*

## *The Unique Challenge for Secondary Educators*

JANE L. POWERS
BARBARA JAKLITSCH

### *The Need for Educational Services*

Over the past decade, the growing recognition that a significant percentage of the homeless population in the United States consists of children and families (McChesney, 1986; U.S. Conference of Mayors, 1987; U.S. Congress, 1986) has brought about legislative initiatives and the desperately needed services of housing, counseling, medical care, and education (e.g., Stewart B. McKinney Homeless Assistance Act of 1987). Despite increased attention from the media, policymakers, and practitioners, one segment of the homeless population has remained largely invisible and underserved: homeless adolescents. Difficult to locate, perhaps living underground, homeless adolescents can be extremely hard to reach because they tend not to trust adults and traditional service systems. The absence of services for these troubled youth is particularly notable in an area critical for helping them break out of the cycle of poverty, hopelessness, and despair: education.

Although the Stewart B. McKinney Act (1987) established a national policy requiring that each state educational agency provide homeless children and youth access to a free and appropriate public school education, adolescents have often not been the recipients of these educational services. On review of state plans and model programs, very few states have developed programs and services for the education of homeless adolescents after the eighth grade (e.g., Zeldin & Bogart, 1990). Almost all educational services are designed to meet the needs of younger homeless children, from kindergarten through eighth grade. Provision for secondary education is virtually ignored.

Studies have demonstrated that most homeless adolescents do not attend school; those who do are below grade level for their age (Ely, 1987; Shaffer & Caton, 1984; U.S. General Accounting Office, 1989). As a consequence of being homeless, these youth tend to miss significant amounts of school. They fall behind, become discouraged, and eventually drop out of the system. Rather than offering opportunities for advancement, schools become a place of humiliation and failure. Even if motivated to attend school, many homeless youth are denied access to education because they lack a permanent address or do not live with their families (Bucy, 1987). The lack of proper documents, such as proof of immunization, grade reports, and special education evaluations, often required prior to registration, can also prevent young people from attending school. Homeless youth who do not live with their families face even greater obstacles in obtaining records because they are not likely to have the necessary identification documents or the required information to obtain them. Estranged guardians often refuse to provide the necessary documents. Some states even require students to be registered in school by a legal parent or guardian or require a parent's signature to reenroll students after they have been suspended or have dropped out (Ely, 1987; Stronge & Tenhouse, 1990).

These barriers to school attendance and lack of secondary educational services for homeless adolescents are costly for both our young people and our society. The high school years are critical in preparing youth for their transition to adulthood and the assumption of adult roles and responsibilities. Schools are the primary vehicle for socializing youth and for providing the requisite academic and vocational skills and training that will lead to their eventual independence. Without a high school education, homeless adolescents are at a significant disadvantage in the labor market and may be denied the opportunity of becoming productive, contributing members of society. Instead these young people may become a drain on society, perpetually depending on public services; they could become a threat to society if drawn into criminal activity or the illegal economy.

## Recognition of the Problem

Although homelessness among adolescents is not a new social problem, over the past several decades it has increased in volume, scope, and visibility. During the 1960s, the number of young people running away from home rose significantly. Most of these youth took to the streets as a form of rebellion and political protest. The runaway population primarily consisted of middle-class youth, and the majority had homes to which they could return. The problems faced by runaways generated sufficient concern for Congress to pass the Runaway Youth Act (1974), which created a funding stream for providing grants and technical assistance to communities and nonprofit agencies for meeting the needs of runaway youth outside the juvenile justice system.

During the 1970s, agencies serving runaway youth began to observe changes in the makeup of the runaway population. The phenomenon of *throwaway youth* began to emerge, referring to those young people who had been forced to leave their homes with the intent they not return. These youth had no homes or families to which they could return. It became clear that these throwaway/homeless youth were different from traditional runaways: They were in need of more intensive and more comprehensive services and were at much greater risk because they were disconnected from family and lacked support. In response to the recognition that many runaways were really throwaways, Congress reenacted the Runaway Youth Act in 1980, broadening its scope and renaming it the Runaway and Homeless Youth Act (P.L. 96-509). As involvement with the population intensified and services grew, so did knowledge about the complexity of the problems faced by runaway and homeless youth, their increasing numbers, the seriousness of their home situations, and the dangers and exploitation to which they are subject while on the run (Janus, McCormack, Burgess, & Hartman, 1987).

During the 1980s, economic and social forces, reductions in human services, and lack of affordable housing contributed to a significant rise in familial and youth homelessness. Street perils, such as crack and AIDS, have further compounded the problems faced by the population of homeless adolescents. Current epidemiological data on homeless youth are imprecise because of the transient nature of this population and the fact that many are not connected to shelters, schools, or human service systems. Be that as it may, recent attempts to measure the extent of the problem suggest that each year in the United States at least

500,000 (Finkelhor, Hotaling, & Sedlak, 1990) to 1 million (Solarz, 1988; U.S. Department of Health and Human Services, 1984), and perhaps as many as several million youth between the ages of 10 and 17 are living on the streets, in abandoned buildings, or in welfare hotels (National Network of Runaway and Youth Services, 1988).

These numbers, which may underestimate the true prevalence of the problem, are alarming in view of the lethal risks associated with life on the street and the degree to which the lives of young people are jeopardized and their futures cut short. Ill-equipped to survive on their own, homeless adolescents are easy targets for victimization and exploitation. To secure food and shelter, increasing numbers of street youth resort to prostitution, the drug trade, and other forms of criminal activity (Janus et al., 1987). The vast majority of homeless teens are at high risk for such self-destructive behaviors as suicide (Shaffer & Caton, 1984; Yates, MacKenzie, Pennbridge, & Cohen, 1988), substance abuse (Robertson, 1989; Shaffer & Caton, 1984; Yates et al., 1988), mental health problems (Mundy, Robertson, Roberts, & Greenblatt, 1990; Solarz, 1988), and physical health problems, including AIDS.

## Reasons for Youth Homelessness

Adolescents become homeless for a myriad of reasons. Although some are part of homeless families, the vast majority are "unaccompanied youth" living independently of their families. Some of these young people are on their own because of the lack of shelter facilities for families. Although families constitute 30% of the homeless population, the federal government reports that only 8% of shelters nationwide can accommodate families. Consequently homeless families are forced to separate in order to receive shelter (Foscarinis, 1987). Many of the shelters that do serve families will not accept older children, particularly adolescent boys who are considered too disruptive to other shelter residents. The dysfunctional nature of their families can cause adolescents to become homeless. A large percentage of unaccompanied homeless youth are fleeing from violent and abusive home situations; others have been subject to severe neglect and have for all intents and purposes been abandoned as they were "pushed out" of their homes and "thrown away" by their families (Bucy, 1987). Although these throwaway youth are predominantly adolescent males (Powers, Eckenrode, & Jaklitsch, 1990), female adolescents may be forced to leave home because of teen pregnancy and parenthood. It has become clear to service providers that many of these young people come from families that are so torn apart by economic and marital problems, substance abuse, domestic violence, and mental illness that going home is not a viable option. A large number of youth who are living on the streets have spent many years in foster care or substitute care, where they may have been subject to frequent disruptions and a cycle of multiple placements (Barth, 1988; Cook, 1986; Festinger, 1983). Although unprepared to function independently, these youth may have ejected themselves prematurely from placement and run to the streets.

### Unique Problems of Homeless Adolescents: Implications for Educators

Even under the best of circumstances, working with adolescents can be challenging within and outside of the classroom. Their rebelliousness, defiance of authority, testing of limits, and sometimes obnoxious behavior can be trying for the most patient and understanding educator. Take away stability, security, and the basic necessities for survival— add an abusive, dysfunctional family; a hostile, exploitive street life; and an anonymous service delivery system: The end product is a hornet's nest of problems that most educators would find difficult. An understanding of the problems faced by homeless adolescents and recognition of the difficulties in working with them may shed light on how to plan for and more effectively meet their educational needs.

The terms *runaway* and *homeless* frequently are used interchangeably, but some important distinctions have educational implications. *Runaways* have viable families to which to return, while the truly *homeless* youth do not. Homeless youth are believed to have greater service needs and to be at greater risk, but a single runaway incident is serious, and every effort should be made to resolve responsibly the problems that led to the behavior. A young person who is a chronic runaway is choosing street life over home life and therefore should be treated as a homeless youth who will need more intensive services. One of the difficulties in planning for the education of these youth is related to whether the young person ultimately will return home. It must be decided whether (a) it is worth keeping the youth in his or her home school (which may require extensive travel) or (b) educational plans should be developed without concern for geographic location.

The length of time a young person has been homeless is another significant variable to be considered in determining educational needs. The longer youth have been on the street, the harder they may be to reach and to serve. Young people who have become homeless as adolescents are most likely to have had recent educational disruption, while youth who have experienced intermittent homelessness over several years are likely to have had more extensive educational disruption and be in greater need for services. The population at greatest risk for educational failure is the emerging group of younger adolescents who have been homeless most if not all of their lives as they continue the pattern of unaccompanied homelessness into adolescence.

**Life on the Street**

For many homeless youth, the street has replaced the school as a source of education and identity. Having experienced limited academic success, these youth may be lured by the rewards of street culture. In a world of violence, instability, and poverty, the most important skill to master is survival. Successful survival on the street can result in status, power, and money. Many homeless adolescents have become involved in prostitution and the drug trade to support themselves and survive (Cohen, 1987; Janus et al., 1987). It is not uncommon for these youth to earn hundreds of dollars in the course of one night, selling either drugs or their bodies. The incentives to go to school are minimal in light of the "rewards" of the street. Role models on the street are people who have achieved status through illegal means, not as a result of their education. It is not an easy task to motivate young people to leave the street, to enter the classroom, and above all, to value education.

One consequence of street culture that has major implications for educating adolescents is substance abuse. Drugs are an integral part of life on the street. Drug involvement may prohibit young people from attending school at all. Those young people who do attend school are much more likely to be under the influence of drugs or alcohol that will affect their performance in the classroom and their abilities to focus, comprehend, and learn.

**Developmental Lags**

Adolescence is a time of tremendous changes in physical, psychological, cognitive, and social development. Ideally these changes are facilitated by both the school and the family. Homeless adolescents are at a double disadvantage, having the support of neither families nor school; they are likely to fall behind developmentally and not complete the normal tasks of adolescence (e.g., form their identity). Research has demonstrated that homeless children experience significant developmental delays (e.g., Bassuk & Rubin, 1987; Fox, Barrnett, Davies, & Bird, 1990; Rescorla, Parker, & Stolley, 1991). Adolescents also are likely to suffer from general developmental delays as a consequence of homelessness. The lack of basic resources—food, shelter, clothing, a place to study, and a stable family—take their toll on academic performance. Prolonged periods of absence or constant change in schools results in discontinuous instruction and may create learning gaps that necessitate remediation. Because of their inability to adapt to a "normal" classroom, some young people may be expelled before they have had adequate special education testing and assistance.

It is important for educators to recognize that at any given moment they may be dealing with an adolescent who is at multiple developmental levels, depending on his or her life experience. A 16-year-old youth may function socially like an 11-year-old, intellectually like a 9-year-old, sexually like a 25-year-old, and emotionally like a 3-year-old. Educators need to assess developmental level constantly in order to respond appropriately to a young person's needs. Such assessments may be particularly difficult to identify if masked by physical size and maturity, bravado, or a hard exterior.

### Emotional and Psychological Problems

The experience of being homeless may cause young people to feel confused, insecure, and out of control of their lives. Under these stressful emotional conditions, learning can be extremely difficult if not impossible. Among the homeless youth population currently seen by educators and service providers, a large percentage have experienced physical abuse, sexual abuse, and/or neglect (Farber, Kinast, McCoard, & Falkner, 1984; Garbarino, Wilson, & Garbarino, 1986; Janus et al., 1987; National Network of Runaway and Youth Services, 1988). Some have been abused in placement, in the very settings designed to protect them. The resulting barriers to academic success are compounded when the consequences of being homeless are considered in consort with the common effects of maltreatment, some of which are discussed below.

*Depression.* Researchers have found that depression is one of the most common psychological effects of both adolescent homelessness (Mundy et al., 1990; Shaffer & Caton, 1984; Yates et al., 1988) and maltreatment (Browne & Finkelhor, 1986; Farber & Joseph, 1985; Fisher, Berdie, Cook, & Day, 1980; Moran & Eckenrode, 1987). Although depression may be variously disguised during adolescence, it is nevertheless the prevailing condition and must be addressed. Depression can result in poor academic performance and can cause youth to be distracted, lack motivation, and be indifferent to their situation. Other consequences of depression include substance abuse, sexual acting out, withdrawal, and such self-destructive behaviors as self-mutilation and suicide.

*Low self-esteem.* The erosion of self-esteem frequently occurs among homeless adolescents and is often associated with depression. It is common for these young people to engage in behaviors that reinforce a poor self-image, particularly in a school setting. They may blame themselves for their situation, and this continuing distortion of reality further contributes to the lowering of self-esteem to the point of immobilization. They approach situations feeling inferior even if they mask it with bravado. It is not easy for these youth to give up the comfortable view of themselves as worthless and to view themselves with a more positive self-image (Gil, 1983).

*Loss of trust.* Homeless youth have learned to anticipate a lack of stability and not to trust adults. If they have experienced abuse or neglect from an early age, they may find that trust is impossible. Their experiences with parental figures have taught them not to rely on adults for support, guidance, and protection. Those youth who have been in care or placement from early ages have learned to distrust adults, having been betrayed by a system in which seemingly caring adults more often than not disappear from their lives (Raychaba, 1988). Homeless youth are not likely to have experienced the healthy attachments with adults that help an individual cope with stress, frustration, and fear and that provide the foundations on which future relationships are built. They are likely to have tremendous difficulties attaching to anyone or getting their needs met. In a school setting, such young people may have difficulty learning in small group settings or even in one-to-one situations. These youth may test relationships until the most patient teacher is exhausted.

*Feelings of futurelessness.* Raised in homeless, substance-abusing, and violent families, these young people may have tremendous feelings of hopelessness. Having learned to expect little or nothing of what they hoped for as children, they find it difficult to see beyond the present and have little faith in the future (Jaklitsch & Beyer, 1990). An attitude of "why bother" may interfere with their ability to focus on school and to perceive any value in education. The very nature of the school setting as a place of preparation for adulthood is in conflict with the feelings of futurelessness that are caused by the experience of being homeless.

*Survivor guilt.* Many of these young people may act as if their family situations have established a ceiling on their future success. Some believe that they are destined for a life of violence and instability. This world view effectively prevents young people from being more successful than their families. Unconsciously they view success as a criticism of their families' limitations and feel that it would be disloyal for them to go beyond their place in life. These feelings, described by Beyer (1986) as "survivor guilt," can prevent homeless adolescents from succeeding academically.

## Behavioral Problems

The physical and environmental realities of being homeless can contribute to behavioral problems. Physical illness, poor hygiene, and malnutrition can result in listlessness, withdrawn behavior, and physical conditions that are not conducive to learning. Educators working with homeless adolescents are likely to confront violent behavior, which can take several different forms.

*Aggression.* The combination of homelessness and maltreatment can cause adolescents to feel tremendously angry. They may direct their anger outward, which results in violent outbursts and aggressive behaviors. When they are in school, these behaviors frequently lead to rejection by teachers and difficulties with peers, resulting ultimately in suspension or expulsion. They might also turn their anger inward and engage in self-destructive behaviors, including suicide.

*Suicide.* Suffering from depression and without hope for the future, homeless adolescents may not want to continue living. Several studies have reported high rates of suicidal behavior among unaccompanied homeless youth (Janus et al., 1987; Mundy et al., 1990; Shaffer & Caton, 1984). Maltreated adolescents are at particular risk for suicidal thoughts and attempts (Anderson, 1981). It is essential that school personnel be trained in identifying and handling suicidal behavior. Immediate action should be taken with young people who communicate suicidal thoughts and or have a specific suicide plan.

**Stigmatization**

Adolescence is a time of heightened self-awareness, when young people are greatly concerned about their body image and appearance. The lack of cleanliness, clothing, and physical attractiveness as a result of being homeless can be disconcerting and painful for these youth. Many feel different, are ridiculed by their peers, and may be ostracized for being a "shelter kid" or homeless. Rather than face this kind of humiliation and stigmatization, many young people choose not to go to school or remain as anonymous and detached as possible.

**Teen Parenthood**

Given their risk for sexual exploitation, homeless female teens are extremely vulnerable to premature pregnancy and parenthood. Homeless pregnant teens are among the highest risk group for low birth weight babies and high infant mortality rates. Extensive work has been done in the area of teen pregnancy, and programs and innovative models have been developed to keep teenage mothers in school. These programs have addressed the issues of ensuring child care that is critical to a teen mom's educational participation and success.

*Program and Policy Recommendations*

Clearly, hurdles remain to be overcome in providing educational services to adolescents, but they are not insurmountable. Many homeless teenagers want to attend school. In 1984, the New York Psychiatric Institute conducted a study of all adolescents using youth shelters in New York City and found that 69% of these youth wished to finish high school and 41% hoped to graduate from college (Shaffer & Caton, 1984). Some homeless youth find school a haven—as a place to belong, to be "normal," and to be like everyone else. A study of survivors of abuse relates the story of a young man who had been pushed out of his home and was living on the streets. Though struggling to survive on a daily basis, he nevertheless managed to attend school every day, claiming that it provided the only source of stability and security in his life (Powers & Jaklitsch, 1989). Another survivor from this study, a 17-year-old homeless female who had spent years on the street as a prostitute and suffered from a severe substance abuse problem, had the following to say about school:

I used to cry when we got snow days because I wanted to go to school. I got my GED in 1983 and I've gone to college for criminal justice, I have gone through two semesters for criminal justice because . . . someday I want to become a lawyer. At the present moment I don't have any plans. One of these days I am sure I will just get tired of working and go to school again. One of these days, I am going to become a lawyer. But I am happy right now, stable . . . I'm definitely in control. I'd like to be a criminal lawyer, and I want to work with kids. I would like to defend kids, because I feel some of them get bad deals . . . like me. (Powers & Jaklitsch, 1989, pp. 77-78)

The provision of educational services to homeless adolescents can be facilitated in several ways, some of which are described below.

## Improved Networking and Communication

The community-based agencies that typically serve homeless youth include runaway and homeless youth programs and adult shelters, as well as independent living, substance abuse, and prostitution/street outreach programs. These programs often hire young staff who when appropriately trained can relate more easily to and better assist homeless youth. Well-established programs often have a reputation "on the street" as a place that can help young people without judging them or forcing them to compromise their self-control or self-determination. Educational services will be enhanced if educators and service providers collaborate through interagency task forces, youth study, or interdisciplinary teams on both a community and individual case basis. If homeless young people are to remain involved educationally, it is essential that schools develop working relationships with the agencies that provide services to troubled youth.

## Education and Training of School Personnel

In communities and school districts that have a significant number of homeless youth, education and training on the topic of homelessness and specifically homeless adolescents should be offered to school personnel. Such training could be provided by community-based agencies that have experience working with homeless youth. Training models that encourage the coordination of services, such as bringing together service providers and educators to share their general expertise, can be particularly effective around the issue of homelessness.

It is important for teachers to be aware of and to understand the problems faced by homeless adolescents. They need to provide a safe and secure environment for these youth and to encourage them to stay in school. If informed teachers who are aware of the ostracism experienced by homeless students can sensitize their colleagues, administrators, and community leaders to the issues of homelessness, some of the pressure homeless students feel from their peers might be minimized.

### Relaxation of Legal Barriers

The previously mentioned legal barriers to educating homeless youth must be addressed. This can be achieved through greater coordination with community agencies, followed by legislative and regulatory advocacy. Some states have legal advocacy groups that have the information and expertise to assist with these efforts. Although existing networks and organizations that advocate for the homeless have adopted this challenge, the struggle to relax the legal barriers to educating homeless children and youth continues.

### Alternative Schools

Alternative high schools may be a viable option for meeting the educational needs of homeless youth. Alternative schools can provide homeless adolescents with increased individual attention and specialized counseling services. Many alternative schools work closely with community agencies and provide instruction on social skills, self-esteem, conflict resolution, and other special subjects designed to address behavior management issues that may hinder learning.

The employment of special tutors represents another approach often used in runaway and homeless youth shelters. Some school districts are willing to provide special tutoring services for shelter programs that serve homeless youth. This can allow for more integrated services as the tutors can function as part of the shelter program.

### Mentoring Programs

Studies that have examined factors contributing to the resiliency of at-risk youth who have overcome adversity and have succeeded despite poverty and dysfunctional home conditions have reported a clear and consistent finding: Resilient youth somehow have found and maintained a positive relationship with adults other than their parents (e.g.,

Werner & Smith, 1982). This finding has led to an increased appreciation of the *mentoring* concept, which is based on a young person building a one-on-one relationship with a caring, nurturing adult. Because homeless youth are particularly distrustful of adults, especially adult authority figures, mentoring programs may be extremely valuable if carried out in a nonthreatening, nonauthoritarian manner.

## Increased Opportunities for Counseling Services

Special counseling services should be offered to adolescents that will help them deal with the physical, social, and emotional stresses of being homeless.

## Life Skills Training

Homeless adolescents are in need of practical "life skills" in the areas of employment, money management, housing, household management, health, and community resources. Such skills can be taught in a variety of settings. Many schools and shelters are focusing increasingly on teaching life skills so that young people are equipped with the basic knowledge to function on their own. In some settings, life skills training can be a vehicle for teaching other basic skills, such as decision making, problem solving, and goal setting and planning.

Several available curricula and materials are designed specifically for teaching life skills to homeless adolescents. For example, OASIS Center, Inc., a youth-serving agency in Nashville, Tennessee, developed a useful resource entitled *Meeting Life's Challenges: A Youth Worker's Manual for Empowering Youth and Families.* Published in 1988, this manual is distributed by the University of Oklahoma, National Resource Center for Youth Services. Another useful resource that was written specifically for homeless youth is *Heading Out: A Guidebook for Living on Your Own.* This manual was developed in 1987 by Laura Castleman for The Sanctuary, a runaway and homeless youth program in Royal Oak, Michigan.

## Youth Involvement

Homeless young people often feel powerless and out of control. These feelings can be addressed by involving the youth in the planning and provision of services, particularly around their education. Models for this approach include youth advisory boards, youth drama groups, and peer counseling programs. Involvement in educational planning and decision making may help homeless adolescents regain control and encourage them to want to go to school.

## Model Programs for Homeless Adolescents

We have identified two model programs that provide educational services to homeless adolescents. These programs demonstrate how some of our recommendations have been implemented in an actual program setting.

Career Education Center, New York City

250 West 18th Street, New York, NY 10011 (212) 727-7200. Contact Sherry Zekowski

The Career Education Center (CEC) in New York City educates homeless youth at 27 sites throughout Manhattan, the Bronx, Queens, and Brooklyn. The key to the success of this program lies in its flexibility, responsiveness, and ability to collaborate with institutions as diverse as the La Mama Experimental Theater Company, and Time, Inc. Currently serving more than 800 homeless adolescents, the program offers educational advocacy, as well as an exceptional high school and GED curriculum, in addition to a hands-on vocational program that provides a vehicle for entry into the business world.

In recognition of the various special needs, living situations, and barriers that exist for homeless youth, the Career Education Center's goals are to

support students living in hotels or shelters and still registered in district schools

return nonattending students to their school of register and provide follow-up to ensure success

secure school placements for students not returning to previous school of register

provide credit-bearing, GED, and basic literacy courses for students in transition

In many cases, CEC's educational programs are situated at shelters, hotels, group homes, and hospitals. Providing services away from school settings has been a key factor in the success of these educational programs. Teachers use an individualized program in conjunction with group-work to provide students with the opportunity to relate with each other and to achieve a sense of positive group affiliation. In addition to meeting the individual educational needs of homeless youth, the CEC enhances the learning process through a variety of innovative approaches. In one group home, 50 teen mothers and 25 formerly homeless senior citizens are linked in an intergenerational program supported by Fordham University's social work students. In another program, homeless youth are linked with corporate mentors, while in the "adopt a school" program, adolescents serve as tutors and big brothers or big sisters to elementary school children. Through these and other creative strategies, such as cultural awareness programs, CEC is working with students, parents, staff, and the communities to improve the quality of student academic and vocational achievement and to increase the self-esteem of the homeless adolescent population.

The Kansas Children's Service League Emergency Shelter
2600 East 23 Street, Topeka, KS 66604 (913) 234-5424. Contact Michael Patrick

In Topeka, Kansas, the Kansas Children's Service League Emergency Shelter provides comprehensive educational services to its residents, in addition to its care of temporary housing services. Staff place strong emphasis on encouraging young people to attend their home school. The youth's home school first is contacted by staff to inform guidance counselors, teachers, and other school personnel of the youth's temporary residence. The shelter transports the young people to and from their home schools (within four school districts). Although the ride can take up to 2 hours, staff believe it is critical to maintain the continuity because they "don't want to have another familiar place taken away from these children."

Tutoring and educational counseling services are provided during the afternoon at the shelter, with assistance from the Topeka Public School District. The young people receive homework support, as well as supplementary activities designed to create enjoyable learning experiences. In addition, the Kansas Department of Education provides an on-site life skills education support program for all youth that covers the topics of finances, sex education, GED preparation, basic skills instruction, employment, and cultural awareness. This program offers a range of needed educational services through bringing together agencies, organizations, and individuals. Funding is provided from a variety of public and private sources.

## Conclusion

Hope persists for keeping adolescents off the street and for homeless adolescents to have viable futures. That hope lies in education. Homeless adolescents must have opportunities to return to school, to complete their GED, and to enter vocational training programs. Many of these young people are bright and have untapped strengths and potential. When comprehensive services are provided for them, homeless adolescents can achieve. It is the challenge of secondary educators to provide those services and to ensure that homeless adolescents have opportunities not only to survive but to succeed.

## References

Anderson, L. (1981). Notes on the linkage between the sexually abused child and the suicidal adolescent. *Journal of Adolescence, 4,* 157-162.

Barth, R. (1988). *On their own: The experiences of youth after foster care.* Berkeley: University of California, School of Social Work, Family Welfare Research Group.

Bassuk, E. L., & Rubin, L. (1987). Homeless children: A neglected population. *American Journal of Orthopsychiatry, 57*(2), 279-286.

Beyer, M. (1986, September-October). Overcoming emotional obstacles to independence. *Children and Youth Today,* pp. 8-12.

Browne, A., & Finkelhor, D. (1986). Impact of child sexual abuse: A review of the research. *Psychological Bulletin, 99,* 66-77.

Bucy, J. (1987, February 24). *The crisis in homelessness: Effects on children and families.* Testimony for the hearing before the Select Committee on Children, Youth, and Families, House of Representatives 100th Congress, First Session, Washington DC.

Cohen, M. (1987). *Identifying and combatting juvenile prostitution: A manual for action.* Norman: University of Oklahoma, National Resource Center for Youth Services, and the National Association of Counties.

Cook, R. (1986). *Independent living services for youth in substitute care* (Contract #OHDS 105-84-1814A). Washington, DC: U.S. Department of Health and Human Services, Administration for Children, Youth, and Families.

Ely, L. (1987). *Broken lives: Denial of education to homeless children.* Washington, DC: National Coalition for the Homeless. (ERIC Document Reproduction Service No. ED 292 897)

Farber, E., & Joseph, J. (1985). The maltreated adolescent: Patterns of physical abuse. *Child Abuse and Neglect, 9,* 201-206.

Farber, E., Kinast, C., McCoard, W., & Falkner, D. (1984). Violence in families of adolescent runaways. *Child Abuse and Neglect, 8,* 295-299.

Festinger, T. (1983). *No one ever asked us. . . . A postscript to foster care.* New York: Columbia University Press.

Finkelhor, D., Hotaling, G., & Sedlak, A. (1990). *National incidence study of missing, abducted, runaway, and throwaway children.* Washington, DC: Office of Juvenile Justice and Delinquency Prevention.

Fisher, B., Berdie, J., Cook. J., & Day, N. (1980). *Adolescent abuse and neglect: Intervention strategies* (DHHS Publication No. OHDS 80-30266). Washington, DC: Government Printing Office.

Foscarinis, M. (1987, February 24). *The crisis in homelessness: Effects on children and families.* Testimony for the hearing before the Select Committee on Children, Youth, and Families, House of Representatives 100th Congress, First Session, Washington, DC.

Fox, S., Barrnett, R., Davies, M., & Bird, H. (1990). Psychopathology and developmental delay in homeless children: A pilot study. *Journal of the American Academy of Child and Adolescent Psychiatry, 29,* 732-735.

Garbarino, J., Wilson, J., & Garbarino, A. (1986). The adolescent runaway. In J. Garbarino, C. Schellenbach, & J. Sebes (Eds.), *Troubled youth, troubled families* (pp. 41-56). Hawthorne, NY: Aldine.

Gil, E. (1983). *Outgrowing the pain.* San Francisco: Launch.

Jaklitsch, B., & Beyer, M. (1990). *Preparing for independence: Counseling issues with the maltreated adolescent.* Norman: University of Oklahoma, National Resource Center for Youth Services.

Janus, M., McCormack, A., Burgess, A., & Hartman, C. (1987). *Adolescent runaways: Causes and consequences.* Lexington, MA: Lexington.

McChesney, K. Y. (1986). Families: The new homeless. *Family Professional, 1,* 13-14.

Moran, P., & Eckenrode, J. (1987, July). *Personality variables related to depression in maltreated adolescent females.* Paper presented at the Second Family Violence Research Conference, Durham, NH.

Mundy, P., Robertson, M., Roberts, J., & Greenblatt, M. (1990). The prevalence of psychotic symptoms in homeless adolescents. *Journal of the American Academy of Child and Adolescent Psychiatry, 29,* 724-731.

National Network of Runaway and Youth Services. (1988, January). *Preliminary findings from the National Network's survey of runaway and homeless youth.* Testimony before the U.S. House of Representatives Subcommittee on Human Resources.

Powers, J., Eckenrode, J., & Jaklitsch, B. (1990). Maltreatment among runaway and homeless youth. *Child Abuse and Neglect, 14,* 87-98.

Powers, J., & Jaklitsch, B. (1989). *Understanding survivors of abuse: Stories of homeless and runaway adolescents.* Lexington, MA: Lexington.

Raychaba, B. (1988). *To be on our own.* Ontario, Canada: National Youth in Care Network Press.

Rescorla, L., Parker, R., & Stolley, P. (1991). Ability, achievement, and adjustment in homeless children. *American Journal of Orthopsychiatry, 6,* 210-220.

Robertson, M. (1989). *Homeless youth: Patterns of alcohol use.* A report to the National Institute of Alcohol Abuse and Alcoholism. Berkeley, CA: Alcohol Research Group.

Runaway Youth Act of 1974, Title III of the Juvenile Justice and Delinquency Prevention Act of 1974, (P.L. 93-415) U.S. House of Representatives.

Runaway and Homeless Youth Act. (1980). P.L. 96-509.

Shaffer, D., & Caton, C. (1984). *Runaway and homeless youth in New York City: A report to the Ittleson Foundation.* New York: New York State Psychiatric Institute and Columbia University of Physicians and Surgeons, Division of Child Psychiatry.

Solarz, A. (1988) Homelessness: Implications for children and youth. *Social Policy Report, 3,* 1-16.

Stewart B. McKinney Homeless Assistance Act of 1987, P.L. 100-77, Subtitle B, Education for Homeless Children and Youth, P.L. 100-77, 42 USC, 11431-11435.

Stronge, J., & Tenhouse, C. (1990). *Educating homeless children: Issues and answers.* Bloomington, IN: Phi Delta Kappa Educational Foundation.

Tower, C., & White, D. (1989). *Homeless students.* Washington, DC: NEA Professional Library.

U.S. Conference of Mayors. (1987). *Status report on homeless families: A 29-city survey.* Washington, DC: Author.

U.S. Congress. (1986). *Homeless families: A neglected crisis* (63rd Report by the Committee on Government Operations, October 9). Washington, DC: Government Printing Office.

U.S. Department of Health and Human Services, Office of Human Development Services Administration for Children, Youth, and Families. (1984). *Runaway youth centers: FY 1984 report to Congress.* Washington, DC: Government Printing Office.

U.S. General Accounting Office. (1989). *Homeless and runaway youth receiving services at federally funded shelters* (GAO/HRD-90-45). A report to Senator Paul Simon, Washington, DC.

Werner, E., & Smith, R. (1982). *Vulnerable, but invincible: A longitudinal study of resilient children and youth.* New York: McGraw-Hill.

Yates, G., MacKenzie, R., Pennbridge, J., & Cohen, E. (1988). A risk profile comparison of runaway and non-runaway youth. *American Journal of Public Health, 78,* 820-821.

Zeldin S., & Bogart, J. (1990). *Education and community support for homeless children and youth: Profiles of fifteen innovative and promising approaches.* Washington, DC: Policy Studies Associates. (ERIC Document Reproduction Service No. ED 322 249)

*8*

# Educating Special Needs Homeless Children and Youth

LORI KORINEK
CHRISTINE WALTHER-THOMAS
VIRGINIA K. LAYCOCK

*Vignette: Julio*

Julio is an energetic 6-year-old. He and his 21-year-old mother, Elena, have been living in a Salvation Army shelter in Kansas City for about 2 weeks. The shelter will allow them to stay 30 days. At that time, they will be required to move to another shelter in the area. Last year they lost everything in a fire. Since then, they have lived with relatives in Chicago, on the streets, and in several other Midwestern shelters.

Elena is concerned because Julio has missed a lot of school so early in life. She also is worried about a hearing problem he has had since infancy; he has had many ear infections. Often he does not answer when she talks to him, and he has difficulty understanding many things that people say. His speech and language are like that of children who are considerably younger.

Currently Julio attends a school program for children at the shelter where two Kansas City teachers, an aide, and several community volunteers serve 30 to 50 students daily. Additional school district personnel (e.g., special educators, English as a second language [ESL] teachers, psychologists, social workers, librarians) provide instructional materials and other assistance as needed to help shelter students.

133

During an initial interview with Julio's mother, his teachers learned about his hearing and school attendance problems. Elena brought a copy of Julio's school records from the school he attended in St. Louis. These records noted Julio's language and speech problems, as well as some related problems (e.g., in following directions, task completion, group participation). A summary report from his previous teacher recommended an evaluation for special education.

Julio's current teachers quickly observed Julio's communication problems. In class, he is reluctant to speak and frequently resorts to gesturing and/or hitting to get what he wants. The severity of his problems has prompted the teachers to refer Julio for a special education evaluation. The evaluation process was explained to Elena, and she gave permission for testing. A multidisciplinary team comprised of teachers and a psychologist from a nearby school will conduct the evaluation. Julio's strengths and weaknesses in areas of concern (e.g., hearing acuity, language, academics, cognitive, social-emotional, and adaptive behavior) will be evaluated. This process in all likelihood will take several months to complete. In the meantime, his teachers have requested assistance from school division specialists. They have observed Julio in class and have suggested a number of classroom interventions that can be implemented immediately to help Julio.

Julio's teachers talk with Elena almost daily. They keep her apprised of his performance through these conversations and with written weekly summaries of his progress. His teachers stress to Elena the importance of parent-teacher teamwork. Working together will enable them to develop a more appropriate education program for him. The teachers have asked Elena to keep them apprised of her immediate and long-range plans. This will enable them to identify a contact person at the next school Julio will attend. With Elena's permission, they can send formal and informal information about Julio to the new school. This will greatly facilitate the evaluation process. Prior planning before Elena and Julio move will enable his teachers to arrange support services at the next school which will help Julio make a smoother transition into that learning environment.

### Vignette: Denise

Unlike Julio, Denise no longer attends school. She is tall, thin, and appears much older than her 13 years. Before she was 9, she lived in seven different farming communities in North Carolina. After years of physical violence, her parents separated 3 years ago. Last year she moved to Virginia Beach with her mother and her two younger brothers, ages 4 and 9. Her mother worked as a hotel maid for several months until she developed pneumonia. Three months later her family was evicted from their apartment and began living in their car near the beach.

According to Denise's mother, May, Denise has always had school problems. Reading and writing have been especially difficult for her. May reported that Denise fell farther behind each time the family moved. Over the years, several teachers have suggested "special testing," but May does not remember whether the testing was ever completed or whether Denise ever received special help for her learning problems.

Denise's 9-year-old brother goes to school regularly, but Denise has not attended school during the last 6 months. She claims to be "too busy" for school. She also expresses some concern about her lack of the "right kind" of clothes for school. May acknowledged that Denise is a lot of help taking care of her younger brother, so she does not "push" school at the present time. She also collects soda cans daily to turn in for money. May says that when the family can get another apartment, Denise will go back to school.

* * *

## Defining Special Needs Students Among the Homeless

As these vignettes illustrate, several factors mitigate against homeless students with disabilities receiving education, let alone *special* education services. These factors include the unpredictability of their moves, their short durations of residence, the difficulties in transferring records, the instability of parental/family situations, and the discontinuity of general education programs, as well as those specifically designed to serve the homeless (e.g., Bassuk, 1985; Human Resources Administration of New York City [HRANYC], 1985; Rafferty & Rollins, 1989; U.S. Department of Education, 1989; U.S. House of Representatives, 1986).

*Special Education Characteristics*
*of Homeless Children and Youth*

Although homeless students frequently have functional characteristics in common with other special populations, including those who qualify for Chapter I, speak English as a second language, are migrants, or frequently change programs for whatever reasons (e.g., chronically ill students, juvenile offenders, foster children), homeless children and youth with handicapping conditions constitute a unique subpopulation with special needs. Daily, homeless students confront poverty, poor nutrition, limited access to health care, alcohol and narcotics abuse, transiency, and removal from familiar environments (Schumack, 1987; U.S. Department of Education, 1989). Infectious diseases such as tuberculosis and whooping cough run rampant among uninoculated children. Many homeless children and youth risk hearing loss because of untreated ear infections, which in turn may lead to learning problems (Reed & Sautter, 1990). All of these factors undermine homeless students' efforts to attend school regularly, to complete homework, to remain attentive in classes, and to benefit from their education without special assistance and support. Results of a study by the U.S. Conference of Mayors (Waxman & Reyes, 1990) indicated that approximately 20% of the homeless are children; fewer than half attend school. Although one study (Bassuk, 1985) reported 29% of the homeless students sampled had been in special education, no current, reliable, national estimates of the number of homeless students qualifying for or receiving special education are available.

Rubin (U.S. House of Representatives, 1986) testified that homeless children manifest a wide range of emotional, social, and cognitive difficulties and delays. Bassuk (1985), who did in-depth interviews with 51 homeless mothers and 78 children in Boston, found that 47% of the preschoolers showed severe developmental impairments, and 54% of the school-age individuals had repeated grades. Over 50% of the children in the study were clinically depressed, most with suicidal thoughts and severe anxiety. Bassuk also found that homeless children and youth manifest more problem behaviors than do nonhomeless students diagnosed "emotionally disturbed" or recommended for psychiatric evaluation.

Reported behavioral problems among homeless children and youth vary greatly, but the following are commonly reported: aggression, withdrawal, listlessness, apathy, increased acting out, restlessness, depression, moodiness, and low frustration tolerance (Bassuk, 1985; HRANYC, 1985; U.S. House of Representatives, 1986). Shelters with overcrowding and little privacy exacerbate the emotional, behavioral, and academic difficulties.

Due to the stresses of moving and lack of security, especially for younger children, homeless children are likely to regress developmentally (Kliman, 1968) and be anxious and insecure (Gewirtzman & Fodor, 1987). They may share some of the effects of rootlessness noted among migrant children: little sense of space or possessions, difficulty completing projects, and a view of life as temporary and beyond their control (Coles, 1976). Migrant and homeless children frequently lack experience playing with toys, blocks, games, and other items necessary for development of perception and spatial relationships (New York State Department of Education, 1989). These characteristics—difficulty with task completion, lack of internal control, and perceptual problems—are also typical of students labeled "learning disabled" (Lerner, 1988).

### Provisions for Students With Disabilities Under the McKinney Act

Among the provisions of the Stewart B. McKinney Homeless Assistance Act of 1987 (P.L. 100-177) is the mandate that every homeless child and youth shall have access to a free, appropriate, public education consistent with the services provided to students who are residents of the school division. These services specifically include any for which students meet the eligibility criteria, including special education for students with disabilities, compensatory education for the disadvantaged, programs for students with limited English proficiency, vocational education, and services for gifted and talented students. The act also requires that states develop plans to meet the educational needs of homeless children and youth. These plans are to (a) authorize the state educational agency, the local educational agency, the parent or guardian of the homeless child or youth, or the applicable social worker to make the determinations related to the requirements of the law; (b) include procedures to determine school placement; and (c) include procedures to resolve disputes that may arise related to placement.

## Organizational Obstacles
## to Special Education Service Delivery

Organizational procedures typically followed in schools often delay or effectively eliminate the delivery of education services to homeless populations. Access to special education services presents an even greater challenge to the homeless. To qualify for special education services, a child or youth must proceed through a series of steps intended to protect student and parent rights to privacy, confidentiality, and due process, while identifying specific problems that prevent him or her from benefitting from general education. This process is designed to secure a free, appropriate public education in the least restrictive environment (one in which students with disabilities are educated with nonhandicapped students to the maximum extent appropriate and suited to students' individual needs). Special education may also include related services—any programs/services necessary to help students with disabilities benefit from special education (e.g., audiology, transportation, occupational and physical therapy). Special education procedures are dictated by federal law (P.L. 94-142, EHA, 1975) and subsequent amendments (e.g., Public Law 99-457, 1986; Public Law 101-476, IDEA, 1990). Although no comparable federal legislation mandates services for students who are gifted, many states require similar procedures for service delivery to these students (Houseman, 1988). To the extent that procedures for gifted education programs have been modeled after those for special education, homeless students and families may encounter similar organizational obstacles.

### Handicapping Conditions and Definitions

The handicapping conditions for which children or youth are eligible to receive special education services include autism, deafness, blindness, developmental delays (birth through age 5), hearing impairments, multiple handicaps, mental retardation, traumatic brain injury, other health impairments, orthopedic impairments, severe emotional disturbance, severe/profound handicaps, speech and language impairments, and specific learning disabilities. With every condition, the disability must adversely affect educational performance to be considered handicapping and to qualify students for special educational services.

The handicapping conditions most likely to be evidenced by school-aged populations, including homeless children and youth, are specific learning disabilities (SLD), speech and language impairments, mild to moderate mental retardation (MR), and serious emotional disturbance (SED) (U.S. Department of Education, 1990). According to federal regulations accompanying P.L. 94-142, a *specific learning disability* is a disorder in the basic psychological processes involved in understanding or using language, which may manifest itself in difficulties listening, thinking, speaking, reading, writing, spelling, or calculating/ reasoning in math. The term does not include students who have learning problems that are primarily the result of visual, hearing, or motor handicaps, of mental retardation or emotional disturbance, or of environmental, cultural, or economic disadvantage. A *speech or language impairment* is a communication disorder such as stuttering or impaired articulation, voice, or language. *Mental retardation* means significantly subaverage intellectual functioning (at least two standard deviations below average on an IQ test) existing concurrently with deficits in adaptive behavior and manifested during the developmental period. *Serious emotional disturbance* refers to one or more of the following characteristics exhibited over a long period of time and to a marked degree: an inability to learn that cannot be explained by intellectual, sensory, or health factors; an inability to build or maintain satisfactory interpersonal relationships; inappropriate types of behavior or feelings under normal circumstances; a general pervasive mood of unhappiness or depression; and a tendency to develop physical symptoms or fears associated with personal or school problems.

Even a cursory review of these definitions highlights the problematic nature of distinguishing the effects of homelessness from the effects of these possible handicapping conditions. For example, the exclusionary clause in the SLD definition suggesting that student problems are not primarily the result of environmental or economic disadvantage, the requirement that problem behavior be exhibited over a long period of time in the SED definition, and the specification of what constitutes "adaptive" behavior under the MR definition often give rise to questions of eligibility for special education for homeless students. Ironically, various elements in these definitions could be used to exclude homeless students from special education services, in direct violation of the spirit of the legislation intended to ensure that all students with special needs receive an appropriate education. The conditions under which homeless students live undoubtedly exacerbate the negative effects of any disabilities they may have. Consequently these students may be more in need of special education than students with the same disabilities who are not homeless. Even when school personnel are well intentioned, the length of the special education referral and eligibility process, described in the next section, may effectively prevent homeless students from receiving services.

### The Special Education Process

Procedures for determining eligibility for special education include referral and multidisciplinary assessment with parental/guardian permission. If the student is found eligible, an individualized education program (IEP) is developed and the student is assigned to the general and/or special education classroom(s) where his or her program can best be implemented in the least restrictive environment.

*Referral.* Anyone suspecting that a student needs special services can refer him or her via the school principal or designee. The law mandates that a Child Study Committee (CSC) comprised of teachers, the principal or his or her designee, and specialists (e.g., psychologists, social workers, special educators) review the referral information, existing student records, and classroom performance indicators to determine whether a multidisciplinary assessment for special education is warranted.

The CSC must meet within 10 administrative days of the student's referral to decide how the child can best be helped. Alternative instructional or behavioral management methods for the classroom may be suggested as the most appropriate starting point, and the committee will set a time line to review progress. If the committee feels that formal, multidisciplinary assessment for special education is needed, the special education administrator for the school must be notified within 5 administrative days of the CSC meeting. The special education administrator then will notify the parents in writing, requesting permission to complete a formal assessment. This notice must be in the parents' native language and include a description of the action and assessment, reasons, other options considered, and the parents'/guardians' procedural rights.

*Evaluation.* If the parent or guardian gives informed written permission, a multidisciplinary evaluation is conducted to gather more information about the student and his or her learning needs. The evaluation includes (a) assessment of the student's educational performance, (b) a medical examination, (c) a sociocultural evaluation of the home, as well as school and community factors that may affect his or her performance in school, and (d) a psychological evaluation to determine the student's intellectual and emotional-social development. In addition, the student must be assessed in other areas related to his or her suspected disability. All tests should be suited to the child being tested, the examiners must be qualified, and no single test can be used as the sole criterion for determining eligibility for special services.

*Eligibility.* Once the multidisciplinary evaluation is completed, an eligibility committee of qualified school personnel reviews all the information and determines whether the student is eligible for special education and/or related services. This decision must be made within 65 administrative days after the CSC initially requested the evaluation. If the student's parents or guardians disagree with the eligibility decision, they may request a due process hearing within 45 days.

*Individualized Education Program (IEP).* When a student is found eligible for special education and/or related services, an individualized education program (IEP) specifying services the student will receive must be developed within 30 calendar days of the eligibility determination. If the student is being considered for special education for the first time, the team that develops the IEP must include a member of the evaluation team or a representative of the school division, and one or both of the student's parents or a guardian. The student's current teacher must also be involved in subsequent IEP meetings. The parents' role in these meetings is to help plan their child's educational program and to give their permission for the IEP to be implemented. The completed IEP must include a statement of the student's present level of performance, annual goals, and short-term objectives; specific educational and related services he or she will receive; a description of how much the student will participate in general education programs; and criteria, methods, and time lines that will be used to evaluate the student's progress. Once the IEP is developed, the student is assigned to the classroom(s) where the program can best be accomplished. The choices range from the general education classroom with minimal supportive services, to special classes, to special day schools or residential schools. The student's IEP and placement must be reviewed annually, and a comprehensive reevaluation is required every 3 years.

**Unique Obstacles for the Homeless**

This review of the special education process and definitions mandated by P.L. 94-142 and P.L. 101-476 for educating students with disabilities serves as a context for analyzing the many unique problems faced by homeless children/youth that may complicate or delay referral, eligibility, and delivery of special education services to these students. In addition to the residency, health, and transportation requirements, frequent and often unpredictable moves impede the transfer of formal school records. Consequently transitions from one school to another often lack meaningful instructional and social continuity. Students face the prospect of starting over again and again with teachers, peers, placement tests, classroom rules, and instructional materials. While this is a difficult task for any student, for homeless students with additional learning and behavior problems it will likely prove insurmountable. In addition, teachers who notice these difficulties in performance may attribute them to frequent absenteeism and homelessness rather than to a true handicapping condition.

Procedural safeguards designed to protect the due process rights of students with disabilities and to provide maximum involvement of parents set an evaluation pace that makes it difficult to qualify these students for services. Even with maximum cooperation from school personnel and families, the referral and eligibility process is likely to take 3 to 4 months to complete. Educators and administrators may question the value of pursuing special education services, given common patterns of short-term enrollment by homeless students. Fruitless past efforts may lead school divisions serving these students to approach the special education process slowly rather than expeditiously to avoid commitment of limited resources.

Special education legislation also recognizes the critical role of parents in securing services for their children with disabilities. In the case of homeless students with special needs, parental involvement may be limited for a variety of reasons or be nonexistent in the case of the 12% of homeless individuals who are unaccompanied youth age 18 and under (Waxman & Reyes, 1990). The McKinney Act requires that an advocate be appointed as soon as possible to expedite service delivery to homeless children and youth. The Individuals with Disabilities Education Act (IDEA) governing special education, however, considers the appointing of a surrogate parent as a last resort after repeated, documented attempts to involve the natural parents or guardians in each step of the process.

The provisions of the McKinney Act are designed to expedite educational service delivery, recognizing the need for personnel to act quickly in light of the frequent school changes among homeless students. IDEA, on the other hand, is structured to protect the rights of students and their families. Consequently school personnel are required to follow important, albeit time-consuming, procedures to ensure these rights are not violated. This is but one example of the need for implementation guidance (Jennings, 1989) and clarification to resolve the contradictions inherent in the current legislation. Meanwhile collaboration between service providers and schools dealing with homeless students is imperative.

## *Important Program Considerations*

As currently structured in most schools, special education is difficult to access for homeless students with suspected disabilities. Recognizing the obstacles that exist, responsive programs will be characterized by high levels of collaboration, administrative leadership, peer involvement, in-service training, expedited access to records and services, individualized programming, and transition planning.

### Collaboration

The complex needs of homeless students require mobilization and coordination of a full array of services within the school and community. General agreement exists that the effectiveness of education for the homeless hinges on a high level of collaboration among professionals interacting with students and their families (Gewirtzman & Fodor, 1987; Scott & Cranston-Gingras, 1991; Stronge & Tenhouse, 1990). Basic needs for food, clothing, and shelter must be addressed before students can benefit from educational offerings. Because the schools and shelters tend to occupy the most central positions in the network of health and human service agencies providing assistance to the homeless, they can assume shared leadership in promoting interagency collaboration.

Parent involvement in the educational process is viewed as critical (Massachusetts Organization of State Funded Shelter Providers [MOSFSP], 1986; McCormick, 1989). Parents can provide valuable information about the educational programs their children experienced in other settings. For students with suspected or identified disabilities, parent reports of their functioning in school and community environments are especially helpful.

Even if parents do not have copies of evaluation reports or IEPs, they may be able to provide the names of teachers or administrators who can be contacted for that information. To the extent that parents perceive the schools as sensitive to their needs and committed to serving their children, they are likely to participate more actively in assessment, program planning, and implementation.

Service providers need to recognize the numerous concerns these parents have about their families at this time. Current life situations may preclude significant parent involvement, and reluctance of some parents to participate should not be misinterpreted as lack of caring. Professionals need to work diligently to keep parents apprised of their child's performance, to elicit parent counsel, to respect their rights, and to avoid shortsighted judgments about the parents' lack of concern. In many ways, service to the homeless involves a process of educational programming similar to the development of the individualized family service plan (IFSP) required under P.L. 99-457 for infant and early intervention. Like an IFSP, comprehensive programs should address the concerns, strengths, and coping resources of the family, as well as the child, and incorporate a wide range of child and family support services. In collaborating with families, the goal should be capacity-building or empowering families to develop their own unique strengths and skills in order to negotiate educational and community systems more effectively (Dunst, Trivette, & Deal, 1988; MOSFSP, 1986).

Within schools, a variety of professionals should be involved with students and their families. If school personnel can collaborate as a team, their unique perspectives and collective expertise contribute to more creative solutions to complex problems and more integrated programs for students and families (Chalfant & Pysh, 1989; Friend & Cook, 1990; West & Idol, 1990). A sense of shared responsibility for decision making, program development, and accountability is essential not only within schools but also between the schools that send and receive homeless students. Both the sending and receiving schools have important roles to play in order to promote rather than obstruct student progress.

## Administrative Leadership

Central office and building-based administrators are responsible for articulating the school's commitment to educate all children (McCormick, 1989; U.S. Department of Education, 1991), including the homeless. In particular, administrators should emphasize the school's moral and legal obligation to pursue the special education process as actively as possible whenever a handicapping condition is suspected, even when students are likely to move on at any time. Unless this commitment is communicated clearly from the top down, homeless children and youth are likely to be overlooked.

Administrators can help create structures, such as school-based assistance teams and team teaching, to facilitate communication, collaboration, and flexibility in service delivery to meet diverse students' needs. In part, this involves clarifying responsibilities of school personnel concerning who should serve as primary liaisons for internal and external coordination of services. At the building level, principals also play a key role in encouraging teachers and reinforcing them for their efforts (e.g., through release time for collaboration, assignment of volunteers). At the state level, administrators can become advocates for more coordinated services for the homeless. Communication could be enhanced greatly, for example, by state-operated computerized records management and electronic mail systems to expedite records transfer, facilitate student monitoring, and enable agencies to share information about available resources.

### Peer Involvement

Where a climate of acceptance of individual differences and support for all students is achieved in schools, homeless students are likely to be assimilated more successfully. Many schools and classrooms have procedures in place to welcome and orient any newcomers throughout the school year. Special friends or peer mentors may be appointed to help homeless students ease the transition to a new school and community (Stronge & Tenhouse, 1990). Age-appropriate grade placement is recognized as critical to success even though students may evidence academic delays (Scott & Cranston-Gingras, 1991). Appropriate use of cooperative learning and peer tutoring may facilitate both academic and social integration.

### In-Service Training

Carefully planned staff development programs are necessary to sensitize school personnel to the effects of homelessness and to enhance their ability to educate homeless children and youth. The goal is a shared commitment to their collective roles toward establishing a structured, stable, and nonthreatening environment for students (Gewirtzman & Fodor, 1987). A focus on specific attainable outcomes may help both the professionals and the students they serve not to feel totally overwhelmed by the challenges they face.

Clarification of the special education process and the kinds of accommodations that can be made for transient families is essential. School personnel should be well informed about existing community programs that serve the homeless and should know who is the appropriate liaison person in the school to help mobilize such services.

### Expedited Access to Records and Services

Greater efficiency in the transmittal of educational records is essential to effective educational programming for the homeless. Each school should have a designated contact person, preferably a teacher, counselor, social worker, or administrator known to the family, who is responsible for obtaining records from previous programs and forwarding them along to future programs. This individual has to take a personal interest in the homeless family, be knowledgeable about school division policies and procedures, and be willing to do whatever it takes to ensure that records are available as quickly as possible. Although overnight and electronic mail services can speed records transmittal, personal follow-through remains critical.

Providing parents with copies of educational records and encouraging them to share the records with receiving schools is also a worthwhile practice. Schools should inquire routinely about enrolling students' participation in special education and related services. Parents should be asked not only about IEPs and placements but also about previous referrals or evaluations for special education.

Although schools may be reluctant to accept parent copies of records, services to students can be initiated on the basis of these reports until the official copies can be obtained. Any time students have an active IEP, it should be honored by the receiving school to continue service delivery. Furthermore if referral, child study, or evaluation processes have been initiated in other schools, the receiving school should accept the validity of those efforts and should continue the special education process from wherever it was interrupted by the family's move. Although this may represent a significant departure from general school practice, a cumulative approach may be the only way that some transient children will ever make it all the way through the special education process to the point where services can be delivered (Scott & Cranston-Gingras, 1991).

## Individualized Programs

Even if students are eligible to receive special services, they are still likely to experience most of their educational programs in mainstream environments (U.S. Department of Education, 1990). For most students, the general education curriculum can be adapted appropriately to meet their learning needs. A primary focus should be on the development of basic literacy skills. Students' instructional levels and needs generally can be identified most effectively through curriculum-based measures (systematic assessment using classroom learning activities). Individualizing programs for homeless students may also require many of the varied strategies used for effective instruction, practice, and evaluation of at-risk learners and students with disabilities. Teachers should be especially attentive to motivating homeless students through provision of more explicit connections to real life and previous learning.

While programs in the mainstream center on the general education curriculum, special programs can emphasize functional skills. By analyzing the demands of present and likely future environments, individualized programs can be designed to address areas most critical to student survival, including communication and social skills, personal health and hygiene, nutrition, family life education, stress management, and career-vocational preparation. To the extent possible, students should be taught to be their own self-advocates in educational and community settings.

## Transition Planning

Because a family move is always imminent, planning for the student transitions to the next environment should begin on the first day. Teachers and other direct service providers need to provide careful, even daily, documentation of each student's program and performance. Students themselves can be taught to identify the basic materials they have used (e.g., title of their reading book) and can be encouraged to share this information with their next teachers. If the school personnel understand that a student's enrollment is only temporary, it is important to discuss how the parents, student, and schools can work together to facilitate future moves. Parents may even be asked immediately to sign forms that will be needed to release educational records to the next school. Any time school personnel know where the student will be enrolled next, every effort should be made by the designated contact person to notify the receiving school and to share relevant educational information as quickly as possible.

For adolescents receiving special education and related services, transition planning has additional significance. The 1990 Amendments to P.L. 94-142 require that IEPs for students 16 years of age and older include specific objectives and interagency activities to promote successful transitions to the workplace and/or post-secondary educational programs (P.L. 101-476, 1990). This emphasis on coordinated, sequential experiences to prepare students for employment and independent functioning in the community is a critical component in programming for secondary students. Unfortunately it will be difficult to implement for homeless students.

## Providing Services to Students With Disabilities

Some special education services may be provided in separate schools or programs for homeless children and youth. Arguments for this approach include building students' self-esteem, reducing stigma, and meeting immediate, unique needs (Jennings, 1989; Leslie, Abramson, Robins, & Namuth, 1989). On the other hand are compelling reasons to try to serve homeless students with disabilities through more integrated school programs. Since 1975, public schools have been legally responsible for child find activities to identify students with disabilities. This includes referrals, assessment, eligibility, and service delivery described in the special education process. Federal and state funds are appropriated to assist localities in serving these children. Thus the process and funding to help serve special needs students have been "institutionalized" in public school settings, whereas resources available through the McKinney Act may be limited and subject to the vagaries of future funding. The McKinney Act has been described as "crisis legislation" designed to meet immediate needs but lacking provisions needed to meet long-term educational needs of homeless students (McGonigel, Kaufmann, & Doherty, 1991). Public schools must offer a complete range of services (e.g., speech and language, occupational therapy, physical therapy, transportation) in addition to special education. Separate programs may offer some individualized special education but may not have access to the variety of services needed by homeless students with disabilities. Furthermore students served in self-contained programs for the homeless face yet another transition when they have to return to a general school setting.

Regardless of program setting or obstacles to service delivery, all teachers and administrators have legal and ethical responsibilities to develop appropriate programs for homeless students with disabilities by utilizing formalized special education procedures. While this process is under way, schools can respond more immediately to student needs by use of existing school support services and personnel resources.

### School-Based Assistance Teams

Because of widespread problems in schools today, many states have adopted "prereferral" procedures to help struggling students and their teachers (McCarney, 1988). The CSC team or other designated master teacher teams within schools can work with the teachers of these students to develop appropriate classroom interventions for their academic and/or behavioral problems (Chalfant & Pysh, 1989). Special education teachers and other support personnel (e.g., school psychologist, nurse, social worker) may not be core members of assistance teams; however, they can be asked to participate on assistance teams as needed. These classroom interventions are implemented, monitored, and discussed by the teacher and the assistance team over time to evaluate their effectiveness. Modifications are made as needed. If the teacher and the team decide that the interventions have not significantly improved the student's performance, other action will be taken (e.g., parent-teacher conference, special education evaluation).

Prereferral assistance has been shown to provide effective help for students and teachers, and it has been successful in reducing the number of referrals for special education (Chalfant & Pysh, 1989). This process can provide immediate help for homeless students with possible disabilities while the evaluation for special education is being conducted. Classroom data collected during this process can provide the professional staff with valuable information regarding student performance. These data can also help staff members determine whether special education referral is genuinely warranted. Initial problems exhibited by students transitioning into new classrooms may be eliminated when teachers employ appropriate interventions.

**Classroom Collaboration**

Today many school specialists (e.g., special educators, school psychologists, school counselors, reading specialists, art and music teachers) are providing fewer services outside the general education classroom and more assistance for students and their teachers within the classroom (Bauwens, Hourcade, & Friend, 1989; West & Idol, 1990). This instructional approach enables general educators and appropriate specialists to plan and team teach together in a more collaborative manner. The benefits of these relationships are many. Ongoing interaction between these professionals helps ensure appropriateness of the instruction and practice that students receive. If two teachers work together during the critical periods of instruction, greater flexibility in the instructional groupings is possible. Team teaching can provide more opportunities for teachers to work individually or in small groups with students needing additional assistance. Collaboration also enables the educators to monitor students' academic and social performance more accurately.

Instructional collaboration is particularly useful in schools that serve large numbers of homeless and other at-risk students. This approach allows specialists such as special educators to have early, ongoing contact with students experiencing learning and behavior problems before they qualify for formal special education services. Working together daily, professionals will be more likely to share their observations and intervention ideas. As a team, they may be more successful in quickly identifying student needs and in mobilizing available school and division resources to aid these students.

*Conclusion*

Homeless students with disabilities constitute a unique subset within today's school population. They are children and youth who have many educational needs. Unfortunately these needs often are unmet because of school laws, frequent family moves, and poor channels of communication. Although it is difficult to estimate how many homeless students have disabilities that impede their ability to learn effectively, it is reasonable to assume that a disproportionately high number would qualify for special education because of the tremendous physical, psychological, and social problems they face.

Administrators and teachers must work together with families and supporting community agencies to ensure that these students receive the educational services to which they are entitled. Because of the special education students' complex problems, service providers need to recognize the importance of collaboration and teamwork as they develop appropriate programs for these students. While it is difficult for schools to provide special education for homeless students with disabilities, such factors as administrative leadership, communication within and across public agencies, in-service training, and use of existing school resources (e.g., school-based assistance teams and program specialists) can facilitate the development and delivery of more appropriate educational programs for these students.

## References

Bassuk, E. L. (1985). *The feminization of homelessness: Homeless families in Boston shelters.* Unpublished manuscript, Harvard Science Center, Cambridge, MA.

Bauwens, J., Hourcade, J. J., & Friend, M. (1989). Cooperative teaching: A model for general and special education integration. *Remedial and Special Education, 10*(2), 17-22.

Chalfant, J. C., & Pysh, M. (1989). Teacher assistance teams: Five descriptive studies on 96 teams. *Remedial and Special Education, 10*(6), 49-58.

Coles, R. (1976). *Uprooted children.* Pittsburgh, PA: University of Pittsburgh Press.

Dunst, C. J., Trivette, C. M., & Deal, A. (1988). *Meeting the individual needs of families: Principles and guidelines for practice.* Cambridge, MA: Brookline.

Friend, M., & Cook, L. (1990). Collaboration as a predictor for success in school reform. *Journal of Educational and Psychological Consultation, 1*(1), 33-40.

Gewirtzman, R., & Fodor, I. (1987). The homeless child at school: From welfare hotel to classroom. *Child Welfare, 66*(3), 237-245.

Houseman, W. (1988). *The 1987 state of the states gifted and talented report.* Topeka, KS: Council of State Directors of Programs for the Gifted.

Human Resources Administration of New York City (HRANYC). (1985). *Longitudinal study of homeless families: Preliminary findings.* New York: Policy and Program Development, Human Resources Administration.

Jennings, L. (1989, February 8). Report to sharpen policy debate on homeless. *Education Week,* p. 19.

Kliman, G. (1968). *Psychological emergencies in childhood.* New York: Grune & Stratton.

Lerner, J. (1988). *Learning disabilities: Theories, diagnosis, and teaching strategies.* Boston: Houghton Mifflin.

Leslie, C., Abramson, P., Robins, K., & Namuth, T. (1989, January 23). Can a shelter be a school? *Newsweek,* p. 51.

Massachusetts Organization of State Funded Shelter Providers (MOSFSP). (1986). *A service model for homeless families.* Boston: Author.

McCarney, S. B. (1988). *The pre-referral intervention manual.* Columbia, MO: Hawthorne Educational Services.

McCormick, K. (1989). *An equal chance: Educating at-risk children to succeed.* Alexandria, VA: National School Boards Association.

McGonigel, M. J., Kaufman, R., & Doherty, D. M. (1991, August). *Social change in the 90's: Supporting families in crisis.* Symposium conducted at the Child Development Resources Summer Institute, College of William and Mary, Williamsburg, VA.

New York State Department of Education. (1989). *New York State plans for education of homeless children and youth, 1989-91.* Albany: Author.

Public Law 94-142, The Education for All Handicapped Children Act, 1975. Codified at 20 U.S.C. 1401-1420, 29 November, 1975.

Public Law 99-457, Amendments to the Education of the Handicapped Act, 1986. Codified at 20 U.S.C. 1400-1485, 8 October, 1986.

Public Law 101-476, Individuals With Disabilities Education Act (IDEA), 1990. Codified at 20 U.S.C. 1400-1476, 30 October, 1990.

Rafferty, Y., & Rollins, N. (1989). *Learning in limbo: The education deprivation of homeless children.* Long Island City, NY: Advocates for Children of New York.

Reed, S., & Sautter, R. C. (1990). Children of poverty: The status of 12 million young Americans. *Phi Delta Kappan, 71*(10), K1-K12.

Schumack, S. (Ed.). (1987, September). Homelessness: A barrier to education for thousands of children. *Center for Law and Education, Inc., Newsnotes, No. 38,* pp. 1-4.

Scott, J., & Cranston-Gingras, A. (1991, April). *Special education for migrant students with handicaps.* Paper presented at the 69th Annual Council for Exceptional Children Conference, Atlanta, GA.

Stewart B. McKinney Homeless Assistance Act of 1987 (P. L. 100-177).

Stronge, J. H., & Tenhouse, C. (1990). *Educating homeless children: Issues and answers.* Bloomington, IN: Phi Delta Kappa Educational Foundation.

U.S. Department of Education. (1989). *Report to Congress on the education of homeless children and youth.* Washington, DC: U.S. Department of Education, Homeless Children and Youth Program.

U.S. Department of Education. (1990). *Twelfth annual report to Congress on the implementation of the education of the handicapped act.* Washington, DC: Author.

U.S. Department of Education. (1991). *America 2000: An educational strategy.* Washington, DC: Author.

U.S. House of Representatives. (1986, February 4). *The crisis in homelessness: Effects on children and families.* Hearing before the Select Committee on Children, Youth, and Families, 100th Congress. Washington, DC: Government Printing Office.

Waxman, L. D., & Reyes, L. M. (1990). *A status report on homeless families in America's cities: A 29-city survey.* Washington, DC: U.S. Conference of Mayors.

West, J. F., & Idol, L. (1990). Collaborative consultation in the education of mildly handicapped and at-risk students. *Remedial and Special Education, 11*(1), 22-31.

# 9

# *Educational Support Services for Homeless Children and Youth*

### JOSEPH F. JOHNSON, JR.

Amazingly some homeless children and youth are successful in school in spite of their chronically unmet basic needs. Many homeless children, however, have difficulty concentrating, attending regularly, or feeling motivated to participate in school activities because basic needs have not been adequately addressed. Through supportive services that address the physiological, safety, affiliation, and esteem needs of homeless students, schools can increase the likelihood that these students will attend and be successful in school.

## *Supportive Services Addressing Physiological Needs*

The nature of homelessness deprives many children of basic physiological necessities. The need for food, shelter, clothing, and health care may be extreme for some homeless youngsters, and the extent of these needs may vary tremendously. For instance, homeless children living in cars, campgrounds, or other out-of-doors environments typically will have more severe needs than those who live in shelters. Variation in the extent to which different shelters are able to respond to the physiological needs of homeless students may be considerable. Nonetheless, by identifying and attempting to respond to these needs, schools can increase the likelihood that homeless students will attend school regularly and achieve success in school.

## School Meal Programs

Hunger is a common experience for many homeless children and youth. Inadequate meals and missed meals are the frequent consequences of poverty and the lack of amenities of a home. Wright and Weber (1987) reported that nearly 2% of homeless children suffer from nutritional deficiencies that were commonly thought not to exist in the United States. Homeless families or homeless youth often do not have money to buy food. Even when money is available, the facilities for food preparation may be limited (if any). Often transportation is not available to suburban grocery stores, forcing shopping at drug stores or expensive city markets. Rarely do homeless individuals have access to food storage facilities, so the purchase of perishable food items (milk, meats, fresh vegetables, etc.) may result in wasted money or jeopardized health (Kozol, 1988). Where they exist, community food programs are frequently underfunded. In some cases, homeless families are only able to use food bank programs a limited number of times. Even though some shelters prepare meals for their guests, and soup kitchens are available in some communities, most programs do not provide three meals a day and frequently do not provide adequate fresh vegetables, fruit, meat, and milk. Consequently very few homeless children eat nutritionally balanced, adequate, and regular meals (Waxman & Reyes, 1987). School meal programs can substantially improve the nutritional health of homeless children and youth. For some children, the meals provided at school may be the only healthful food eaten. Some school meal programs, however, may do a poor job of responding to the hunger needs of homeless students. For instance, some school meal programs do not include breakfast. In some schools, breakfast is provided but only during a narrow span of time that may not coincide with the arrival of homeless children because of bus schedules, shelter problems, or other transportation difficulties. In some schools, homeless students may not have access to school meal programs until paperwork is processed that confirms the families' eligibility for school meal services. Such paperwork may take several days to process—a time frame, given the transient nature of homelessness, that may completely exclude some students' participation.

Section 722(e)(1)(D) of the McKinney Homeless Assistance Act requires states to ensure that homeless students who meet relevant eligibility criteria have access to federal, state, and local school meal programs. School meal programs are most likely to meet the needs of homeless students when provisions are made for emergency access to services. Policies and procedures should be in place that ensure that homeless children get access to school meal services on the first day of school attendance. Furthermore schools that do not already do so should consider providing breakfast programs. Noon is a long time to wait to eat, especially if the last full meal was eaten at noon the previous day. Beyond these provisions, the most effective school meal programs will include provisions for children who come to school late or who, because of a lack of evening meals, are hungry at mid-morning or mid-afternoon (Mihaly, 1991). Nutritious snacks provided at various times during the school day can help ensure that students are able to devote maximum energies to school tasks. Good school meal programs may also help maintain the health of homeless students and result in decreased absenteeism and increased motivation to attend school regularly.

**School Health Services**

Factors related to homelessness endanger the health of thousands of children and youth. Edelman and Mihaly (1989) noted that lack of health insurance or funds for medical care; inadequate diet; lack of access to bathing facilities; exposure to the elements; shared living, eating, and bathing quarters; and inadequate sleeping arrangements pose substantial risks to the health of homeless children. Frequently the health problems of homeless children are neither diagnosed nor treated (Redlener, 1989). Therefore medical problems tend to worsen or become chronic.

A study by Wright and Weber (1987) compared the health needs of homeless children with those of other children in a national medical survey. The study reported incidence rates of health problems for homeless children which were substantially higher than the incidence rates for other children. For instance, homeless children had upper respiratory infections, eye disorders, ear disorders, anemia, and serious skin disorders at rates twice as high as for other children. Similarly, homeless children were ten times as likely to have dental problems and four times as likely to have gastrointestinal disorders. Almost 16% of the homeless children aged 15 or younger already had one or more chronic health condition.

In a study of families in shelters in New York City, Rafferty and Rollins (1989) found that 30% of the parents indicated that their children's health had gotten worse since becoming homeless. And 38% of the parents reported that their children had problems with ear infections; 26% reported asthma; 24% cited diarrhea; and 23% reported skin rashes.

In some cases, health problems afflicting homeless children and youth are related to alcohol and drug abuse and sexual activity. As a means of survival, some homeless children and youth are lured into prostitution. As a means of escape from the trauma of homelessness, some turn to alcohol or drug abuse. Wright and Weber (1987) reported that, of the homeless girls aged 13 to 15 who participated in their study, 9% were pregnant; 24% of the homeless girls aged 16 to 19 were pregnant. Other serious health problems, such as AIDS and sexually transmitted venereal diseases, are thus concerns for homeless children and youth.

Many of the health problems that afflict homeless children will result in increased rates of school absenteeism. Even when unhealthy children remain in school, physical discomfort may limit their ability to listen, concentrate, or fully participate in learning activities. Schools can increase the likelihood of school success for homeless students by providing comprehensive school health services.

Comprehensive school health services should begin with a thorough health assessment by the school nurse or school nurse practitioner when a homeless student enrolls in school (Chauvin, Duncan, & Marcontel, 1990). In addition to general health appraisal, screening for vision, hearing, and dental problems should take place. When appropriate, the school nurse should provide referrals to appropriate professionals who provide services without charge to indigent children. The school nurse should be mindful that transportation might be necessary to get the child to the service provider. Follow-up should occur to ensure that essential services are provided in a timely manner.

Frequently, homeless children have been immunized; however, documentation of immunizations may not be readily available. In many schools, the lack of documentation of immunizations prevents the enrollment of homeless children and youth. In most states, however, grace periods can be provided (Johnson, Davidson, Edwards, Jackson-Jobe, & Linehan, 1990). Only in cases of epidemics should the grace period be denied. The school nurse should assist in verifying previous immunizations. If immunizations have not been obtained or additional immunizations are needed, the school nurse should assist in making arrangements to ensure that the appropriate immunizations are acquired. Ideally the immunizations should be administered at school. Minimally the school nurse should assume an advocacy role in helping ensure that appropriate immunizations are provided.

Health education and counseling are critical roles for school nurses in the provision of services to homeless children and youth. Depending on the child's age and situation, critical issues for instruction and counseling may include diet, personal hygiene, lice, sexually transmitted diseases, HIV infection, alcohol and drug abuse, and pregnancy. Education and counseling should be directed toward helping children assume responsibility for their health maintenance (Chauvin et al., 1990).

In some cases, homeless children or youth may not have access to such personal hygiene items as toothbrushes, deodorant, or other supplies. As previously noted, homeless children may not have a place to bathe. These children may become reluctant to attend school if they suspect that their teachers or peers might notice their lack of cleanliness. School nurses can provide access to essential personal hygiene supplies. The use of wash basins or shower facilities may be extremely helpful to those children who lack such facilities because they sleep in a car, under a bridge, or in some other substandard location.

In providing health services, it is important to avoid stigmatizing or bringing undue attention to the living arrangements of homeless children. Health services should be provided in a confidential setting. School health personnel should take note of the sensitivities of homeless students and provide services in a manner that does not generate fear or embarrassment (Texas Education Agency, 1991a).

To increase the likelihood of homeless children succeeding in school, school health personnel may also need to assume a case management role related to the physiological needs of homeless children. School health personnel should assume responsibility for assessing health needs, providing available services as needed, making referral to other community agencies when services are not available in the school, and providing follow-up to ensure that all physiological needs are being addressed adequately. To accomplish the case management function well, school health personnel must become familiar with all of the community services that might address the physiological needs of homeless students. School health personnel must become familiar with each homeless student, identifying unique attributes and needs so that appropriate services can be planned and implemented.

**School Clothing**

The nature of homelessness causes many children to have an extremely limited supply of clothing. Families may have only the clothes they can carry with them in their search for shelter. As children grow and as clothes become outworn, money may not be available for replacements. The lack of clothing can be a health concern. Lack of appropriate shoes, coats, and jackets may leave homeless children unprotected in inclement weather. In addition, the lack of clothing is a social concern. Students may not want to come to school if they are teased because they wear the same shirt everyday or because their clothes are dirty or of inappropriate sizes or styles (Johnson et al., 1990).

Frequently shelters and other agencies maintain clothing closets to assist homeless individuals. Sometimes, however, the majority of the clothing is for adults. Rarely are coats, good shoes, and such items as children's underwear or socks available. Of course, communities vary in the extent to which they have become sensitive and responsive to this need.

Schools can participate in efforts to ensure that homeless children have appropriate school clothing by maintaining their own clothing supplies. Some schools involve Parent-Teacher Associations in helping maintain a supply of appropriate clothing. Some schools involve local businesses, seeking donations of tennis shoes, socks, and other apparel. Other schools have used federal Elementary and Secondary Education Act (ESEA) Chapter One funds to provide emergency clothing to low-income children.

A critical issue in the provision of clothing is the method of dissemination. Some children might be extremely embarrassed to have their classmates know that they have received donated clothing (Texas Education Agency, 1991a). In some cases, homeless children and youth have been observed to avoid acquiring desperately needed clothing or shoes because of fear of embarrassment. School staff can respond to this issue by placing clothing supplies in a confidential place. In some schools, homeless students are shown the clothing closet and are given permission to get items whenever they feel the need, without seeking permission. Such a procedure can increase the extent to which needed items are acquired and used.

In a similar way, unnecessary stigmatization can be avoided by seeking clothing supplies that represent a variety of styles. For instance, when a Houston Independent School District counselor received a donation of several dozen pairs of identical tennis shoes, she quickly realized that the tennis shoes would get very limited wear as soon as students began to suspect that the shoes would be recognized by peers as "homeless shoes" or "poor kids' shoes." The counselor consulted with the benefactor and exchanged some of the shoes for a greater variety of styles.

## Supportive Services Addressing Safety/Security Needs

The ability to feel safe and secure eludes many victims of homelessness, most noticeably children and youth. The vulnerability created by life on the street, in shelters, or in other temporary living quarters creates significant stresses. Frequently, homeless individuals live in inner-city areas where shelters, soup kitchens, and other services are more accessible. As such, gang violence, drugs, prostitution, assaults, murders, and rapes surround the everyday existence of thousands of homeless children. Perhaps even more frightening, some homeless children must also face daily fears of domestic violence that may take the form of parental fights; physical, emotional, and sexual child abuse; and kidnapping.

In addition to fears related to safety, many homeless children are plagued with insecurities concerning their immediate future. Not only must homeless children worry about who might hurt them or their family members, but they might also have persistent worries about sleeping arrangements, food, money, and other critical survival issues. Even when physiological needs are addressed adequately, serious concern may exist about the extent to which those needs will continue to be met tomorrow (Johnson et al., 1990).

The lack of safety and security in their lives outside of the school day may cause some homeless children to experience difficulty focusing on the learning tasks presented during the school day. Extreme safety and security concerns may cause some homeless children to avoid going to school at all. Supportive services can address some of these safety and security issues and increase the likelihood that homeless children will attend and be successful in school. School can become a safe haven for homeless children—for some, their only refuge from an otherwise unsafe and unstable world.

### Transportation Services

School districts typically provide transportation to students who live beyond a certain distance from the school campus. The assumption is that children who live within a specified radius (usually 1 to 2 miles) can either walk to school, ride to school in the family car, or pay for public transportation. All of these assumptions are incorrect for many homeless children. Homeless parents may be unable to walk consistently with their children because of work schedules, appointments for social services, shelter work assignments, job interviews, or other activities; a family car may not be available, and bus fare may seem like a distant luxury to many homeless families (Johnson et al., 1990).

Getting to and from school may pose significant dangers to many homeless children and youth. Even when the walk is short, it may cross areas of gang activity, drug traffic, and other criminal activity, especially for those students living in urban areas. In cases where children are homeless because of domestic violence, the walk to and from school may increase the possibility of kidnapping. In some cases, an abusive father may follow the child home to locate and further abuse the mother.

Section 722(e)(5) of the McKinney Homeless Assistance Act requires that homeless children be provided transportation services comparable to those provided to other students. Thus if a homeless student is otherwise eligible for transportation services based on state or local policies or procedures, transportation must be provided. The fact that a student's temporary residence is a shelter or a campground does not alter any district responsibility to provide transportation.

Beyond the requirements of law, some schools have responded to the needs of homeless children by providing bus transportation in response to safety concerns. In some cases, where the area surrounding the shelter presents hazards to walking, bus transportation is provided even though the shelter is within a relatively short distance from the campus. Some school districts provide additional bus stops along existing routes; other districts provide special bus routes to offer transportation for homeless children; still other districts provide tokens for public transportation or arrange for transportation through other community or public agencies.

It is important to ensure that transportation services are provided safely yet without stigmatizing homeless students. Some schools integrate bus routes with homeless and nonhomeless students but arrange bus stops that are not directly in front of the shelters. As a result, attention is not drawn to the students' living accommodations (Texas Education Agency, 1991a). It is also important to ensure that children are safe while waiting for the school bus. In some cases, arrangements can be made with shelter personnel to help supervise a bus stop.

When special bus routes are needed, schools should take care to label the route and the bus with the generic area of the bus route (e.g., downtown), as opposed to using terms associated with a shelter or with homelessness. Students may become very creative in finding ways to avoid riding a bus that has been overtly or covertly labeled "the shelter bus."

If tokens for public transportation are provided, care should be taken to ensure that children are likely to be safe while waiting for and while riding the public transportation system. This may be of particular concern for young children. It may be necessary in some cases to provide tokens for parents to ride along with their children. It is important to keep in mind, however, that some homeless parents may be unable to accompany their children to school because of work schedules or other obligations or problems.

Getting to and from school should not be a risk to a child's safety. By providing transportation, schools can decrease the stress in the lives of students and increase the likelihood of regular student attendance. The provision of transportation can also respond to the social/affiliation needs of homeless children, as will be discussed later in this chapter.

### Before- and After-School Programs

Frequently, homeless children have nowhere to go and nothing to do in the hours immediately before and/or after school. Many shelters open at 5:00 p.m. or later and close at 6:30 a.m. or earlier. Edelman and Mihaly (1989) reported that some shelters in Washington, DC, required homeless children and their parents to remain off of the premises between 7:30 a.m. and 7:30 p.m. Homeless children are frequently on the street during the times when neither the shelter nor the school campus is open. During these times, homeless children may be most vulnerable to the ills of inner-city life. Also during these times, homeless children may be without protection from inclement weather.

Even when shelters are open for a greater portion of the day, homeless children may not have any organized activities in which to participate or even a safe place to play. Sometimes, homeless parents are not available to meet their children when school adjourns because of job interviews, work schedules, social service appointments, or other problems or commitments. Thus the early morning and late afternoon hours frequently bring boredom, if not danger, to the lives of homeless children and youth.

Schools can respond to the need for safety and constructive activity by ensuring that homeless children and youth have access to before- and/or after-school programs. Such extended-day programs may provide recreational activities, field trips, academic enrichment, counseling, experiences with fine arts, athletics, case management services, homework assistance, leadership development, self-concept building activities, snacks, and transportation.

Some extended-day programs, such as the Denver Public Schools After School Program and the New York City Board of Education Extended School Day Program, were designed in response to the needs of homeless students although they are open to other students at the school (McCall, 1990). By integrating homeless students with nonhomeless peers, the potential is less for stigmatizing and isolating homeless students.

Section 722(e)(1)(E) of the McKinney Homeless Assistance Act requires states to ensure that homeless students who meet relevant eligibility requirements have access to existing federal, state, and local before- and after-school care programs. This does not require that new extended-day programs be established. It does require, however, that homeless children have appropriate access to existing programs that may meet their needs.

Extended-day programs may address many of the needs of homeless students. By providing nutritious snacks and protection from inclement weather, they may respond to the physiological needs of homeless students. By providing opportunities to interact positively with peers, they may respond to the social needs of homeless students. By providing tutoring, homework assistance, and academic enrichment, such programs may respond to the esteem needs of homeless students (Johnson & Wand, 1991). Yet for many homeless students, the most important facet of extended-day programs is that they extend for a few more hours the safe haven provided by school—a few more hours of peace, and fewer hours of worry or fear.

### Record-Handling Services

In situations of domestic violence, the manner in which a school handles the records of a homeless child may be of extreme importance to the life and well-being of the child and members of the child's family. In several situations, abusive parents/spouses have used schools to help track, find, and harm children and spouses who are homeless as a result of domestic violence (Texas Education Agency, 1991b).

For instance, a woman may take her children and flee an abusive situation, moving to a shelter in a nearby city. Enraged, the abusive husband may seek to find and harm the woman or the children. The husband may go to the children's school and ask the names of school districts that have requested the children's school records. Armed with such information, the husband sometimes is able to locate and further harm his wife or children.

Schools can help respond to these dangers by exercising caution in the handling of records of children who are homeless as a result of domestic violence. The Family Educational Rights and Privacy Act (FERPA) requires that parents be provided access to their children's records. Therefore, in some cases, schools may not have the right to deny an abusive parent information concerning the whereabouts of his or her children. Schools can intervene, however, in several ways to help ensure the safety of children fleeing from domestic violence.

First (when domestic violence is suspected), some schools delay responding to requests for records for 72 hours. This gives the abused spouse time to acquire protective orders that can legally prevent the disclosure of information about the spouse or children to the perpetrator. Second, in the absence of protective orders, some schools notify police, the receiving school, and the domestic violence shelter when information has been given to an abusive spouse. These two steps alone can enhance the safety of many children fleeing domestic violence situations (Texas Education Agency, 1991a).

## Homebound Services

In some cases, the threat of domestic violence is so severe that school attendance provokes a substantial risk for further violence or kidnapping even though all other reasonable precautions have been taken. Many homeless children in this situation simply do not attend school. They remain in the shelter or in some other location all day.

For families at severe risk of domestic violence, schools can respond to safety needs by providing homebound educational services. A teacher can be sent to the shelter to provide instruction when too great a risk is incurred by children attending school on the public school campus. Homebound services may be provided like the services provided for children who are hospitalized or bedridden. The goal should be to integrate the student into the regular school program as soon as it is reasonably safe to do so.

*Supportive Services Addressing Social/Affiliation Needs*

A home provides much more than a roof; it provides a sense of belonging and a sense of identity. Generally, when a child becomes homeless, he or she has lost much more than a place to sleep. Frequently homelessness separates children from favorite toys, pets, relatives, and friends. In interviews of homeless elementary students, over 95% said that they missed their friends more than anything else (Johnson, 1991).

After the tremendous sense of loss associated with becoming homeless, children are frequently thrust into a busy, confusing world that has little time or intent to address their needs for belonging and affiliation. Some children are traumatized severely by these losses. Some react aggressively; others quietly isolate themselves. In either case, students are not likely to benefit fully from education without appropriate attention to their social needs.

### Outreach Enrollment Programs

Feelings of rejection can surround the lives of homeless individuals. Often they have been rejected by their families, friends, communities, and various social service agencies who could not help or did not help in their time of need. It is not surprising that many homeless families anticipate rejection from the public schools. Whether because of previous experiences, misinformation, or fear of the system, many homeless parents do not pursue the enrollment of their children in public school. Ultimately these parents assume that the school does not want their children. Through outreach enrollment programs, schools can send a different message to homeless parents and their children. Schools can help parents understand and believe each child's enrollment and attendance is important to the staff of the school (Texas Education Agency, 1991a).

Outreach enrollment programs can take many forms. Some schools simply provide shelters with all of the necessary enrollment forms so that parents know that their children are welcome and expected. Terrence Quinn, the principal of Public School 225 in Rockaway Queens, New York, takes coffee and donuts to the local shelter in his attendance area and personally talks to parents to convince them to enroll their children (Quinn, 1989). Parents come to understand that the school staff value them and their children.

At Burnet Street School in Newark, New Jersey, an attendance counselor position was created to coordinate with shelters, the health department, and other schools to get homeless children enrolled. The attendance counselor visits shelters and hotels for homeless persons on a daily basis to help ensure that homeless students are enrolled in school (Zeldin & Bogart, 1990).

Through a variety of techniques, schools can help parents overcome the expectation of rejection. Posters and brochures advertising the school and the programs offered by the school can be placed in shelters, soup kitchens, and other agencies that serve homeless parents or homeless children. Maps, school bus schedules, school calendars, and similar information can be posted in shelters. School personnel can provide workshops for homeless parents in which the parents are encouraged to enroll their children. Such strategies as these may help homeless parents feel a sense of belonging within a school community, perhaps for the first time in their lives.

**Transportation for Continuity**

By providing transportation, schools can respond to some of the safety needs of homeless children, as well as address many of their social needs. As required by Section 722(e)(3) of the McKinney Homeless Assistance Act, if it is in the best interest of the child, a homeless student must be allowed to return to attend the school of origin (the school the child attended before becoming homeless or the school in which the child was last enrolled). Congress acknowledged that continuity is important to the educational success of many homeless students. By being able to continue attending the school of origin, many homeless children can maintain a sense of affiliation and continuity in at least one important aspect of their lives.

Unfortunately, despite policies that allow students to return to the school of origin, few states have policies that provide the transportation needed to make attending the school of origin practical. In other words, few homeless children can take advantage of this provision of the law because they do not have access to transportation (Friedman, 1991). As a result, as homeless children move from place to place in search of housing, they must also move from school to school.

Even though Section 722(e)(1)(G)(i) of the McKinney Act requires states to address the transportation needs of homeless children in their state plans, few resources are available to ensure that the need is addressed adequately. A few states, however, have dedicated a significant amount of state and local resources to ensure that homeless students are realistically able to attend their schools of origin. For instance, New Jersey has enacted legislation that ensures transportation for homeless students to the school of origin if such is in the best interest of the homeless child (Johnson & Wand, 1991).

Another option for increasing continuity for homeless students is the modification of school attendance zones. Some cities have several shelters. Frequently, homeless families travel back and forth among these shelters as shelter stay limits expire or as possibilities for jobs or permanent housing seem to appear and disappear. In some cases, school districts can decrease the number of times that homeless children transfer between schools by assigning several shelters to the same attendance area.

Figure 9.1 illustrates a city with 12 shelters in the attendance zones of 12 different elementary schools. As students move from one shelter to another, they are likely to be assigned to a different school with each move. Providing transportation to the school of origin could be a logistical nightmare. Figure 9.2 illustrates the same city with each of the 12 shelters assigned to one of three elementary schools. Regular transportation can be planned and provided efficiently between the shelters and their attendance area school, minimizing safety concerns and attendance problems. Furthermore, as students move among the shelters, the number of school transfers is likely to remain low. Even when students move to a shelter out of the attendance area, the opportunity to provide transportation to the school of origin is greater because of the smaller numbers of schools.

When it is in the best interest of the homeless child to attend the school of origin, strategies that provide needed transportation can have a dramatic effect on the life of a child. Such transportation services require planning and the commitment of human and fiscal resources. Perhaps more than any other supportive service, transportation to the school of origin allows a homeless student to maintain patterns of academic, social, and emotional development. In an otherwise chaotic, unpredictable world, school can be the constant on which future growth is supported.

**Buddy Programs**

Entering a new school can be a difficult event for any child. For children who have been repeatedly uprooted and placed into new school environments, the experience can be traumatic. In the face of such trauma, some children will have difficulty becoming fully involved in

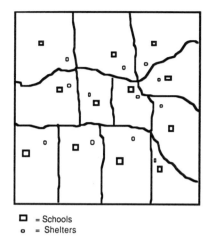

☐  = Schools
o  = Shelters

**Figure 9.1**. Twelve Shelters in Twelve School Zones.

learning processes. Schools can reduce the trauma and facilitate the social-
ization of homeless children by instituting buddy programs. These simple
programs provide new students with a "buddy" who assumes responsibility
for introducing the student to the new school, its rules and routines, and
other students. Buddy programs provide an uncomplicated strategy for
integrating homeless children into the school community (Texas Education Agency, 1991a). An important feature of many buddy programs is
that they are available for all new students. Thus homeless students are
not stigmatized when assigned a buddy. In fact, in some schools, care
is taken to provide some homeless students the opportunity to be a
buddy to other new students (Johnson, 1991).

**Mentor Programs**

Like buddy programs, mentor programs are designed to help children
feel a sense of acceptance at school, a sense of belonging. Whereas buddy
programs provide the new student with the attention of a peer, mentor
programs generally provide the attention and support of an adult.

City Park Elementary School in Dallas, Texas, has a mentor program
that has provided support to many children. All adults on the campus
(including secretaries, custodians, food service workers, teachers,

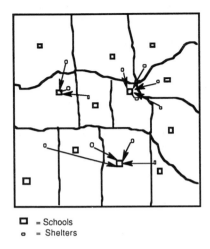

**Figure 9.2**. Twelve Shelters in Reconfigured School Zones.

classroom aides, volunteers, and the principal) may serve as mentors. Mentors are required to make at least one personal contact a week with their assigned students. Contacts typically are more frequent, however. Mentors sometimes write notes to their students. Sometimes mentors can be seen walking their students around the campus at recess. Some mentors provide extra assistance to their students on homework or other school assignments. Some even take their students to lunch at a nearby fast-food restaurant. In City Park's program, as in other mentor programs, a mentor's primary responsibility is to help the student feel valued as a part of the school community. Students at City Park come to feel a strong sense of belonging and attachment, and they know that they are important (Johnson, 1991).

**Counseling Programs**

Many homeless children adjust to the stresses of homelessness with minimal difficulty. For some students, however, the trauma of homelessness may be overwhelming. These students may have little capacity to focus on learning tasks because of the many feelings associated with their homelessness. Their capacity to make friends or to be a friend to other students may be impaired by the trauma of multiple separations.

Redlener (1989) explained that many homeless children experience depression, while some develop serious psychiatric and behavior problems. Bassuk and Rosenberg (1988) found that 31% of homeless children were clinically depressed. School counseling programs can help ensure that the social-emotional needs of homeless children are adequately addressed by offering these students an opportunity to express appropriately their feelings and frustrations, resulting in improved school behavior, self-esteem, and interpersonal relationships.

School districts have provided a variety of counseling interventions in response to the needs of homeless children. Coeur d'Alene Elementary School in Venice, California, (Los Angeles Unified School District) provides a psychologist to assist homeless students with social-emotional issues. The psychologist frequently works with students in small groups but also sees students on an individual basis. Some of the groups are designed for children with aggressive or impulsive behaviors, whereas other groups focus on the needs of children who seem withdrawn or introverted. Students are encouraged to refer themselves for individual counseling when tension mounts (Castanon, 1990).

Just as the school nurse may assume case management responsibilities for the physiological needs of homeless students, school counselors and social workers may assume case management responsibilities for the social-emotional needs of homeless students. The counseling program should ensure that needed counseling and psychological services are delivered by the staff at either the school or other agencies within the community. Assumption of case management responsibilities requires (a) knowledge of the resources available to meet student needs, (b) knowledge of the guidelines and procedures for accessing those resources, and (c) a commitment to pursuing and acquiring services that may address the social-emotional needs of homeless children and youth.

**Training for School Personnel**

Most educators have never visited a shelter. Their perceptions of homeless persons may have been formed by television images and the one-dimensional portrayals witnessed on inner-city street corners. Without training, educators may have neither an awareness of nor a sensitivity to the needs of homeless students. As a result, the lack of understanding may make school a less inviting place for homeless children. Many school districts have initiated training programs to help school personnel become aware of the situations surrounding homeless children and their families. For instance, the Massachusetts Department of Education sponsored a series of workshops during the 1989-90 school year to provide educators an opportunity to meet with shelter providers and to learn about the special needs of homeless children (McCall, 1990). The workshops were designed to communicate the facts and refute the myths about homeless children, to explain the similarities between homeless children and their nonhomeless peers, to provide teachers with strategies for helping homeless students develop friendships at school, to explain the nature of the school difficulties some homeless children may experience, and to suggest ways that school personnel can be involved in supporting homeless families (Johnson, 1991). The Region XIX Education Service Center in El Paso, Texas, conducted a similar workshop during the 1990-91 school year for school district personnel and other service providers. This workshop included a field trip for participants to local shelters, allowing some educators to see the inside of a shelter for the first time. The staff of the Harbor School in San Diego, California, hold regularly scheduled meetings with the staff of the St. Vincent de Paul Family Shelter. At these meetings, the special needs of individual students are discussed, coordination problems are discussed and resolved, and plans are shared for future activities (Johnson, 1991). At City Park Elementary School in Dallas, Texas, an ongoing staff development program includes workshops from professionals who provide services to homeless students, tours of nearby shelter facilities, and staff meetings in which school personnel help each other respond to the special needs of homeless students (Johnson, 1991).

By providing opportunities for school personnel to better understand the needs of homeless children, schools can promote an environment in which homeless students feel accepted. Training should be directed toward all professional and paraprofessional staff who encounter homeless children, including teachers, aides, administrators, secretaries, custodians, and bus drivers. Training programs can help eliminate insensitive procedures or remarks that may unintentionally have a devastating effect on homeless children. With greater understanding comes greater acceptance. For many homeless children, the feeling of being accepted in a normal, healthy environment may be tremendously rewarding, spawning new and powerful interests in school and learning.

## *Supportive Services Addressing Esteem Needs*

The desire to feel successful and competent is just as strong in homeless children as in other children. Homeless children want to be recognized for their attributes and achievements. They seek a sense of accomplishment; they look forward to succeeding in school, just as other children do. The situations surrounding homelessness, however, may make it difficult for some homeless students to feel successful and competent in school. When school does not provide for the esteem needs of students, students may seek to have those needs met in other arenas of life. For homeless children and youth, alternative arenas other than those provided by street life may be few.

All of the support services previously discussed may in various ways address the esteem needs of homeless children. For example, in addition to meeting the need for protection from inclement weather, appropriate shoes are likely to help children feel better about themselves. Similarly the attention provided through an after-school program may help children feel better about their school performance, as well as responding to their needs to have a safe place to go until the shelter opens. A few services that may specifically address the extent to which homeless students feel successful and competent in school remain to be discussed.

### Expedited Evaluation

In some cases, homeless children may need special education services or other special programs in order to benefit from education. Access to these services may be limited because of the length of time involved in acquiring evaluations. Homeless children often move before special education evaluations are completed (Johnson et al., 1990). In some schools, teachers are told bluntly not to refer homeless children for special education programs because the students are not likely to remain at the school long enough to complete the evaluation process. "Why go through all of the paperwork and trouble? He's only going to be here for a month," is the explanation given at some schools where personnel may not understand that the child's entire school year may be a series of month-long enrollments. For other special programs, such as those for gifted and talented students, some schools only offer screenings or evaluations at a certain time of the school year. Homeless children may not gain access to certain programs because they did not arrive at the time of year that screenings or evaluations were offered.

Expedited evaluation services can help ensure that homeless students promptly receive needed services. Evaluation may determine the need for such special programs as bilingual education, special education, or programs for gifted/talented students. Evaluation may also determine the appropriate focus of regular classroom placement. For instance, evaluation may help a teacher immediately determine the appropriate reading program for a child or identify the skills that should be the focus of math instruction for the child. The transition room at Emerson Elementary School in Madison, Wisconsin, provides evaluation services to determine each student's academic level prior to placement in regular classrooms (McCall, 1990). At Coeur d'Alene Elementary in Venice, California, the psychologist provides an academic evaluation for each child during the first week of school attendance to help teachers better address the academic needs of homeless students (Castanon, 1990).

Schools may also use funds provided by Section 723 of the amended McKinney Homeless Assistance Act to provide diagnosticians or psychologists to expedite the evaluation of homeless students. Schools thereby can develop systems to rapidly screen, evaluate, and place homeless students who need special services. Alternative screening and evaluation systems can also be developed to respond to the needs of homeless students who were not present during formal screening periods. For instance, at City Park Elementary, the teacher for the laureate program (program for gifted and talented students) regularly visits classrooms to observe new students who may benefit from the program. Although screening and evaluation for the program take place annually, students can be screened, evaluated, and placed anytime during the year (Johnson, 1991).

By expediting evaluation, schools can reduce the frustration experienced by inappropriately placed students. When these students promptly receive needed evaluations, each student is more likely to benefit academically and to experience a sense of accomplishment at school.

### Tutoring/Individualized Academic Attention

For some homeless children, frequent transfers between schools have resulted in gaps in sequences of academic skills. Some students may have been earning good grades in school, but after a prolonged period of homelessness and transiency, grades may falter, along with the student's sense of accomplishment in school. Rafferty and Rollins (1989) found that, on average, children missed 5 days of school each time they moved into a new shelter facility. For some homeless children, lack of language development opportunities and early cognitive stimulation may result in school difficulties. These children may have excellent potential for intellectual growth, but such potential may not be readily apparent in school because of the lack of prior learning experiences.

Tutoring services may help many homeless students achieve success in school. At Coeur d'Alene Elementary, a tutor works closely with classroom teachers to identify the learning needs of homeless students. Tutoring activities are designed to increase the likelihood that homeless students are successful despite gaps in prior learning (Johnson, 1991). At some schools, efforts are made to decrease the adult/teacher ratio in classrooms to allow teachers to better respond to the individual learning needs of homeless students. Classroom aides, volunteers, and peer tutors are used in some classrooms to increase the amount of individual attention directed to each student. In some schools, such as City Park Elementary, low adult/teacher ratios are maintained to ensure that teachers have adequate opportunity to respond to the academic needs of homeless students (González, 1991).

The extra attention directed to academic needs can make a dramatic difference for some homeless students. The difference between success and failure may be only 15 minutes of one-on-one tutoring twice a week, a little extra time for the teacher to explain a prerequisite concept, or an aide who can listen to a child read for a few minutes each day.

**Funds for School Supplies and Fees**

Many homeless children may have the capacity to excel in any of a variety of extracurricular activities. Unfortunately sometimes these children are not able to participate because of the costs associated with participation (e.g., fees, dues, uniforms). In addition, many homeless children may have the capacity to excel academically in school, but sometimes they do not have a full opportunity to demonstrate their competencies because they do not have appropriate school supplies or money for lab fees, field trips, or other costs related to instruction (Johnson et al., 1990).

Schools can help ensure the success of children in school by providing school supplies and resources to allow homeless children to participate fully in school activities. It is important that provisions be made without drawing undue attention to homeless students. For instance, school supplies, gym uniforms, or other resources might be distributed at the shelter so that students will have these items when they arrive at school (Texas Education Agency, 1991a).

## Summary

All students have physiological, safety, affiliation, and esteem needs. Traditionally schools have sought to respond to certain needs, while assuming that other needs might be addressed adequately by parents or by other community resources. Today hundreds of thousands of home-less students in America are coming to school with physiological, safety, affiliation, and esteem needs that require more of schools than ever before. Students who on most nights acquire their dinners from park dumpsters need school meal programs. Students who must remain on crime-filled city streets until their shelter opens at 6:00 p.m. need extended-day programs. Students who suffer from the emotional trauma of losing their friends, pets, furniture, toys, and clothing, along with their homes, need counseling services. Students who have been to six or seven schools in a year need tutoring services to fill in the academic gaps created by their transiency.

Throughout American public schools, one can find school mission statements, conference themes, banners, posters, and buttons that pro-claim, "All children can learn." The proclamation is made not simply to acknowledge the neurological capacity of children to acquire, pro-cess, and use knowledge. Rather the proclamation is an expression of a commitment to ensure the learning of each child to the maximum of the child's potential. In light of the number of children who are not learning in school, who are dropping out of school, or who cannot even gain admittance into school programs, it may be suggested that the commit-ment expressed by the words *All children can learn* is more evident in rhetoric than in practice. Yet the opposite is true in some schools.

The evidence is clear that homeless children are learning in public schools where their needs are being addressed appropriately. On any given day, one fourth of the students at City Park Elementary in Dallas are homeless. The school has the highest rate of transiency of any school in the city, yet test scores are among the highest in the district (González, 1991). At Coeur d'Alene Elementary in Los Angeles, even though as many as 50 students on any day come to school from shelters and motels, an atmosphere of learning exists; discipline problems are rare (Johnson, 1991). An assumption evident in both policy and practice says, "Every child will learn here: no exceptions!"

As America's public schools confront an increasing population of homeless students who present increasingly complex needs, schools have a choice. On the one hand, school staff can contend that they cannot or should not expand their services to address the needs of homeless children and youth. Perhaps other social service agencies should assume these responsibilities. Perhaps parents should be expected to do more. Perhaps the resources simply are insufficient. Perhaps the school cannot handle any more responsibilities. On the other hand, school staff can contend that they truly can make a difference. Perhaps the resources can be found. Perhaps it is primarily a change in attitude that is required. Perhaps school staff can ensure that today's homeless children will not be tomorrow's homeless parents. Perhaps there truly is not a choice.

## References

Bassuk, E. L., & Rosenberg, L. (1988). Why does family homelessness occur? A case-control study. *American Journal of Public Health, 78*(7), 783-788.

Castanon, C. C. (1990). Working with homeless children fraught with hope. *Communique: National Association of School Psychologists, 18*(1), 1.

Chauvin, V., Duncan, J., & Marcontel, M. (1990) Homeless students of the 90's: A new school population. *The School Nurse, 6*(3), 10-13.

Edelman, M. W., & Mihaly, L. (1989). Homeless families and the housing crisis in the United States. *Children and Youth Services Review, 11,* 91-108.

Friedman, L. (1991). *Small steps: An update on the education of homeless children and youth program.* Washington, DC: National Law Center on Homelessness and Poverty.

González, M. L. (1991). School-community partnerships and the homeless. *Educational Leadership, 49*(1), 23-24.

Johnson, J. F. (1991). *Educating America's homeless children in the least restrictive environment.* Unpublished dissertation, University of Texas.

Johnson, J. F., Davidson, D., Edwards, J., Jackson-Jobe, P., & Linehan, M. (1990). *Position document on the re-authorization of Subtitle VII-B of the Stewart B. McKinney Homeless Assistance Act.* Baltimore, MD: National Association of State Coordinators for the Education of Homeless Children and Youth. (Available from Maryland Department of Education, Office for the Education of Homeless Children and Youth, 200 W. Baltimore St., 4th floor, Baltimore, MD 21201)

Johnson, J. F., & Wand, B. E. (1991). *Homeless, not hopeless: Ensuring educational opportunity for America's homeless children and youth.* Baltimore, MD: National Association of State Coordinators for the Education of Homeless Children and Youth.

(Available from Maryland Department of Education, Office for the Education of Homeless Children and Youth, 200 W. Baltimore St., 4th floor, Baltimore, MD 21201)

Kozol, J. (1988). *Rachel and her children: Homeless families in America.* New York: Crown.

McCall, K. P. (1990). *Educating homeless children and youth: A sample of programs, policies, and procedures.* Cambridge, MA: Center for Law and Education.

Mihaly, L. (1991). *Homeless families: Failed policies and young victims.* Washington, DC: Children's Defense Fund.

Quinn, T. (1989). My hard encounter with the reality of homeless children. *The Executive Educator, 11*(12), 17-29.

Rafferty, Y., & Rollins, N. (1989). *Learning in limbo: The educational deprivation of homeless children.* New York: Advocates for Children of New York.

Redlener, I. E. (1989, October 4). *Unacceptable losses: The consequences of failing America's homeless children.* Testimony before the U.S. Senate's Committee on Labor and Human Resources, Subcommittee on Children, Family, Drugs, and Alcoholism.

Texas Education Agency. (1991a). *Campus self-assessment guide for the education of homeless students.* Austin: Author.

Texas Education Agency. (1991b). *Texas state plan for the education of homeless children and youth, 1991-1993.* Austin: Author.

Waxman, L. D., & Reyes, L. M. (1987). *The continuing growth of hunger, homelessness, and poverty in America's cities: 1987.* Washington, DC: U.S. Conference of Mayors.

Wright, J. D., & Weber, E. (1987). *Homelessness and health.* Washington, DC: McGraw-Hill.

Zeldin, S., & Bogart, J. (1990). *Education and community support for homeless children and youth: Profiles of 15 innovative and promising approaches* (Contract LC 89089001). Washington, DC: Policy Studies Associates.

# PART III

# *Education for the Homeless*

## Access and Equity Issues

## 10

# Ensuring Access to Education

## The Role of Advocates for
## Homeless Children and Youth

JOAN ALKER

Widespread homelessness became a feature of the American landscape during the 1980s. While there have been homeless persons throughout the 20th century, shrinking incomes and declining welfare benefits, combined with increased housing costs and a shortage of 4.2 million low-income units by 1990, pushed unprecedented numbers of men, women, and children out of their housing during the 1980s (Dolbeare & Alker, 1990). While it is impossible to state with any precision how many persons are homeless, estimates range from 600,000 to 3 million on a given night. A recent study of homeless families reported the frightening projection that as many as 2 million American children may experience homelessness over the course of a year (Mihaly, 1991). Nationwide, families with children constitute approximately one third of the homeless population (Waxman & Reyes, 1990).

### Trends in National Advocacy
### for Homeless People

In response to this growing crisis, activism around the rights and needs of homeless people increased during the late 1970s and early

1980s (see Hombs, 1990). Two groups have played a prominent role on the national scene since that time: the National Coalition for the Homeless (NCH) and the Community for Creative Non-Violence (CCNV) (see Rader, 1986).

The National Coalition for the Homeless was formed in 1982 and remains the major grass roots organization working with and for homeless people across the United States. The National Coalition for the Homeless works to end homelessness through public education, organizing, litigation, and advocacy. The initial membership included representatives from 40 cities and regions across the country—predominantly from large urban areas (Hope & Young, 1986). By 1991, reflecting the spread of homelessness across the country, the National Coalition's Board of Directors had grown to 75 persons from 42 states, the District of Columbia, and Puerto Rico. The board is composed of homeless and formerly homeless persons, service providers, researchers, and other advocates for homeless people.

The Community for Creative Non-Violence was founded in 1970 by a Catholic priest, Ed Guinan. Initially focused on antiwar efforts, CCNV soon shifted its focus to domestic issues, specifically poverty and homelessness, after the Vietnam War ended in the mid-1970s. Since that time, CCNV has provided direct services and has advocated for and with homeless people on both local and national issues. Today CCNV members live and work in the large 1,400-bed shelter that CCNV obtained from the federal government after a dramatic fast by CCNV activist Mitch Snyder on the eve of the 1984 presidential election.

Both of these groups came to national attention after early efforts to obtain decent shelter for homeless persons in New York City and Washington, DC, respectively. In New York, a right to shelter was secured by a successful lawsuit, *Callahan v. Carey* (1979), brought by then volunteer attorney Robert M. Hayes, who became the National Coalition's first counsel. In Washington in 1976, CCNV began a campaign to obtain shelter for all who needed it. This campaign culminated in the passage of Initiative 17, the "D.C. Right to Overnight Shelter" in 1984.[1]

While early efforts were focused on obtaining decent shelter, both groups became quickly committed to the goal of decent housing as a right. During the late 1980s, the most important activities for the advocacy community focused on passage of the Stewart B. McKinney Homeless Assistance Act in 1987 and the Housing Now! march on Washington in October of 1989, organized by CCNV, the National Coalition for the Homeless, and the National Low Income Housing Coalition. The

Housing Now! march brought more than 250,000 people to Washington, calling for the restoration of funds cut from the federal housing budget during the Reagan years and helping ensure passage of the National Affordable Housing Act of 1990, the first substantial piece of housing legislation in 15 years.

## The Stewart B. McKinney Homeless Assistance Act of 1987

Although several limited federal programs (see "President signs," 1987) to serve homeless people existed prior to the passage of the Stewart B. McKinney Homeless Assistance Act in July 1987, this legislation represented the first real recognition by the federal government that homelessness was a problem deserving of national attention and was passed over the objections of the Reagan administration. Originally titled the Urgent Relief for the Homeless Act, the bill subsequently was renamed for one of its key sponsors, the late Rep. Stewart McKinney (R-CT). It authorized just over $1 billion to be spent over the course of 1987 and 1988 (although Congress appropriated only 50% of this amount)[2] for emergency aid, including emergency shelter and food assistance, transitional housing, health and mental health care, job training and education programs, and a few very small permanent housing programs. The McKinney Act was not intended by its architects to end homelessness but rather was an important first step in responding to the emergency needs of homeless people to prevent them from literally dying on the streets.

Passage of the bill followed intense lobbying efforts by the National Coalition, CCNV, and others. To symbolize the plight of homeless people and to urge passage of McKinney, CCNV activist Mitch Snyder and homeless advocate Michael Stoops slept on a grate outside the Capitol from Thanksgiving Day in 1986 through April 1987. The less conventional tactics of CCNV and the more traditional lobbying of the National Coalition, as well as lobbying from state and local organizations generated by both groups, combined for an effective strategy.

### Education Provisions of the McKinney Act

Several advocacy groups played important roles in the development of sections of the McKinney Act that were designed to address some of the educational needs of homeless children. In addition to the National

Coalition for the Homeless, these included the Children's Defense Fund (CDF), a national nonprofit organization that performs research and advocacy on behalf of low-income and minority children, and the Center for Law and Education (CLE), one of 16 national support centers funded by the Legal Services Corporation. Also, many mainstream education groups, such as the National Association of State Boards of Education, became involved in the debate although often with views at odds with NCH, CDF, and CLE.

In 1987, a survey of shelter providers on the educational needs of homeless children and youth was undertaken by the Center for Law and Education, the Homelessness Information Exchange, the National Coalition, and the National Network of Runaway and Youth Services (Ely, 1987; Jackson, 1990). The study found that one third of the shelter providers interviewed knew of instances in which homeless children or older youth living on their own had been denied access to school as a result of local enforcement of residency laws or guardianship requirements.

In 1987, residency laws were the major barrier to the enrollment of homeless children. Children with no fixed address had extreme difficulty in proving residency in a school district. Families who moved to a shelter in another district in the middle of the school year were unable to demonstrate intent to reside permanently in the district in which they were temporarily living and often were unable to continue their child's education in the original district due to distance or inadequate transportation. Because school funding is based on residency requirements, many schools were unwilling to be flexible on this issue.

Another obstacle was the need for a legal guardian's signature during the enrollment process. This poses clear problems for runaways and older homeless youth living on their own. But guardianship requirements also pose problems for younger homeless children for a number of reasons. Many homeless families move frequently—successive short stays with family or friends, relocation in an attempt to find work, and sometimes as a result of shelter policies that limit the length of shelter stays. Children are sometimes separated from their parents, particularly older boys who often are denied entry into family shelters, but also because parents may leave a child with a friend or relative to ensure continuity in the child's schooling. These practices may result in a child not living with his or her legal guardian.

The survey also identified transportation, the slow transfer of school records, and the denial of special services to homeless children as significant problems. A second study of state education officials conducted by the Center for Law and Education revealed that most had little or no knowledge of the numbers of homeless children in their states or the problems they faced (Jackson, 1990).

Both of these studies resulted in the inclusion of two provisions to address the educational needs of homeless children and youth in the original McKinney Act. The first established small formula grants to states that submitted acceptable state plans for the education of homeless children and youth. Grants were allocated on the basis of the formula used for the Chapter One program, which provides remedial educational services to disadvantaged children. Each state was required to establish an office of the State Coordinator for the Education of Homeless Children and Youth, which would be responsible for writing and implementing the state's plan. The submission of the state's plan was to be accompanied by data on the number of homeless children in that state and the percentage of those children attending school. States were also required to revise residency requirements to ensure that these did not pose a barrier to the enrollment of homeless children.[3]

In addition, the bill included a small program of competitive grants for exemplary programs, authorized at $2.5 million but not funded until 3 years later.[4] Money allocated through the larger formula grant program was not authorized to be spent on direct services, but grants made to exemplary programs could be used for virtually anything, including direct services to meet the educational needs of homeless children.

Both of the education sections were the result of compromises between traditional education groups and advocates for homeless children. In fact, from the National Coalition's perspective, the education provisions were among the most controversial of the McKinney Act. Many of the original provisions developed by advocates for homeless children were watered down significantly, partly as a result of opposition from education groups. Such mainstream education groups as the National Association of State Boards of Education and the Chief State School Officers objected to being required to ensure homeless children access to school and services without receiving any new funding.

Initially the National Coalition had proposed that states that did not revise residency laws and ensure that homeless children have access to school would lose all of their federal education funding. Naturally education groups were vehemently opposed to this provision, and it was soon dropped. As a result of the powerful opposition of the education groups, virtually no mandates remained in the final version of the McKinney Act. The only penalty attached to a state that did not revise its residency laws was ineligibility for the small amount of McKinney funds provided through Section VII.

School choice was one of the most contested issues during construction of the original McKinney programs. The advocacy community had sought to obtain a choice for homeless parents to keep their child in the school he or she was attending before becoming homeless or to enroll the child in the school district in which the family currently was residing. Many education groups, battling the issue of school choice on a number of other fronts, vehemently opposed this position. The result was that the original McKinney Act gave local education agencies the power to make this decision and only required the state plan to establish a mechanism by which disputes regarding a child's school placement were to be resolved.

As expected, state efforts on behalf of homeless children, as a result of the 1987 McKinney Act, were varied. Only small incentives were offered to participate in the program; states could easily pass up the $50,000 minimum allotment that more than half received in the early years, although almost all elected to apply for funding. Initially the Department of Education was extremely slow in implementing the program and offered little oversight or guidance on states' plans. In December 1987, following a lawsuit brought by the National Coalition, a settlement was reached with the department on a timetable for implementation of the program. Despite the agreement, the department continued to distribute funds slowly, with little monitoring of or technical assistance to states. The Government Accounting Office reported in 1990 that the Department of Education still had done little to oversee its program (U.S. General Accounting Office, 1990).

Much of the variability in state programs can be attributed to the amount of funding a state receives and the energy and effectiveness of its state coordinator. Some states enacted their own legislation that specifically addressed residency barriers to enrollment. Most, however, did not. From the perspective of homeless parents and those working with them to have their children enrolled, many problems remained at local schools. Staff at most schools were unaware of the McKinney Act and its requirement that residency laws be revised; in many instances, the necessary information may have made it no farther than a school system superintendent's office. Rarely had knowledge of McKinney directives trickled down to teachers and, perhaps more importantly, to school secretaries or enrollment personnel, who are often the first and possibly the last person to come into contact with a homeless child trying to enroll in school.

## 1990 Changes to McKinney Education Provisions

The original McKinney programs were authorized to continue for 2 fiscal years. Because the Department of Education was so slow in starting up its program, by the time the McKinney Act was ready to expire or be renewed in 1988, little evidence could be found on the merits or drawbacks of the education piece. Unlike the highly publicized passage of the original McKinney Act in 1987, the greatest threat to the 1988 reauthorization of McKinney programs was the difficulty of attracting Congressional attention to an issue they had so recently addressed. The bill did pass, however, and the programs were reauthorized for another 2 years. The education programs remained virtually unchanged except for a few technical amendments. Thus most McKinney Act programs, including the education provisions, were scheduled to expire in 1990. Early that year, the National Coalition convened a series of working groups to develop recommendations on the reauthorization of McKinney programs. One of these groups was devoted solely to Subtitle B of Section VII, the education provisions of the McKinney Act. Organizations participating in the education group included the Center for Law and Education, the Children's Defense Fund, the Child Welfare League, the National Governor's Association, and the National Law Center on Homelessness and Poverty. This group met regularly to discuss policy changes to the education provisions and submitted comments on legislative drafts. Many of these comments were incorporated into the final draft of the Stewart B. McKinney Homeless Assistance Amendments Act of 1990.

### Improved Climate for Change

It was clear from continuing reports of homeless children and youth not attending school or being denied access to needed services that the education provisions of the McKinney Act needed substantial improvement. In March of 1990, the Department of Education reported to Congress that 28% of homeless children were not attending school regularly. Advocates for homeless children believed that the proportion of children not attending school could be much higher and saw the reauthorization as a significant opportunity to expand McKinney mandates.

A 1990 study of service providers in 20 states by the National Law Center on Homelessness and Poverty confirmed these fears. In the study, 60% of providers reported that residency requirements were still a problem despite the explicit requirement in the 1987 McKinney Act that the states review and revise residency requirements if these were acting as a barrier to the enrollment of homeless children. Also, 70% of those surveyed reported that difficulties with record transfers were keeping children out of school; 55% reported that homeless children were being denied access to comparable services, including special education and school meals; and 40% mentioned guardianship requirements as posing barriers.

In addition to these findings, the climate for substantive change was much improved over the original passage of the McKinney provisions. First, the McKinney Act had required states to collect data on the numbers of homeless children that were and were not attending school. Even though the quality of these data varied widely from state to state, the process of their collection was often the first introduction to the issue for many school systems. Staff in many school systems were simply unaware that homelessness was a problem in their districts. Others closed their eyes to it. McKinney data collection efforts played an important role in establishing that homelessness among children was a national problem of substantial proportions.

Second, the position of education groups changed markedly between passage of the original McKinney Act and the 1990 reauthorization. Such groups as the National Association of State Boards of Education that previously had been opposed to the McKinney provisions remained neutral or were supportive of program expansion. Equally important was the increasingly active profile of the McKinney-appointed State Coordinators for the Education of Homeless Children and Youth, who in 1989 formed the National Association of State Coordinators for the Education of Homeless Children and Youth (NASCEHCY).

In January of 1990, NASCEHCY issued its first position paper, which included lengthy recommendations for improvements to the McKinney Act. These included expanded directives to states to review and revise all policies and barriers, including but not limited to guardianship requirements, that were preventing homeless children and youth from enrolling in school. These recommendations were unusual, coming from a group that would be required to implement additional mandates and in many cases reflected the frustration that state coordinators experienced as a result of efforts to advocate with varied success on behalf of homeless children within their own state education bureaucracies.

The paper also called for the authorization of substantially increased funding to provide services, including transportation, expedited record transfer, tutoring, school personnel sensitivity training, clothes, and a range of other services that state coordinators had not been able to provide with original McKinney funds as a result of the prohibition on the funding of direct services.[5] Finally the paper called for the modification of the existing data collection requirements by focusing on the numbers of children being served in schools rather than a head count of homeless children in each state.

State coordinators were particularly frustrated by the McKinney requirement to count homeless children, because of the notorious difficulty and controversy that any count of homeless people causes. A well publicized example of the difficulties of counting homeless people was the Census Bureau's attempt to count "selected components" of the homeless population as part of the 1990 Census. Critics charged that the Census Bureau had missed as many as two thirds of the persons they were trying to count (see National Coalition for the Homeless, 1991).

Many homeless people, including homeless children, who are often stigmatized by their peers, do not want to be identified as homeless. Others are notoriously hard to find as a result of transitory or hidden life-styles. In addition, disagreements always arise about who should be considered homeless. The most salient issue for children surrounding the definition of homelessness is whether families that are living doubled or tripled up with friends or relatives should be considered homeless.

**Summary of New Provisions**

The state coordinators' position paper and the work of the advocates' education working group became the starting point for many of the discussions that ensued between advocates and Congressional offices on drafting the new legislation. After months of preparation, the changes to the education provisions were enacted when the McKinney Act was reauthorized in the fall of 1990. The final form of the law reflected many of the recommendations of NCH's education working group and the state coordinators' position document, with a few important exceptions.

The new statute expanded the list of barriers that states must review and revise from the original focus exclusively on attendance laws to include "other laws, regulations, practices, or policies that may act as a barrier to the enrollment, attendance, or success in school of homeless children and homeless youth."[6] State plans are also now required to address enrollment delays caused by transportation, immunization, and residency requirements, the lack of birth certificates or school records, and guardianship issues.[7]

The formula grant program was amended to allow for the provision of direct services with a vastly increased authorization ceiling of $50 million, and the exemplary grants program was terminated. States continue to receive funding based on the Chapter One formula but now are authorized to make grants to local education agencies on a competitive basis for a wide range of activities, including tutoring, excess transportation costs, school supplies and documentation costs, school personnel sensitivity training, and the education of homeless parents about the rights of their children. Local education agencies must use at least 50% of their grants for "tutoring, remedial education, and other education services."[8] Throughout the bill, coordination with existing services for other children is emphasized, and funds may be used to expand the number of places for homeless children in existing programs for all low-income children, such as Chapter One and Headstart.

The school choice issue was revisited, and the law was marginally improved. The new law requires local education agencies to take into consideration a parent's request for school placement. The data collection requirement was modified so that state coordinators now are required to count homeless children every other year, and the Department of Education is charged with obtaining a national estimate.

Undoubtedly the most contested issue surrounding the education of homeless children in local communities is the creation of separate school settings for homeless children. The 1987 McKinney Act was silent on this point. The 1990 McKinney Amendments, however, while not prohibiting the use of funds for separate schools, made it very clear that Congress did not favor the use of federal funds for separate schools. This is evident throughout the law, starting with the statement of policy, which now includes a statement that "homelessness alone should not be sufficient reason to separate students from the mainstream school environment."[9]

**Issues for Advocates**

*Mainstreaming Versus Separate School Settings*

Separate schools for homeless children are often referred to as "transitional schools" and usually provide educational services on-site at a shelter or transitional housing facility for homeless families. Advocates for homeless children, working on developing the new McKinney education program, were wary of recent trends toward creating separate school settings for homeless children. Indeed the opposition is virtually unanimous from advocacy groups and most McKinney state coordinators to the idea of the federal government encouraging separate schools as a matter of policy or priority for funding.

This was a concern for several reasons. First, the most potent fear was the specter of a return to a segregated system of education, determined this time not by race but by a child's housing status. Second, while successful programs with high visibility serving homeless children may receive a good deal of private funding today, these school settings could face serious shortfalls in already scarce resources when the tide of charitable giving turns away from homeless families. Advocates for homeless children believe that homeless children, like housed children, have a right to an appropriate public education. The public school system, while certainly struggling on a number of fronts, holds out the most promise, in the long term, as the setting in which a homeless child will receive the best education.

Education groups had a natural interest in opposing the funding of separate schools because it most likely would channel resources away from public school systems to nonprofits that established on-site programs for homeless children. In addition, most education groups today believe that mainstreaming, whenever possible, is in the best interest of any child with or without special needs.

For an advocacy group like the National Coalition for the Homeless, the position is more difficult. Because the coalition represents many service providers working with homeless families, the recognition is clear that most service providers who establish schools in their shelters do so out of frustration with the lack of responsiveness of the local school system to the needs of homeless children. Many children appear to do better in these environments than in unsupportive public school settings and are certainly better off than those who are not attending school at all. At the local level, it is often much easier to establish one's own project than to do battle with an entrenched and generally underfunded public education bureaucracy. This heightens the importance of effective advocacy for homeless children and the need for homeless parents and advocates for homeless children to be conversant with the educational rights of homeless children and the resources available to them.

The overriding concern for NCH, however, was that homelessness should not be viewed as an educational condition, and a certain set of educational assumptions should not be made about a child simply because he or she is homeless. Many of the problems experienced by homeless children trying to obtain an education are similar to those experienced by other poor but housed children. High mobility, stressful domestic living conditions, hunger, poor health, and other conditions associated with poverty affect poor housed and homeless children alike. Homeless children cluster at one end of the spectrum of residential instability that confronts most poor families living in America today. The public school system should be encouraged to adapt to the needs of poor children in general and, in the case of the McKinney Act, to the needs of homeless children.

## Use of Direct Service Funds

As originally conceived, the direct service program established by the 1990 McKinney Amendments gave state and local education agencies complete flexibility in determining how those funds would be spent. This flexibility reflected the varying degrees of success that local communities had achieved in enrolling homeless children in public schools. The Education and Labor Committee in the House of Representatives included a provision that at least 50% of the funds be used for tutoring as described above. The committee was concerned that, without this restriction, the majority of funds would be used for transportation, clothes, school supplies, and other services that were not perceived by the committee to be directly educational.

Initially the committee had suggested that 90% of the McKinney funds be used for tutoring and remedial education. Advocates for homeless children objected strongly to this proposal for two reasons. First, it was pointed out that many homeless children are not attending school and need transportation or clothes before they can enroll and be tutored or receive other educational services. Second, advocates were concerned that this provision would encourage the use of funds for separate school programs, which often provide tutoring, if funds for transportation or other services needed to enroll children in public schools were not available. The objections of advocates prompted the committee to lower the requirement to 50%, a partial victory because advocates had recommended that it be dropped altogether.

*Data Collection Requirements*

The new McKinney data collection requirements are somewhat confusing and reflect the incorporation of both the House and Senate versions of the bill. State coordinators had requested that they no longer be required to count homeless children. The Senate version of the bill removed the burden from state coordinators altogether and required the Department of Education to come up with a report to Congress on the possible methodologies to count homeless children on a national basis. The department was instructed to establish an advisory panel with representatives of advocacy organizations, state and local education agencies, and federal agencies to work with the department on the development of the report. The National Coalition proposed the inclusion of this panel to ensure that Congress, state coordinators, and such groups as the National Coalition had some role in the contentious and often highly politicized issue of counting homeless children.

The House version reduced the data collection requirement for state coordinators to every other year, and the law now allows states to use random sampling techniques and not to try to count every child. The law does not make clear what relationship, if any, should exist between the state and national counts or why both are necessary.

**Conclusion: Action Shifts
to the Local Level**

The new McKinney education provisions have created a window of opportunity for advocates and educators to ensure that homeless children enroll and succeed in public schools. While it is impossible to say how much money the program will receive, early indications suggest that the increase in its appropriation will be sizable.[10] How these additional funds are spent will play a critical role in determining the shape of future educational strategies to address the needs of homeless children.

Advocates for homeless children played a critical role in ensuring that the new law best serves the needs of homeless children. While outstanding issues certainly remain for advocates to pursue at the federal level (most importantly, working to ensure that the program is funded), much of the important advocacy for homeless children now must happen at the state and local level through the development of the state plan and the policies of local school districts. Local and state advocates for homeless children should contact their state's McKinney education coordinator in order to become involved in the process of drafting the state plan—the document that will set broad policy parameters for addressing the educational needs of homeless children. In addition, advocates and service providers at the local level often may have to alert local schools to the provisions of the McKinney Act and the rights they afford to homeless children, as well as simply to educate school personnel about the realities of homelessness in their communities.

Thus one of the most important tasks remaining for national advocacy groups is to provide information about the new McKinney Act directives and successful programs serving homeless children to those working at the state and local levels to ensure that homeless children receive the education they need. For many homeless children, school may be the only stable setting in their daily lives. Few would deny that any group of children is more in need of education than those without a place to call home.

## Notes

1. The right to shelter was rescinded by an action of the District of Columbia City Council, which was upheld narrowly by District voters in November 1990. See "Shelter referendum," 1990.

2. The amount of funds that are spent on federal programs is determined by Congress in a two-stage process. Authorizing legislation determines how much can be allocated to a program in upcoming fiscal years and establishes how that money will be spent. The actual amount that a program receives is determined through the appropriations process, which occurs every year.

3. See Sections 721 and 722 of P.L. 100-77.

4. Section 723 received funding in FY90 but was subsequently terminated in the reauthorization of the McKinney Act in 1990.

5. The Department of Education allowed some states to embark on "pilot projects" that usually involved the provision of some direct services to children, but this was done at the department's discretion.

6. P.L. 100-645 Section 612 (a)(2)(A), which amends Section 721 of P.L. 100-77.

7. P.L. 100-645 Section 612 (b)(8)(G).

8. P.L. 101-645 Section 612 (c), which amends Section 723 of P.L. 100-77 (b)(1).

9. P.L. 101-645 Section 612 (a)(3).

10. In June 1990, the House Appropriations Committee allocated $37 million for FY92, a substantial increase over the $7.2 million the program received in FY91 and the only McKinney program to receive an increase over the previous year's funding level. In early July, the Senate Appropriations Committee gave the program $25 million. The final appropriation will probably be somewhere between these two levels.

## References

*Callahan v. Carey,* (NY Superior Court, Dec. 5, 1979).

Dolbeare, C. N., & Alker, J. C. (1990). *The closing door: Economic causes of homelessness.* Washington, DC: National Coalition for the Homeless.

Ely, L. (1987). *Broken lives: The denial of education to homeless children.* Washington, DC: National Coalition for the Homeless. (ERIC Document Reproduction Service No. ED 292 897)

Hombs, M. E. (1990). *American homelessness: A reference handbook.* Santa Barbara, CA: ABC-Clio.

Hope, M., & Young, J. (1986). *The faces of homelessness.* Lexington, MA: Lexington.

Jackson, S. (1990). *The education rights of homeless children.* Washington, DC: Center for Law and Education.

Mihaly, L. K. (1991). *Homeless families: Failed policies and young victims.* Washington, DC: Children's Defense Fund.

National Coalition for the Homeless. (1991). *Fatally flawed: The Census Bureau's count of homeless people.* Washington, DC: Author.

National Law Center on Homelessness and Poverty. (1990). *Shut out: Denial of education to homeless children.* Washington, DC: Author.

President signs $1 billion bill to aid homeless. (1987, July 24). *New York Times,* p. 1.

Rader, V. (1986). *Signal through the flames: Mitch Snyder and America's homeless.* Kansas City, MO: Sheed & Ward.

Shelter referendum loses by a slim margin. (1990, November 7). *Washington Post,* p. A3.

U.S. General Accounting Office. (1990, December). *Homelessness: Access to McKinney Act programs improved but better oversight needed.* (GAO/RCED-91-29) Washington, DC: Author.

Waxman, L. D., & Reyes, L. M. (1990). *A status report on hunger and homelessness in America's cities: 1990.* Washington, DC: U.S. Conference of Mayors.

# 11

# Educational Climate for the Homeless

## Cultivating the Family and School Relationship

### MARIA LUISA GONZALEZ

Education for any homeless child presents seemingly insurmountable challenges to the school because this child's most basic needs are not being met in the home. Yet the school's instructional requirements can be meaningless. Homework assignments, passing exams, or sitting attentively may become nonsensical to the child. The problems are exacerbated when the school staff's perception is that the family lacks interest in the education of their children. Therefore family support and involvement may be ignored.

Educators have long accepted that two domains must be developed in the education of the total child: the academic and the psychosocial. Before adequately addressing the academic domain of the homeless child, the psychosocial domain needs to be considered. To do this, a family-school relationship must be cultivated (Stronge & Tenhouse, 1990).

In this chapter, the obstacles to the family-school relationship will be explained as the incompatibilities of poverty, mobility, and societal perceptions. Once these incompatibilities are understood by the school personnel, the educational climate benefitting the homeless student can be promoted. In addition, the chapter addresses educational climate in terms of a supportive model, which provides a framework that enables schools to create a nurturing climate with the stability, security, and nurturance needed by the students. Finally the chapter describes strategies adopted from successful practices for homeless students. These recommendations involve the demonstration of concerns that school personnel have in educating homeless students, creativity in addressing their needs, and commitment in developing a warm, supportive climate for all students to succeed.

## The Theory of Incompatibilities

The *theory of incompatibilities* was proposed during the late 1970s by Cardenas and Cardenas (1977) to explain the incompatibility existing between schools and Mexican American children, as well as economically disadvantaged students. They discussed five areas of incompatibilities. Only three, however, directly relate to the plight of the homeless: poverty, mobility, and societal perceptions. Each represents challenges to the schools that must be addressed to meet the educational needs of the homeless child.

### Poverty

The deprivational effects of poverty related to the homeless are lack of proper housing, lack of proper clothing, and malnutrition, which subsequently can result in poor health. Poor health conditions may cause students to be absent from school more often than other children. Constant absenteeism places them farther and farther behind academically. Moreover very poor children often are deprived of print and communicative media and intellectually stimulating toys. The result is that homeless children may lack in cognitive experience rather than in ability.

Poverty also results in students' embarrassment about going to school without shoes or with tattered clothing. It is the compounding effects of poverty that present educational dissonance for student, family, and school. Take, for example, the case of the Gaites family, who reside in a condemned apartment building with no running water or electricity. The mother, a single parent, lost her job due to a serious drug addiction. The children occasionally bathe at a relative's house. Because of the mother's own deteriorating health and desperate economic condition, the children's only source of food is the two meals they receive during school days. In the winter, the children suffer from constant colds due to the lack of heating.

In the summer, they suffer from dysentery due to lack of running water. Their poor health makes them continually absent from school. When they do attend, they are listless, unmotivated, and withdrawn.

## Mobility

Due to the severe financial struggles and the difficulty for adults to secure jobs, which is most often the case with homeless families, mobility represents yet another incompatibility between the homeless and the schools. Because the homeless are constantly on the move, it is difficult for students to adjust to the numerous schools they attend during their academic lives. This constant change creates program discontinuity, and it is difficult for students who are transferred to several schools each year to acquire even the basic skills. Mobility can also create a disjointed life-style that ultimately affects the children psychologically (Bassuk & Rubin, 1987).

Take, for example, the case of the López family, who move from one rural area to another. The father, unable to secure a permanent job, goes from town to town, performing odd jobs. The family lives in a school bus. They camp out during good weather, and at other times they sleep inside the bus. The López children attend an average of three to four schools a year and are not cognitively stimulated by their parents, who have limited schooling. Their constant mobility exacerbates their academic needs.

## Societal Perceptions

It is difficult for homeless students to feel welcome in a school if they perceive differences in socioeconomic status and academic ability, as well as other conditions that poverty inflicts on the young. When a child does not feel a sense of belonging, learning is not attainable. Less than inviting attitudes may be apparent in school personnel and in other students. The staff may be fostering negative attitudes on both their part and the part of the homeless students, by convincing themselves and their clientele that quality education for the homeless is impossible.

Take, for example, the case of the Jones family, who reside in a temporary shelter in a suburban area of a large city. The family was on a cross-country trip to look for employment when their car broke down. Without money, they sought shelter for the homeless. All four children enrolled reluctantly in the neighboring school. They had no school supplies and felt out of place with the clothing they had. The parents and children were embarrassed to mention that they were staying at the shelter, because of the stigma attached to being homeless.

The incompatibilities inhibit a child's academic development and psychosocial growth. These can be addressed in an educational climate for the homeless that cultivates a positive family-school partnership. To create such a climate requires a strong supportive model that will provide positive educational experiences by bringing school and community together.

## The Supportive Model

The staffs in most schools can successfully address the needs of homeless students if they develop an environment that will provide the homeless children with the support they need. The supportive model (see Figure 11.1) can present the framework to meet these needs. It consists of several concentric circles, centering on the school staff's priority: the students' psychosocial and academic development. Different entities, from the educational staff to the community, focus on the students' development and the attainment of parent/guardian participation. These levels of support are the instructional and building staff, the support service, and the community. All levels of support rely on the coordination provided by the principal's leadership. The arrows of training and communication represent how critical a role both processes play when different groups work together for a positive educational experience. District leadership, on the other hand, offers the background whereby the entire supportive system is centered. Thus the supportive model relies on the support given from level to level. It focuses on the students by providing the training needed and by ensuring effective communication across the levels.

### Student Academic and Psychosocial Development

All levels of support need to work in conjunction by surrounding the student in a stable, nurturing, and highly stimulating climate within the school. School staff must become aware of such basic services as food, health, shelter, and clothing needs. A child is not ready to learn without these basics (Bassuk & Rubin, 1987; Whitman, Accardo, Boyert, & Kendagor, 1990). How can a child concentrate on learning the essentials if she or he feels hungry, sick, cold, or improperly clothed? Once these

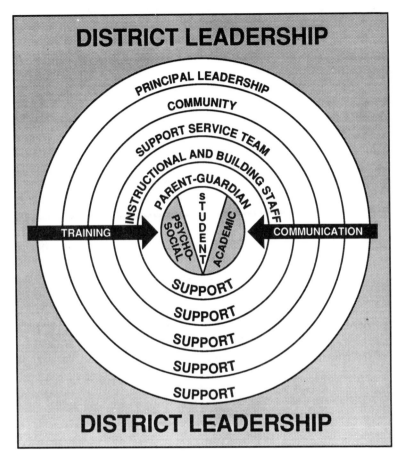

**Figure 11.1.** The Supportive Model.

basic needs are met, the academic program should foster an instructional climate that will encourage the homeless child to learn. Nothing builds self-esteem like success; therefore a stimulating program that motivates children to learn strengthens the psychosocial area. Further, psychosocial development is encouraged with the support given by all school staff, service staff, and school volunteers. Within the optimal climate for the homeless, every adult and every peer in the school setting will play an important part in raising the student's academic level and self-esteem.

## Principal Leadership

The education of homeless students calls for resourcefulness and coordination on the part of the principal. It is the principal who sets the tone of the school in accepting the homeless, while working out the wrinkles of incompatibilities that stand between child and school.

The principal continuously assesses, redirecting when necessary, all activities carried out by the different support levels. The main concern is the academic and psychosocial development of all the students, including the homeless. For this to remain the focus, communication across all support levels must be continuous. Without communication, each entity may work with students, duplicating efforts and at times neglecting important facets of schooling. Thus proper communication can enhance the services and education provided to all students.

The principal guides the training for staff and parents. The principal monitors the awareness level of staff regarding the causes and effects of homelessness. Under her or his scrutiny, training is provided to parents, all staff, and the community. Without training, the staff will be wearing blinders, possibly providing services that are not relevant to the homeless and ignoring areas in need of attention. Thus training enriches the activities by all school personnel by making them aware of needs and how to attend to these.

The principal plays an instrumental role by personally assisting in the comprehensive planning of all educational services for the children. She or he, as an integral force for change, assesses how positive these services are and recommends needed modifications. In addition, the principal acts as a strong advocate, ensuring that the rights of the homeless children and families are known and respected. She or he is constantly assessing the school's climate and the quality of a comparable education for the homeless. As instructional leader, the principal becomes an active participant in the education of the homeless. She or he oversees how all levels of the support system are working through constant communication and thorough training. Roland Barth aptly summarizes the principal's leadership role in his book *Improving Schools From Within* (1990): "Principals can orchestrate the school's constellation of unique needs and resources so that everyone gets some of what is needed. And principals have the capacity to stimulate both learning and community" (p. 64).

## Parent/Guardian Support

One cannot provide a supportive climate for homeless children without soliciting the help of the parents. The school staff plays an instrumental role in communicating to the parents the importance of their own responsibility in the development of their children's academic and psychosocial areas, regardless of family economic constraints. Care should be taken, however, when first communicating with the homeless that they are welcome and accepted. A study by Lueder (1989) found that because most parents of at-risk learners had negative schooling experiences, they are apprehensive in becoming involved with their children's schooling. Therefore one can assume that building trust between the homeless parent and school staff is critical. This can be accomplished through activities that help bond parents with their child's school staff (Jones, 1991).

From the beginning, special care must be taken to foster communication between the school staff and parents. This starts with the appropriate staff members providing an orientation that familiarizes the parent with school personnel, philosophy, and services. The staff members must create a nonthreatening atmosphere conducive to parental communication and involvement.

Research on parents' expectations of schools affirms that parents want a "personal touch" in lieu of an air of professionalism (Lindle, 1989). Therefore it is critical for school staff to understand that parents seek partnership with the schools instead of patronage. Sometimes school staff feel that parents, especially those who are poor, do not care. Yet the research conducted by Epstein shows that they do hold high aspirations for their children (Brandt, 1989). Many times school personnel may not take the time to communicate carefully to parents how they can assist in their child's development. In general, parents across all socioeconomic levels and ethnicities (Tinajero & González, 1991) care about their children's education. They also feel frustration, however, because they do not know how to assist their children; this is especially true of the homeless.

Training of parents should be coordinated with the training offered by shelter personnel when applicable. Thus conflicts with shelter activities may be avoided. Parental training should always include activities that demonstrate how parents, regardless of where they live, can assist with school work. Other useful training sessions for parents may include the following:

- parenting skills
- parental assistance by subject and grade level
- preventing or overcoming drug abuse
- availability of community services
- improving parents' basic skills
- discipline techniques

These sessions can take place in schools or in shelters. The more the parents go to the school building, however, the more familiar they may become with its purpose: to provide an education for their children regardless of their "home" situation.

Parent training is but a small investment in making the educational process more supportive for the student and, in turn, the school staff. Written communication is important. All notes should go to parents in the appropriate language(s) to ensure that the message is clear. Because of the high rate of adult illiteracy, it is essential that students understand exactly what is being communicated to the family. In the case of shelter residence, shelter personnel should know about upcoming school events and should post notices throughout the shelter, thus encouraging parents to attend. Therefore every possible means should be made to involve the parents in relevant school activities and training. At the school, the necessary modifications should be made to accommodate for differences in work schedules, language, home conditions, and educational backgrounds.

**Building and Instructional Staff Support**

The initial contact that a parent and child have at the school begins in the office and classroom. It becomes imperative that office personnel and teachers be trained to make all families feel welcome (Purkey & Novak, 1988). To better communicate with parents and to establish the feeling of family atmosphere within the school, training should begin with "frontline" office personnel, such as secretaries and clerks, to make all parents feel "at home." They should exhibit sensitivity and knowledge of the legal rights of the homeless child and family in providing a comparable education. In fact, this training should be schoolwide in order for every school employee to demonstrate the proper protocol with homeless students and families. Staff should not view financial differences as deficiencies, nor should the poor and homeless be stereotyped.

Teachers are the key element in the education of the homeless children because they are the ones who have the most contact with those children while they remain in school. Teachers must ensure that a family atmosphere is exhibited in the classroom. Acceptance by nonhomeless children is essential. Other children will more readily accept the homeless if this behavior is modeled by the teachers. A risk-free environment can be more easily created by the teacher through proper training. The training should also involve teachers in the development and correct use of instructional materials.

The stress that teachers face in meeting the psychosocial and academic needs of homeless children requires that they be given additional support, such as stress management or the development of coping mechanisms. The task of educating such highly at-risk students as the homeless may create a strain for some teachers who feel that they are doing all within their power to reach these children. Support can be initiated on the part of the principal who is fully aware of the challenge of educating the homeless. Instructional planning meetings held by teachers on a weekly basis not only help create a strong program but also develop feelings of camaraderie that can provide additional support to the individual teacher (González, 1990).

Proper orientation of new teachers is essential. The principal should inform each staff member of his or her responsibilities. The school's in-service programs should address the characteristics of children of poverty. Instructional staff awareness and sensitivity are crucial in serving the children. By visiting the shelters where the students temporarily reside, teachers may become more sensitized and aware of their plight. Yet care should be taken to avoid patronizing the children, for the homeless children should be afforded structure and stability in the classroom within a nurturing climate.

### Support Service Team

For the program to succeed, it is especially important to have a cohesive team of professionals planning the children's academic success. With high-risk populations, teams should meet regularly to analyze grades, medical records, and teacher observations. Child psychiatrist James Comer also includes teams of mental health professionals to create a supportive climate in his school-reform model (Goldberg, 1990; Gurskey, 1990). These teams should be composed of the principal, nurse, counselor, community liaison agents, teacher representatives, and available district personnel (such as a district psychologist). Contact with organizations dealing with the homeless should be continuous. Personnel from the shelters where the children temporarily reside should be invited to become part of the team. Necessary interventions should be identified, prescribed. and implemented. The interventions must be carefully scrutinized, however, to assess their appropriateness for each particular child. Parents should be apprised of the services being provided that aim to meet any academic or psychosocial need.

Given the important role that these "SWAT" teams of at-riskness play, their training is imperative. Finally training should encompass all the possible interventions (instructional, psychological, and/or medical) that can be implemented to assist individual children.

## Community Support

A school that educates the homeless cannot handle the challenge alone. Community and social agencies, volunteer organizations, and parent groups also must join in this effort. Volunteer efforts from the community can assist in promoting a caring climate in the school when it is not present in the home (Hodgkinson, 1991).

The coordination of all of these programs is not always easy. Nor are these volunteer services available to all schools. Proper training of all people working with children who have been traumatized by homelessness and/or poverty must precede working with the children. This can become a time-consuming task that may be difficult for some schools. Yet it is critical to include volunteers in training efforts.

Different community groups can furnish many of the "extras" that the school does not have the time or money to provide. Groups might assist financially by providing funds for lost books that homeless children many times end up taking with them when they cannot be checked out of a school properly (many times homeless students move from one day to the next). These groups also can provide funds for the materials that teachers need to make learning more exciting, such as instructional games and library books. Student incentives, clothing, and funds for extracurricular activities can also be supplied. Other groups may wish to donate time and effort to provide tutoring classes or to help with after-school recreational activities (González, 1991).

Thus support does not include solely monetary assistance but goes beyond the tangible. The effect that contact by a concerned adult can have on a homeless child through such simple activities as tutoring, playing after-school games, or sitting and having lunch is immeasurable. Through such contact, the children's experiential background and self-esteem are enhanced. Therefore the teaching-learning process is facilitated. In this way, community support is not only experienced by the children, but the entire school also benefits. The community, while working closely with the school, can become an extended family for the poor and the homeless (González, 1991).

## District Leadership

In order for different levels of support to provide a climate conducive for good instruction and successful learning for the homeless, a final element of districtwide leadership is necessary. The National Coalition of Advocates for Students (NCAS) completed a landmark study on immigrant students in 1987 (First, 1988). While the study dealt with immigrant students, its conclusions can readily apply to the education of the homeless, given that both groups are affected by high mobility and poverty. For purposes of this chapter, the conclusions have been adjusted to reflect concerns for homeless students. Therefore the following represent the recommendations that districts may implement in educating homeless students.

- Provide comprehensible information about the schools to homeless parents. This information should be available through the different communication media. Information should be available to all social service agencies and shelters, as well as to any organization serving the homeless.
- Place students in heterogeneous classes and, when children are having difficulties, have an understanding of the strong correlation between grade retention and dropping out of school.
- Create an "intake and assessment center" where several homeless students are. Trained staff will be available to assess both the academic and psychosocial skills of the homeless.

- Organize elementary schools so that children progress through broad age groupings rather than through rigid grade levels; they should organize middle schools so that they resemble elementary schools more closely than high schools.

- Evaluate student progress through use of broadly based assessment techniques rather than standardized tests. Important decisions about the educational future of a child should not be based on a single test score or on professional judgment alone.

- Restructure the curriculum to move away from a scope-and-sequence approach and toward an emphasis on central ideas and themes as focal points of student learning.

- Develop mission statements that express strong commitment to the success of (homeless) students.

- Require administrators and teachers to model respect for all children and adults, regardless of race, language, and economic status.

- Forge links with community-based agencies, advocacy groups, and self-help organizations to ensure the availability of physical and mental health services for (homeless) families.

- Encourage school psychologists to become active advocates for the provision of appropriate educational services for (homeless) children within regular classrooms rather than assume that all academically troubled (homeless) children are best served in special education. (First, 1988, pp. 208-209)

Although these recommendations are directed at the district level, they will positively affect the status of homeless children and their families. Thus each supportive level within the school building will function more easily when central office leadership is attuned to the needs of homeless students and responds in kind.

School staff can use the supportive model as a tool in organizing the components for creating a family-school relationship to educate the homeless. The model describes general principles surrounding a supportive, cohesive environment dedicated to student development. Once the decision has been made to adopt the supportive model, the school staff must take a close look at which specific strategies need to be implemented.

### Strategies That Cultivate
### the Family-School Relationship

Some strategies prove effective in creating a family-school partnership while educating the homeless children (Bogart & LeTendre, 1991;

González, 1990). These strategies can be grouped into three phases of schooling: the entering stage, the schooling stage, and the exiting stage (see Figure 11.2).

## At the Entering Stage

The entering stage is the first chance that a school's staff has to initiate homeless families into a warm school atmosphere. Two components—enrollment and orientation—set the stage for a positive family-school relationship.

*Enrollment strategies.* Enrollment, along with orientation, is the most important step when a child begins in a new school. As soon as a family enrolls in a school, they should be greeted warmly by office personnel. Additionally assistance should be provided in filling out forms. When office staff are trained properly, they can readily identify the homeless by appearance, false addresses, or addresses in condemned areas. They can make notes on forms provided to the advising staff and principal that the family will need special services. The main focus is to make family and child feel comfortable and supported.

*Orientation for parent and child.* Immediately following enrollment, the orientation phase begins. Orientation is the most important step when a child begins at a new school. The principal should make time to meet the child and the parent. The principal, as a model for the rest of the staff, should make each new child feel welcome. The procedures of the school need to be explained to the parents, with care taken to make the parents feel that they are now part of the school community. One helpful hint is to provide the parents with a list, including the school name, the school phone number, and the names of the resource people at the school, such as the principal, nurse, counselor, and teacher(s).

Before a formal meeting is scheduled, parents should be encouraged to meet "unofficially" with the support service team. Part of the orientation should always include meeting the nurse and counselor. Later these professionals, with the help of the support service teams, can assess the child's academic and psychological, as well as physical, needs. For the purposes of orientation, however, clothing and school supplies can be provided by having these items prepackaged and readily available to the families (First & Cooper, 1990; González, 1990).

Part of the orientation phase must involve introduction to the child's teacher and new classroom. The principal should make every attempt to do this personally. This part of the orientation should not be delegated

| Entering Stage | Schooling Stage | Exiting Stage |
|---|---|---|
| • Enrollment<br><br>• Orientation | • Assessment & Placement<br><br>• Instruction<br><br>• Monitoring | • Office Check-Out<br><br>• Formal Farewell |

**Figure 11.2.** School Strategies for the Homeless.

to others, for it is the principal who can dissipate any feelings of apprehension on the part of the newcomers. One technique that has worked is to have the teacher assign a special friend (another student) to assist the child in acclimating to the new environment.

### At the Schooling Stage

The schooling stage is characterized by appropriately assessing and placing the homeless child in the instructional program. The instructional methods that are discussed here proved useful in one school that was considered to have an exemplary program for homeless students (González, 1990).

*Assessment and placement strategies.* The student's academic program should be created under the guidance of the support service team. The teacher's instructional style should be matched with the child's learning style to provide a good beginning for both student and teacher. When a child's background is in question, the best source for information is the parent. The principal should spend a few minutes with the parent, discussing the child's placement, when the child enrolls. In most instances, parents know their children well, and this insight can help mitigate any future problems. The principal and staff should be aware of the strain that high mobility places on the child's development.

To provide an individualized academic program, the principal should ensure that student assessment is conducted carefully and as informally as possible. If the proper records have not been forwarded to the school, assessment should be done by an adult trained in creating a nonthreatening situation. The goal is to see how much the child does know rather than how much the child does not know. This assessment should not take place immediately on enrollment but shortly after a time of familiarization to the new school. Nothing is worse than adding the stress of testing to the already stressful situation of entering another new school.

*Instructional strategies.* The instructional program should be based on strategies that link cooperative learning with those of a literacy-based approach to language arts. This basis will provide the child with the stimulation that is academically and psychosocially needed. Journal writing is recommended not only to strengthen reading and writing skills but also to assist psychologically in letting the child tell his or her own story. If these steps are taken, the homeless children need not be isolated, for, in keeping with the literature, students should not be homogeneously grouped (First, 1988).

Furthermore, to address the lack of instructional materials and assistance, the appropriate school staff members are encouraged to institute before- and after-school programs. These sessions can provide tutoring and/or enrichment activities, especially when a child needs to complete "home" work.

Care should be taken to ensure that one-on-one tutoring is provided when formal and informal assessments indicate such tutoring is necessary. Tutoring can be conducted by peers, teachers, or volunteers.

Because homeless children living in shelters may not have the opportunity to work out their energies on a playground, a well-designed physical education program can help the children positively work out aggression.

Including the homeless student in all school events, academic as well as extracurricular, or during awards ceremonies enhances their instruction. It is important for all students, including homeless students, to feel that they are an integral part of the school and for all the school to see them as such.

*Monitoring strategies.* Continuous monitoring is an essential activity in assessing the services provided to homeless children and their families. These services are monitored to see how well basic needs are being met and how successful the program has been in addressing a child's academic and psychosocial development.

The support service team plays an instrumental role by meeting regularly, sharing information, and assessing each student's status. For example, when school attendance is jeopardized by illness, the appropriate social agencies can be contacted to provide medical services. In schools that serve homeless students, it should be understood that the nurse, counselor, and others will be well versed in accessing those agencies that provide resources to homeless families. Lists of such agencies should be readily available in the school so that information can be provided to parents as well.

Counselors play an important role in addressing the psychosocial area of development. Once recommendations have been made by the support service team, counselors are charged with monitoring the designated interventions. Even if many homeless children do not exhibit problems, counselors still should schedule individual and group counseling sessions on a regular basis.

In some schools, a newcomers' club is sponsored to iron out any feelings of apprehension or anxiety that highly mobile children may experience. Academic monitoring also is conducted with the support service team in coordination with the child's teachers. Weekly monitoring is imperative because a homeless child's length of stay may be temporary. One cannot adequately monitor academic progress, however, without initially looking at how the child's basic needs are being met.

**At the Exiting Stage**

The exiting stage is very important because the process followed in the school should leave a lasting memory of a positive experience. Further, if handled correctly, it can give the homeless family a more positive outlook toward schooling in general. The two components—office check-out and formal farewell—cannot be overlooked. As the child and family depart, they should take with them the idea that school can be a safe, secure, and stable place.

*Office check-out strategies.* Just as enrollment begins in the school's office, so does the final stage end therein. Again the office personnel are advised to treat the family warmly and courteously. Assistance in "closing out" forms should be available. When time permits, final meetings with the nurse, counselor, or other members of the support service team can afford parents the opportunity to ask questions regarding their child's progress.

Parents may be given a short survey, soliciting their input about various school activities, that can be answered either orally or in writing. This survey provides the school staff with necessary feedback to make the necessary modifications for the program's improvement. The main reason for office check-out strategies is to reinforce the idea that school personnel care for the family and its future well-being.

*Formal farewell strategies.* The culminating school activity for a homeless child should be a farewell process. The student should be given the opportunity to obtain autographs and to have a photograph taken with her or his favorite school friend(s), staff, and classmates. The photograph can become part of a child's portfolio, which also contains assignments, journals, and any memorabilia. The child should leave with a list of addresses of teachers, classmates, and other staff, who encourage the child to write. This provides for the possibility of continued contact between school and child.

The final activity is when an instant photo is taken of the child and family while still at the school. The child, in the presence of those who have cared for him or her, places the photograph on the bulletin board that exhibits "Contributions to Our School's Greatness." The parents and child then can identify themselves by writing their names below the photograph. This activity should offer a sense of permanence to the family who is leaving, as well as to those who regret seeing them go. Yet no sooner are they walking out the door when another new homeless family is walking down the hall, looking for the office to initiate the enrollment process.

## Summary

The educational climate for the homeless requires cultivating a relationship between the family and the school. Before cultivating a relationship, however, school personnel must understand the incompatibilities that exist between homeless children and school. Poverty, mobility, and societal perceptions are addressed when the school subscribes to the elements combined in a supportive model. Each level of support—parent/guardian, instructional and building staff, support service team, and community—can be coordinated by the principal. District leadership promotes education for the homeless by providing training, monies, staffing, and positive attitudes. This model provides the school staff with strategies needed to enhance the educational experiences of both homeless child and family.

## References

Barth, R. S. (1990). *Improving schools from within.* San Francisco: Jossey-Bass.

Bassuk, E., & Rubin, L. (1987). Homeless children: A neglected population. *American Journal of Orthopsychiatry, 57*(12), 279-286.

Bogart, J., & LeTendre, M. J. (1991). Keeping homeless children in school. *PTA Today, 16*(5), 23-24.

Brandt, R. (1989). On parents and schools: A conversation with Joyce Epstein. *Educational Leadership, 47*(2), 24-27.

Cardenas, J., & Cardenas, B. (1977). *The theory of incompatibilities: A conceptual framework for responding to the educational needs of Mexican American children.* San Antonio, TX: Intercultural Development Research Association.

First, J. M. (1988). Immigrant students in U.S. public schools: Challenges with solutions. *Phi Delta Kappan, 70*(3), 205-210.

First, P. F., & Cooper, G. R. (1990). Homeless doesn't have to mean hopeless. *School Administrator, 11*(47), 17-20.

Goldberg, M. F. (1990). Portrait of James Comer. *Educational Leadership, 48*(1), 40-42.

González, M. L. (1990). School + home = a program for educating homeless students. *Phi Delta Kappan, 71*(10), 785-787.

González, M. L. (1991). School-community partnerships and the homeless. *Educational Leadership, 49*(1), 23-24.

Gurskey, D. (1990). A plan that works. *Teacher Magazine, 1*(10), 46-54.

Hodgkinson, H. L. (1991). *Beyond the schools: How schools and communities must collaborate to solve the problems facing America's youth.* Arlington, VA: American Association of School Administrators and National School Boards Associations.

Jones, L. T. (1991). *Strategies for involving parents in their children's education.* Bloomington, IN: Phi Delta Kappa Educational Foundation.

Lindle, J. C. (1989). What do parents want from principals and teachers? *Educational Leadership, 47*(2), 12-14.

Lueder, D. C. (1989). Tennessee parents were invited to participate and they did. *Educational Leadership, 41*(2), 15-17.

Purkey, W. W., & Novak, J. M. (1988). *Education: By invitation only.* Bloomington, IN: Phi Delta Kappa Educational Foundation.

Stronge, J. H., & Tenhouse, C. (1990). *Educating homeless children: Issues and answers.* Bloomington, IN: Phi Delta Kappa Educational Foundation.

Tinajero, J. V., & González, M. L. (1991). *Raising career aspirations of Hispanic girls.* Bloomington, IN: Phi Delta Kappa Educational Foundation.

Whitman, B. Y., Accardo, P., Boyert, M., & Kendagor, R. (1990). Homeless and cognitive performance in children: A possible link. *Social Work, 35*(6), 516-579.

*12*

# Educating the Homeless in Rural and Small School District Settings

DORIS HELGE

## The Uniqueness
of the Rural Community Context

Two thirds of America's school districts and one third of the nation's children are rural. Rural economies are extremely diverse, with family farming now comprising less than 4% of America's economic life-styles. Agriculture, small business, manufacturing, industries related to agriculture, timber, petroleum, fishing, resorts, military, Indian reservations, and subsistence economies in wilderness areas are examples of this diversity.

Rural communities have distinct environments and unique strengths and weaknesses. Many rural areas still have a relatively high trust factor, close family ties, and a "sense of community." Extended families may be a resource to programs for homeless individuals, and many rural citizens may be willing to volunteer to help those experiencing difficult situations.

Rural subcultures vary tremendously. They range geographically from remote islands and deserts to clustered communities, and economically from stable, classic farm communities to depressed, lower socio-economic settings and high-growth "boom or bust" communities. The array of rural service programs ranges from isolated agencies or schools serving as few as one to ten runaways or homeless families in a location 350 to 2,000 miles from the nearest full-service shelter, to programs located in small clustered towns or surrounded by other service agencies. Clearly location has tremendous implications for proximity to resources, including specialized services serving homeless, runaway children with serious needs (e.g., drug or sexual abuse therapy).

Figure 12.1 may be helpful in conceptualizing the diversity of rural communities and service delivery systems for homeless youth (foster care; shelters; programs for runaways and pregnant teens; schools; health, mental health, and other service agencies). Each of the variables listed has individual ramifications for service delivery. For example, a rural school's administrative structure has implications for securing resources outside of the school. A district that is part of a cooperative can usually obtain comprehensive health services for pregnant teenagers more easily than can a single isolated district.

Two key variables of service delivery are *population density* (Is the number of children with a given need adequate so that a rural community or service agency can "afford" to hire a specialist?) and *topography* (Does a mountain with untraversable roads at certain times of the year inhibit transportation of services?). Interaction of these two dimensions with that of other community and district variables further individualizes a rural area and its services. Change of one variable in any of the three dimensions further differentiates a given community from others. Because this is an open model, the number of possible types of rural communities is infinite (. . . *N*). In fact, previous research cataloged more than 300 combinations when conducting on-site visits (Helge, 1984). Thus rural service delivery systems must be individually designed.

## Unique Factors Inhibiting Service Delivery
## to Homeless Children and Families in Rural Areas

Media images of homeless urban children growing up in subway stations and sleeping on street grates in ghettos usually do not recognize equivalent scenarios in rural areas. Recent studies (Goode, 1990; Helge, 1990; Loughlin, 1990; Weisman, 1990) have had shocking findings relating to rural children and families who are at risk. In fact, a 1990 study conducted by Helge indicated that rural children fared worse than nonrural children in 34 of 39 statistical comparisons related to at-risk

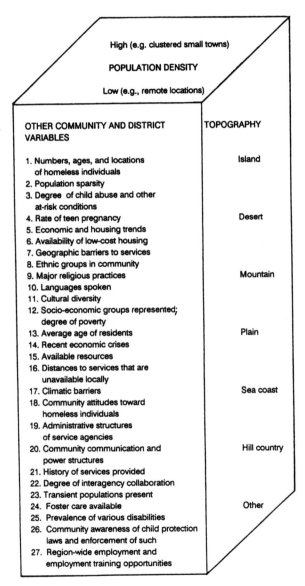

**Figure 12.1.** Dimensions of the Diversity of Rural Community Service Delivery Systems Related to Homeless Students.

student conditions. The analysis suggested that the social and economic strains facing rural students are every bit as bad, perhaps worse, than those facing inner-city youth. Previous national studies have indicated higher dropout and teenage pregnancy rates in rural than in nonrural areas. Some state-specific studies conducted by rural states have also indicated a high rate of at-risk students. The images of rural children leading wholesome, trouble-free lives, compared with youth in more crowded settings, may be in need of revision.

**Personnel Problems**

Many rural areas have large percentages of minority, migrant, and/or English-as-a-second-language (ESL) students but have difficulty attracting educational personnel who are bilingual. A factor further complicating service delivery is the potential difficulty securing funding for and/or attracting personnel who are multilingual.

**Problems Related to Population Sparsity**

Problems of organizing to deliver rural services relate to a basic characteristic of ruralness—how to provide economical, specialized programs in sparsely populated areas. The cost per unit of service is typically higher in a rural than in a nonrural area due to fewer professionals and other human resources available, transportation barriers, and other rural attributes. Because of sparse populations, geographic barriers, related transportation problems, and few specialized resources available, it is necessary to utilize all available agencies and volunteers to appropriately design and deliver services.

Long distances to services including shelters, Red Cross programs, and volunteer centers contribute to difficulties of planning and implementing services. Transportation difficulties relate to lack of funding and difficulties in planning inexpensive transportation systems, in light of long geographic distances, sparse populations, difficult terrain, and climatic barriers. The fact that many rural areas have relatively few industries inhibits finding jobs for homeless individuals.

**Problems Related to Culture and Attitudes**

Many rural areas are known for their close-knit communities, stable family lives, and housing for all citizens (even if it is inadequate for some). Other rural areas are known for high degrees of dysfunctionality of various types, including child abuse, poverty, and homelessness. An example would be rural migrant camps.

The rural tenet of fiercely independent citizens who "take care of their own" in the intimacy of many rural settings can actually contribute to problems. Residents may not be willing to side with an abused or neglected child who is homeless or who chooses to run away from home and against a parent they have known for years. Citizens may be employed by such parents or frequently see them at community functions. A guarantee of confidentiality to a person reporting abuse may be difficult to believe. Citizens may be reticent to use counseling services.

Rural citizens are less tolerant of unconventional behavior unless it is by "one of their own." Local citizens are more likely to "take care of their own" but not to take care of "outsider" homeless mentally ill or other unconventional persons who "drift in." Homelessness in a rural community is unquestionably related to local citizens' attitudes (Belcher & McCleese, 1988).

Homeless rural children and their families may not be readily identified in many rural communities. This is partly because of the rural norm of "taking care of one's own." It is also because rural Americans inherently dislike the labeling of individuals.

Rural areas may have difficulty offering programs and services where youth can readily access them: at home, in schools, and on the street. Street outreach programs may be impractical, community attitudes may inhibit services, and model programs such as "safe place" programs where children can wait until a local social service agency staff member or police officer picks them up may not be practical in rural areas (partly due to difficulties with confidentiality).

**Other Problems**

Other obstacles include the lack of social, psychological, and family counseling services in remote, impoverished rural areas. Many rural communities have inadequate medical and prenatal care, special education, counseling services, foster care, and sex education. A lack of instruction designed to prevent drug and alcohol abuse may also indirectly contribute to homelessness. Career training and vocational education opportunities may be limited. In many rural areas, conditions that can breed homelessness and school failure have worsened in recent years. Statistics long have indicated that rural America has higher rates of poverty than nonrural America. Insufficient low-cost housing and related resources, lack of shelters for homeless and runaway youth and families, and populations too sparse to fund public (secular) shelters all may be part of the problem. Moreover, in many communities, resistance to acknowledgement of the problem may be the most serious obstacle.

Poverty, family instability, depression and suicide, teen pregnancy, and alcohol and drug abuse have increased as farming, timber, coal, and some fishing industries have declined. Recent economic problems not only have exacerbated existing economic difficulties in unemployment, but many persons have also been forced out of mainstream society by circumstances beyond their control. These conditions have occurred at a time when America has experienced an explosion of social problems, such as increases in crime, child abuse, domestic violence, HIV-positive infants, poor single-parent families, fetal alcohol syndrome, crack babies, runaway youth, and the break-up of the traditional American family.

A 1985 study by HUD and the Census Bureau indicated that the shortage of affordable housing is more acute in rural than in nonrural areas. The lack of affordable housing has been a major factor in the increase in poverty and homelessness in the United States (National Network of Runaway and Youth Services, 1991). In addition, citizens in rural areas have a greater tendency to be uninsured or underinsured due to scarce financial resources.

Recent reductions in social service funding and programs in areas that already had inadequate social service infrastructures and that lack related technical assistance have contributed to a rising rate of homelessness. Recent deinstitutionalization also has contributed to increased numbers of rural citizens with mental disabilities returning to small towns and rural areas.

A disincentive exists for many social agencies to adequately cover rural social service needs due to little monitoring required by state or federal agencies and an inadequate voice for sparsely populated rural areas. Funding for travel required to monitor service delivery in sparsely populated agencies is also frequently inadequate.

Rural children, as well as urban youth, are leaving home due to abuse and violence. Many children run away from family conflict, physical and sexual abuse, and other violence. Such children are in great danger of homelessness and of sexual and physical abuse while "on the road." Many (particularly illegal aliens) face language, bicultural, and legal barriers.

Despite common perceptions, rural streets can be quite dangerous for children who are homeless. Dangers include gang activity, prostitution, crime, violence, drugs, poverty, pregnancy, malnutrition, and poor health.

Although, statistically, homeless youth may be from any socioeconomic background, most are from working-class and poor families. Rural areas are known to have greater percentages of individuals of low socioeconomic status.

As society has become more aware of the detrimental effects of child abuse and as schools initiate programs emphasizing that inappropriate touch is illegal, increasing numbers of younger youth have been running away from difficult situations and finding themselves homeless. Homeless runaway youth shelters and crisis intervention agencies in cities provide services to many young people who have left the system of their own volition; in rural areas, such shelters are typically nonexistent. When shelters do exist, they may be full, and rape and theft prevalent. Thus homeless youth are frequently housed in jails, under bridges, and in such places as abandoned railroad stations.

## Problems Specific to Homeless Youth

Adolescents leave home at unusually young ages in many rural areas. Homeless youth may have left home by choice, have been ejected by parents, be runaway street youth, or have left inappropriate or unpalatable foster or institutional care placements.

Regardless of the initial reasons for leaving home, homeless youth often suffer from significant health problems. For some, this is a result of living on the streets with inadequate shelter and food. The leading reported health problem among youth who run away from home is substance abuse (National Network of Runaway and Youth Services, 1991). For some, alcohol and other drugs offer an avenue to relieve pain from the past. For others, it becomes part of a life-style and a coping mechanism for dealing with everyday violence and survival. A General Accounting Office (GAO) report indicated that 22% of all homeless children had alcohol or other drug problems (U.S. General Accounting Office, 1989). Studies reported by the Family & Youth Services Bureau (1990) estimated that 29% had substance abuse problems.

Physical and sexual abuse is reported disproportionately by children who are homeless, particularly those who have run away. These statistics, however, are actually grossly underreported (physical, 31%; sexual, 21%) because much of what has happened to the children is repressed and because generally young people who are aware of their abuse fear the potential involvement of child protective services, repercussions from family members and small communities, and/or that they will not be believed. Studies have indicated that children are not likely to openly discuss their issues of physical and sexual abuse (National Network of Runaway and Youth Services, 1991). The GAO report stated that a minimum of 25% of homeless youth have been physically or sexually abused, 36% have experienced parental neglect, and 11% have been subjected to domestic violence (U.S. General Accounting Office, 1989).

One study found that one fourth of all homeless females aged 16 to 19 were found to be pregnant at the doctor's first visit. AIDS symptoms sometimes do not manifest for 7 years after infection with the HIV virus, and thus AIDS may be much more highly prevalent than is known. AIDS is growing at a higher percentage rate in rural than in nonrural areas (AIDS Prevention and Service Program, 1991).

Homeless youth, having dealt with a series of broken emotional ties with parents or guardians (or parents who are experiencing such problems that they cannot provide shelter) usually experience low self-esteem, alienation, depression, and thoughts of suicide. Because of the abuse they have withstood over the years, some young people are angry, and many are unable to trust anyone. Their past experiences evoke negative reactions to authority figures, which in turn fuels poor relationships with school personnel and conflicts with the law. Because these large institutions are often ill-equipped to interact effectively with these youth and to attend to the hurt behind their anger, these youth become further isolated and alienated.

Young people who engage in survival sex are especially at risk of physical violence, rape, sexually transmitted diseases (including HIV), and pregnancy. Estimates by outreach workers have indicated that as many as 99% to 100% of youth who engage in survival sex have been sexually abused. Selling or trading sex for food and shelter provides an avenue for self-sufficiency for those who cannot support themselves in any other way but comes with great cost and risk for those involved (National Network of Runaway and Youth Services, 1991).

Clearly homeless youth experience a myriad of physical, psychological, and educational problems. These youth have often been failed by their families and communities and are in need of immediate services, such as shelter and counseling. For some, longer term care that stabilizes their living situations and empowers them to live independently is essential.

## Recommendations for Meeting the Needs of Homeless Children and Youth in Rural America

The following recommendations are essential for our society, government, and educational system to meet the needs of homeless children in rural areas.

- The first priority should be the immediate welfare of the students. Teachers, other service personnel, school board members, administrators, and others must understand that the worst thing they can do is ignore a student's problem.
- Federal and state governments tend to recognize and deal with urban problems. The federal and state governments must recognize the extent to which rural populations are at risk for homelessness. Intra- and interagency efforts should address collaborative problem solutions. Federal and state initiatives should be analyzed regarding their ability to address the needs of homeless and at-risk individuals. Federal and state funding for rural at-risk children should be equitable to funding in nonrural areas.
- At the local level, collaboration should involve state and local education agencies and social agencies (foster care, counseling, job training, housing assistance, juvenile incarceration, medical, etc.). Such existing rural outreach systems as cooperative extension and public health agencies, civic groups, parents, and volunteer organizations should also be involved in program planning and implementation.
- Holistic program approaches should be planned that address the housing and other physical needs of at-risk students and their families. In addition, such program approaches should address the emotional, academic, and social needs of students and families in program planning and implementation. Services should be confidential, include prenatal care, and attend to nutritional needs and nutrition education.
- The link between poor self-esteem and at-risk conditions (delinquency, depression, substance abuse, child abuse, teen pregnancy, dysfunctional families, and runaway behavior) should be recognized.

  While homeless children and families need and deserve career guidance, counseling and vocational education, academic tutoring, mentoring programs, health and social services, and other support systems, the most basic ingredient for changing the serious problems of at-risk and homeless individuals is to consistently enhance self-esteem.
- At-risk individuals need to learn skills and to be enabled to identify and express their feelings, validate themselves, and gain a sense of self-worth and personal power.

- Schools should structure ongoing student support systems, such as peer, teacher, and administrative buddy systems and school building case management teams.

- Collaboration between school building personnel and social agencies involved with the child should protect student confidentiality. Partnerships with other community resources, including social agencies, businesses, the justice system, foster care, employment trainers, Job Training Partnership Act (JTPA) programs, and such rural outreach systems as cooperative extension and public health systems, should occur on an as-needed basis.

- In-service for teachers should emphasize processes of enhancing student self-esteem and include methods of developing interdisciplinary assessment and intervention teams. Teachers and other service personnel should be trained to work with families, community agencies, and students, regarding the emotional needs of at-risk students. Each person attending in-service education should be encouraged to take that knowledge back to other personnel in the school and to parents.

- Goals for student development should include the enhancement of the following areas:

    physical needs, including housing, academic abilities, and self-esteem

    ability to self-nurture

    sense of identity

    internal motivation

    sense of responsibility for individual's actions

    control over individual's own life

    ability to find appropriate external support systems and other resources

    physical abilities

    career/vocational goals

- Preventive efforts, including community goal setting, interagency collaboration, school-community partnerships, economic and self-esteem development, career and vocational education services, sex education, prenatal care, nutrition, and counseling, are essential.

- It is essential that the community, including parents, social agencies, businesses, and civic and volunteer organizations be involved. Resources are simply too scarce to attempt to deal with problems in isolation. All community resources are required to handle social problems such as those involved with homeless conditions. It is important that all techniques involving community elements preserve student confidentiality.

- School-business-community partnerships are imperative to solve problems such as finding shelter and implementing effective vocational education. Mentoring can be a volunteer program involving businesspeople, college and high school students, and community members as role models who help students begin to envision their own future and provide much-needed caring and support.

- The justice system, job training/employment agencies, medical profession, child welfare agencies, foster care, police, churches, media, civic groups, and legislatures must play a part.

- It is also essential that the entire community be educated regarding factors in at-risk situations. This is to ensure that many unfortunate situations will not occur and to help in ameliorating current negative conditions. Community education might occur via town meetings, interagency presentations, and involvement with social and fraternal organizations. In small rural communities, presentations may occur at local welcome wagon, garden club, or 4-H meetings or at county fairs. Advanced technologies can be used: satellite training or informational programs regarding recognizing and dealing with such factors as child abuse, runaways, and related conditions of homelessness.

- The following services are recommended as essential to provide services to runaway or other homeless students:

    identification of housing alternatives

    shelter

    residential group homes

    individual counseling

    family counseling

    crisis intervention

    hot line (or equivalent)

    recreational alternatives

    sexual abuse assessment

    physical/sexual abuse counseling

    transportation services

    alcohol and other drug use prevention

    substance abuse needs assessment

    alcohol and other drug counseling

    independent living skills for system use

    street outreach

    educational tutoring

    pregnancy prevention

    safe place programs

    employment training

    HIV-risk needs assessment

HIV prevention

nutrition supplementation and education

transitional living for homeless youth

psychological evaluation

host homes

teen drop-in center

home-based counseling

health screening

foster care

alcohol and other drug outpatient treatment

alternative schools

medical/health services

GED program

day care

residential alcohol and other drug treatment

legal aid

academic services, including mentoring and tutoring

vocational education

community-business-school-social agency partnerships

comprehensive health services

sex education

ongoing peer support systems

career counseling

## Considerations for Service Delivery Planning

As rural communities are so diverse (see Figure 12.1), there is no one appropriate model for rural service delivery.

Just as urban models are not appropriate for rural communities, no one rural service delivery model can be used for the great variety of rural subcultures. It simply cannot be assumed that a practice effective in remote Wyoming ranching territory will be viable on an isolated island, in part of a cluster of New England seacoast towns, or in an agricultural migrant camp. Instead service delivery models must be designed individually for the rural community and service delivery systems in which they will be implemented.

Each of the factors discussed in the section that follows must be considered by those designing the service delivery system for rural children with disabilities. Most important, the interrelationships between them must be assessed. For example, rural communities with equivalent population densities should plan in significantly different ways if one service delivery system is surrounded by mountains with relatively untraversable roads all winter, while the other service delivery system is located in a flat agricultural area with mild winters.

Combinations of factors are critical and should be weighted more heavily than single-factor barriers to service delivery. It is difficult to design an effective service delivery model when a rural area involves multiple cultures that do not necessarily respect each other, and it is more difficult when social services are inadequate and the rates of child abuse, juvenile delinquency, and runaways are high.

The planner should identify which of the variables below are problematic, select those that appear to be most important, and address those variables first. Problems that can be ameliorated quickly (e.g., by gaining the understanding and support of the local power structure, citizens volunteering to build low-income housing) should be. Usually the planner can merely acknowledge factors that are unchangeable givens, such as spring flooding, when designing the service delivery plan.

Rural citizens have, out of necessity, long tended to be problem solvers. The model planner should assess all existing resources. The resulting catalog of current resources should include an identification of "hidden" resources endemic to most of rural America. This would include a community's sense of volunteerism and community spirit.

*Numbers, ages, and locations of homeless individuals.* A key variable in service delivery planning is to understand the current and potential numbers, ages, and locations of individuals who are homeless. Some rural areas tend to be transient, and some are more stable. Particularly in remote areas, some problems virtually are unrecognized until cold winter weather brings death or severe illness and the problem is publicized.

*Population sparsity.* The population per square mile is significant for the model planner. Although a rural area is by definition relatively sparsely populated, services must be planned in a dramatically different manner for a small, clustered township than for schools located on remote islands, vast rangelands, or in the isolated bush villages of Alaska. This is important in determining whether homeless children and families can be clustered for services and in assessing proximity to services.

*Degree of child abuse and other at-risk conditions.* As child abuse and runaways are directly related to homelessness, it is wise to secure information from local and state social service agencies concerning the extent and trends of child abuse and other at-risk conditions. Preventive efforts are essential.

*Rate of teen pregnancy.* As correlations exist between teen pregnancies and inadequately housed or homeless children, the planner will need to contact social service and educational personnel for an understanding of the rate of teenage pregnancy in the area. Preventive efforts concerning teen parenting are advised.

*Economic and housing trends.* The planner will need to be advised regarding economic and housing trends in the area. Such information will assist in determining present and future needs and will assist in publicizing accurate information to other interested persons and agencies.

*Availability of low-cost housing.* Local, state, and federal resources that can potentially assist with housing problems for low-income individuals will need to be understood. The planner may want to identify potential resources and to write grants for low-cost housing. It is also helpful to stimulate interest at the local level to assist with building affordable housing. An example is the Georgia-based Habitat for Housing project in which local citizens volunteer to build houses for those in need; most materials are donated.

*Geographic barriers to services.* Absolute distance from potential services to a homeless individual is frequently complicated by such geographic barriers as mountains, untraversable roads, or the necessity of taking ferries or small planes. An excellent service is virtually unusable to a homeless individual who must secure transportation to reach it.

*Cultural/ethnic groups in the community.* Diverse, close-knit, ethnic groups can complicate a planner's work. For example, in areas with Hispanic migrants, low socioeconomic minorities, non-English-speaking refugees, and other subcultures, cultural customs and mores must be respected. This will ensure that service providers and services are understood and that those eligible take advantage of them.

*Major religious practices.* Some rural areas contain subcultures of religious groups that reject receiving from or developing community services for those of other religious backgrounds. Understanding and addressing local beliefs and customs will prevent problems and ensure appropriate service delivery.

*Languages spoken.* The primary language spoken by the homeless individual has relevance for selecting appropriate personnel, especially itinerant staff who visit rural communities that have life-styles and cultures different from their own. This factor is also extremely important to the administrator who is considering clustering children for services.

*Recent economic crises; degree of poverty in community.* Recent economic difficulties, such as those experienced by migrants, farming communities, and extraction industry workers (timber, fishing, etc.), have had broad implications for the numbers of persons in a given area who may become homeless.

*Available resources.* Community services, including housing, shelter, counseling, career and vocational education, and health and social services, should be identified. The planner must then ascertain what is available and what must be developed.

*Distances to services that are unavailable locally.* Distances to counseling, medical, drug and alcohol abuse, and other services are critical for planning. Existing transportation services available must be determined.

*Climatic barriers.* In areas with severe climates or seasonal problems such as heavy spring flooding, it may be useless that a qualified professional or program is located only 1 hour's distance from the individual. Alternatives must be considered by the planner and may range from technological alternatives to use of local volunteers.

*Community attitudes toward homeless individuals.* Rural citizens are likely to "take care of their own" but not take care of "outsiders" with the same problems. Belcher & McCleese (1988) stated that homelessness in a community is unquestionably related to local citizens' attitudes. Rural citizens are less tolerant of unconventional behavior unless it is that of "one of their own." In that case, they usually will support the homeless individual through extended family or other support networks.

*Administrative structures of service agencies.* An agency that is administratively part of a statewide program may have greater resources available to it than one that is strictly a local volunteer agency. This is particularly true when the isolated agency is located a great distance from state or federal headquarters or when geographic or climatic barriers exist.

*Community communication and power structures.* The planner must understand and positively utilize existing communication and power structures of the local rural community. Informal systems are typically more potent than those that are outlined formally. Informal rules often have significant ramifications for service delivery; they affect such issues as confidentiality of data and willingness for providers actually to serve clients.

*History of services provided.* Past services for homeless individuals in a particular service agency are linked closely not only to available funding and awareness of federal and state regulations but also to community attitudes. In rural communities, key power sources (whether the judge, school board chair, wealthy farmer, minister, or key communicator) have pervasive influences on services.

Rural citizens tend to be highly motivated to provide appropriate services when the initiative is from the local level. They tend to be poorly motivated when they are told they "have to" provide a service. Adept administrators understand and plan to use such inherent rural community attributes, particularly when initiating changes. In rural communities having a unique ethnic heritage, it is important and possible to plan new services that will be palatable to the native heritage and as much as possible preserve the community's self-determination and identity.

*Degree of interagency collaboration.* The cost per unit of many services is higher in rural than in nonrural areas due to fewer human resources available, transportation barriers, and other rural characteristics. Because of sparse populations, geographic barriers, related transportation problems, and few specialized resources available, it takes all available agencies and individuals to appropriately deliver services in rural areas.

*Transient populations present.* Areas with large percentages of transient populations, such as migrant workers, are more prone to have homeless individuals. The planner will need baseline and trend data regarding transiency and related problems (e.g., child abuse, need for interpreters).

*Foster care available.* The availability of quality foster care services is crucial information for the planner. Such information will be particularly helpful when planning services for abused/runaway homeless children.

*Prevalence of various disabilities.* For a variety of reasons, persons with severe disabilities generally do not have lucrative careers. Low income levels, high housing costs, and prejudices of some landlords can contribute to high rates of homelessness for those with severe disabilities.

*Community awareness and enforcement of child protection laws.* A definite correlation exists between the presence, awareness, and enforcement of child protection laws and runaway children. There is also a relationship to the incidence of homeless children. The planner must consider this factor and should be involved in related prevention techniques.

*Regionwide employment and employment training opportunities.* It is critical that the planner have an adequate information base concerning local and regional employment opportunities. This is related to the incidence of homeless individuals. Associated preventive efforts should be implemented.

## Model Development

After considering these factors, the planner is ready to develop a workable service delivery model. No such thing as a pure model for rural service delivery exists. Rather, eclectic approaches are the rule, and numerous variables must be juggled (such as cost vs. intensity of need or availability of alternate services). Variables of the service delivery model that must be manipulated so that the resulting eclectic model has a "fit" are as follows:

> facilities
> financial system
> equipment
> staff development programs
> transportation system
> staffing for services
> community involvement and support
> governance system
> interagency collaboration

Figure 12.2 illustrates the process of designing a rural service delivery model. Factors that may present planning problems that cannot be controlled by the model designer are termed *givens*. Factors that can be manipulated by the planner are termed *variables*. The planner can create an appropriate service delivery model by recognizing givens and controlling variables.

Problems of organizing to deliver rural services relate to a basic attribute of rural districts—how to provide economical services in sparsely populated areas. Strategies for effective interagency collaboration include clarifying each agency's role; developing an implementation plan for coordinating efforts; overcoming turf problems; obtaining resources to implement an interagency agreement (e.g., making that part of an individual's work responsibility); facilitating communication between local, federal, and regional agencies; accessing transportation money to

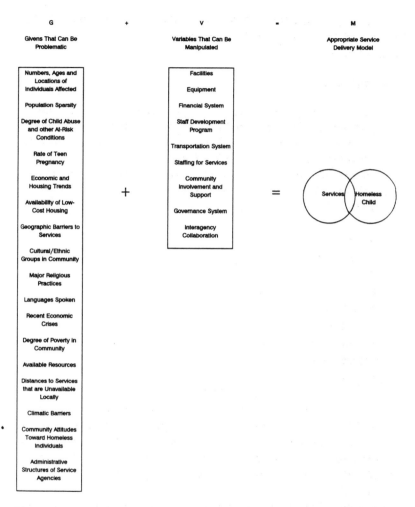

**Figure 12.2**. Consideration of "Givens" and Manipulation of "Variables" Allows the Planner to Create an Appropriate Service Model.

attend interagency meetings; and developing local awareness of community resources available.

Other aspects that are necessary include the following:

including homeless individuals in decision making as community solutions
are designed

providing a continuum of care

developing incentives for local sharing of home and other services

generating community-initiated solutions (an example is use of Habitat for
Humanity, an organization in which volunteers build houses for homeless
individuals)

forming family-community-school-business partnerships

developing incentives for business participation (might include needs for
workers, and positive community publicity)

enhancing interagency collaboration. This should include collaboration between social service agencies that help poor, homeless, and mentally ill
individuals. Such agencies thus would develop a comprehensive plan to
reduce homelessness by getting people into low-cost housing or preventing
them from losing their homes.

developing/using migrant planning and tracking systems

involving/training indigenous personnel (particularly in ESL situations)

starting rent subsidy programs

using local communication and power structures (involvement of rural outreach units, such as cooperative extension, to publicize needs and to build
program support)

using extended families, regional offices of national support agency networks,
and/or use of indigenous workers

## Summary

At-risk children in migrant and Indian communities, the Mississippi
Delta and Appalachian regions, lumber towns, and Alaskan villages
have received media coverage in past years. Homelessness in a variety
of rural areas is becoming an alarming problem. It is time for policymakers, educators, and others to consider carefully the needs of other
rural cultures and their at-risk students.

Homelessness *is* child abuse, and the United States has a generation
of children growing up homeless. This kind of child abuse could be
viewed as intentional by our society because of neglect to change the

situation. It could be said that a society that allows some citizens to have power, money, jobs, and homes and others to be without is actually condoning child abuse.

Strategies designed to provide a continuum of services to urban homeless individuals are inadequate for rural areas. The uniqueness of the rural community context requires service delivery strategies and models distinctively different from those of nonrural areas. Interagency collaboration is essential for successful service delivery.

Because of the tremendous diversity in rural areas, no *one* rural service delivery model exists. A number of community and agency characteristics do exist, however, that a model designer must consider. The planner may then appropriately manipulate such variables as staffing, transportation systems, extended family, and other community involvement to design an individualized model viable for homeless individuals and service agencies, including schools.

## References

AIDS Prevention and Service Program. (1991, Spring). *AIDS LINE, 3*(1), 1.

Belcher, J., & McCleese, G. (1988). The process of homelessness among the mentally ill: Rural and urban perspectives. *Human Services in the Rural Environment, 12*(2), 20-25.

Family & Youth Services Bureau. (1990). *Annual report to the Congress on the runaway and homeless youth program, fiscal year 1989.* Washington, DC: Author.

Goode, S. (1990). The rural school of hard knocks. *Insight, 6*(40), 54-55.

Helge, D. (1984). Models for serving rural students with low-incidence handicaps. *Exceptional Children, 50*(4), 313-324.

Helge, D. (1990). *A national study regarding at-risk students.* Bellingham, WA: National Rural Development Institute.

Loughlin, S. (1990, September 30). AIDS threat becoming real to rural America. *Daily News,* p. 8A.

National Network of Runaway and Youth Services. (1991). *Runaway, homeless & other youth in high-risk situations in the 1990s. To whom do they belong?* Washington, DC: Author.

U.S. General Accounting Office. (1989). *Homelessness and runaway youth receiving services at federally funded shelters* (GAO/HRD-90-45). Washington, DC: Government Printing Office.

Weisman, J. (1990, October 10). Rural America is quietly hurting. *Education Week, X*(6), 10.

# 13

# Programs With Promise

## Educational Service Delivery
## to Homeless Children and Youth

### JAMES H. STRONGE

Concomitant with the contemporary growth of homelessness in American society, educational programs designed to accommodate homeless children and youth have emerged in recent years. Analysis of these educational programs revealed three primary models of service delivery that have been developed or adapted specifically to accommodate homeless children and youth: transitional, mainstreamed, and supplemental support programs (Stronge, 1991).[1] *Transitional* programs are designed specifically to provide an intermediate, or transitional, educational opportunity for homeless students. *Mainstreamed* programs, through various modifications, serve homeless students within the context of regular programs within existing schools. *Supplemental support* programs are characterized predominantly by a part-time, beyond-school-hours mode of service delivery.[2]

An in-depth survey of 40 educational programs for homeless children and youth was conducted in the summer of 1991 in an effort to acquire a better understanding of these programs.[3] This survey, which will serve as the focus for the chapter, revealed a wide array of homeless education programs, many of which can be aptly characterized as programs with promise.

## Characteristics of Homeless Education Programs

### Program Establishment

The development of most homeless education programs parallels the growth in the homeless family population, beginning in the early 1980s and extending to the present. More precisely the vast majority of the programs were inaugurated following the enactment of the McKinney Act in 1987, with most of the programs established since 1989 (see Table 13.1).

Of the programs that are pre-McKinney in origin, most are of the transitional variety. The early development of the transitional programs can be explained primarily as a result of obvious need: Most of the early transitional programs developed in areas where high concentrations of homeless families or independent homeless youth were temporarily housed. The one exception to the transitional model in early program development is that of large urban areas with substantial homeless populations, such as New York City, that began the development of comprehensive, mainstreamed service delivery models in the early to mid-1980s.

Much of the post-McKinney educational programming can be tied indirectly if not directly to the act. Indirectly, the act enhanced public awareness and sensitivity to the unique educational needs of homeless students; directly, the act created a network of state homeless education coordinators who spurred on action at the state and local levels on behalf of the homeless. Perhaps more important, the McKinney Act provided seed money for the inauguration of programs designed specifically to address the educational needs of homeless children and youth. The development of the programs, although obviously facilitated by the enactment of the McKinney Act, appears to have been a reaction to prevailing local circumstances rather than to a proactive advocacy for homeless children.

### Program Location

As would be expected, most transitional educational programs are located on a single site, typically in a nontraditional location (e.g., adjacent to a shelter for homeless families). Mainstreamed programs, by their nature, tend to disperse homeless students throughout the educational organization, often providing special assistance in transporting homeless students to regular school programs. In a few instances, mainstreamed programs transport students from all homeless shelters in the district to a designated public school. Supplemental support programs tend to be

**Table 13.1** Year Homeless Education Programs Established

| Year | Transitional f | Mainstreamed f | Supplemental Support f |
|---|---|---|---|
| Before 1987 | 2 | 0 | 0 |
| 1987 | 0 | 1 | 1 |
| 1988 | 1 | 2 | 1 |
| 1989 | 1 | 4 | 6 |
| 1990 | 4 | 5 | 10 |
| 1991 | 0 | 0 | 1 |
|  | 8 | 12* | 19 |

*One mainstreamed program did not report year of establishment. $N = 40$

fairly evenly distributed between (a) programs that operate on the premises of or adjacent to homeless shelters and (b) programs that are provided before or after regular school hours on regular school campuses (Table 13.2).

**Program Enrollment**

*Program admission.* Special requirements for program admission are reflected in Table 13.3. Numerous programs (42.5% of the sample) had no specific eligibility requirements other than identification of the student as homeless and, as in the case of mainstreamed programs, a requirement that the student be within the age/grade range for which educational services are provided for all students. The greatest restriction across all three program types was that participating students must be residents of a particular temporary homeless shelter (42.5%). In addition, explicit target audience restrictions applied for some transitional and supplemental support programs. For transitional programs, the identified target audience restrictions primarily included older adolescents (e.g., adolescent females, teen mothers); for supplemental support programs, the target audiences tended to be restricted to younger children (preschool or elementary age).

*Length of stay.* When asked whether a limit existed on the number of days that a student may be enrolled in the program, respondents for four, or 50%, of the transitional programs included in the survey indicated that maximum allowable stays did exist, ranging from 30 to 90 days (see Table 13.4). These enrollment limitations tended to correlate with the maximum stay limits imposed by adjacent homeless shelters. None

**Table 13.2** Location of Homeless Education Programs

| Location | Transitional | | Mainstreamed | | Supplemental Support | |
|---|---|---|---|---|---|---|
| | f | % | f | % | f | % |
| Located on a single site | 8 | 100.0 | 2 | 15.4 | 10 | 52.6 |
| Dispersed throughout the educational organization | 0 | 00.0 | 11 | 84.6 | 9 | 47.4 |
| Totals | 8 | 100.0 | 13 | 100.0 | 19 | 100.0 |

$N = 40$

of the mainstreamed programs included in the survey imposed enrollment limitations. Six, or 32%, of the supplemental support programs had established limits on length of enrollment. As with transitional programs, most supplemental support program limitations were tied to the regulations of the corresponding shelter. One supplemental program, however, offered additional flexibility in enrollment requirements, allowing students to remain in the program for up to 4 weeks after families moved from the shelter.

**Program Size**

Program size, as measured by both the maximum number of homeless students that can be accommodated in the program and the average number of homeless students that were served on any given day during the most recent year, reflected considerable diversity. Most programs in the study, including all mainstreamed ones, claimed no limits on the number of homeless students that could be accommodated. Of those transitional and supplemental support programs that identified a maximum capacity, the number ranged from fewer than ten to capacity of an adjacent homeless shelter.

With a few exceptions, the programs tended to provide services to relatively small numbers of homeless students on any given day. It should be noted, however, that data from identified homeless education programs other than those included in this survey suggest a greater variability in enrollment. Available evidence indicates that homeless enrollment for single school/single site programs ranges from <10 to

**Table 13.3**  Admission Requirements for Homeless Education Programs

| Requirements | Transitional f | Mainstreamed f | Supplemental Support f |
|---|---|---|---|
| No specific restrictions other than identified as homeless | 0 | 10 | 7 |
| Resident of temporary shelter | 5 | 3 | 9* |
| Target Audience Restriction: adolescent homeless 18+ teen mother | 3 | 0 | 5* |
| Totals | 8 | 13 | 21 |

NOTE: Multiple restrictions are reflected in some supplemental support programs. Therefore totals are greater than the number of cases. $N = 40$

150+. For districtwide efforts, the range tends to be even greater, from <50 to > 4,000.

## Typology of Homeless Education Programs

### Transitional Programs

Transitional programs are designed specifically to provide intermediate, or transitional, educational opportunities for students who are temporarily displaced from their regular educational programs due to their homeless or temporarily housed condition. Transitional schools designed for pre-high school-age students typically cater either primarily or exclusively to the transitional housing clientele although some do enroll children from other homeless settings (e.g., those sleeping in a car or vacant building). Transitional programs for adolescents tend to be more open in their enrollment policies, often providing citywide services. While each transitional program is distinctive, some characteristics are common to this model: immediacy of service, temporary nature of placements, and emphasis on social and support services.

*Immediacy of service.*  When families become homeless and are forced to leave their former neighborhoods in search of temporary shelter, delays

**Table 13.4**  Homeless Education Program Enrollment Limitations

|                                          | Transitional | | Mainstreamed | | Supplemental Support | |
|------------------------------------------|------|-------|------|-------|------|-------|
|                                          | f    | %     | f    | %     | f    | %     |
| Yes, some limit on total number of days  | 4    | 50.0  | 0    | 0.0   | 6    | 31.6  |
| No limits                                | 4    | 50.0  | 13   | 100.0 | 13   | 68.4  |
| Totals                                   | 8    | 100.0 | 13   | 100.0 | 19   | 100.0 |

N = 40

in reenrollment of their children is common. Problems associated with reenrollment are exacerbated for independent youth (e.g., absence of parent/guardian). Transitional programs are intended to accommodate enrollment of homeless students with minimal delay on their presenting themselves to the schools. To this end, the programs typically are located where the students temporarily reside or congregate (e.g., adjacent to a temporary shelter, in a storefront located in an area frequented by independent homeless youth). The obvious result of these types of policies and practices among transitional schools is that students benefit from a continuation of educational services without undue delays, often with school enrollment available the same day the family or individual appears at the educational site.

The likelihood of immediate enrollment for children with families who are temporarily housed in shelter settings is enhanced because the educational programs are frequently operated in conjunction with the housing facility, often on the campus or adjacent to the facility. The transitional schools typically waive traditional enrollment procedures (e.g., academic transcript from previous school), thus removing some of the impediments that can prohibit or delay reenrollment. In addition, many of the shelters require that school-age children be enrolled in school in order for the family to remain in the shelter. The Harbor Summit School, operated by the San Diego County Office of Education, is a good example of this type of arrangement. Admission to the program is contingent on a student being temporarily housed in the adjacent St. Vincent de Paul-Joan Kroc Homeless Shelter; conversely the shelter requires that school-age children enroll in school.

For independent youth, the educational programs frequently employ a policy of accepting students on a walk-in basis, as well as serving the clientele of the shelter in which the educational program may be housed. In addition, transitional programs designed for independent youth encourage enrollment by making the schooling accessible (e.g., flexible scheduling) and meaningful to the students' present circumstances (e.g., curriculum oriented to living skills or GED preparation). Harbinger House, a program for girls ages 13 to 17 in Framingham, Massachusetts, functions in this manner. The program offers a wide array of services, including individualized academic programs and counseling, within the context of a structured environment. While the program is designed as a short-term residential program and has a maximum limit on the number of days that an individual may stay (45 days), it provides 24-hour accessibility on a year-round basis.

*Temporary placement.* Transitional programs are characterized by the temporary nature of the educational placement. The programs are merely intended as a bridge, connecting students with education until they can return to their former schools or move on to more permanent settings. It is not uncommon for students to enroll in a transitional school on one day and be gone a few days later; moreover many transitional programs do not accept or retain students for more than a predetermined period (e.g., 90 consecutive days). Students may, however, enroll or withdraw (or simply leave) multiple times during an academic year, depending largely on the admission rules of the school (Stronge & Tenhouse, 1990).

The YWCA Family Intervention Center in Kokomo, Indiana, provides a temporary educational alternative for children from violent homes. The center, recognizing the major trauma that battered women and their children face, attempts to minimize the disruption in the children's lives by providing an educational program within the security of the shelter environment. One of the unique features of this program is that it works directly with the child's regular school and classroom teacher. The program provides individualized instruction while keeping the child in textbooks and class work that are familiar to him or her. Thus the child is not considered absent from school, and the academic record does not reflect a change in enrollment until the custodial parent is able to make a school transfer that provides for stability. In many instances, the child returns to her or his original school as the result of a court order enabling the parent and child to return safely to their home or to secure another safe home in the same school attendance area.

*Social and support services orientation.* Transitional programs provide academic services, often on an individualized or ungraded basis.

Due to the frequent absence of educational records and other evidence of past performance, individualization in the delivery of academic services may begin with a personalized assessment of educational achievement and lead to placement in a curriculum that is oriented to the individual. While academic services are rendered, however, a hallmark of the transitional programs is the emphasis on social and support services. In response to demonstrated socioemotional needs of the students, the programs often focus on objectives designed to provide a supportive and stabilizing influence in the students' lives. Provisions for stability, order, and acceptance are viewed as proper goals for education and, therefore, the educational programs are interpreted and designed broadly in an effort to provide a psychosocial safety net (see, for example, Felsman, 1985; Tyler, Tyler, Echeverey, & Zea, 1986). Specific areas of socioemotional support include (a) coping strategies for dealing with stress, crisis, and culture shock; (b) outlets for feelings of anger, frustration, sadness, and so on; (c) social role modeling and developing self-esteem and acceptable social skills; (d) personal and group counseling services; and (e) support for various types of personal needs.

A program that reflects this orientation toward affective education is the Anchorage, Alaska, Vocational Academic Institute of Learning (AVAIL). AVAIL, located in a storefront in a shopping mall, is designed as an alternative school devoted to at-risk teens, including independent homeless youth. The program offers in its philosophy statement: "In order for young adults to become productive citizens . . . we must enhance the self-esteem of young people and empower them to become part of their own solution." To this end, AVAIL includes affective skills as an integral part of its program; this includes classes intended to help students improve self-esteem, improve communication skills, deal with conflict and anger, develop realistic expectations, and learn to make commitments.

Another example of a transitional program with a significant orientation toward socioemotional support are the Shelter Schools operated by the Salt Lake City School District. In addition to more traditional academic services, these shelter schools emphasize family stability through support from the schools and the greater community. Indicative of this social support focus is the availability of services from a wide array of professional staff and volunteers, including pediatric team intervention, educational case worker assistance, school social services, in-school scouting and other enrichment opportunities, and family and personal support through coordinated contributions from the community.

**Mainstreamed Programs**

Mainstreamed programs seek to educate homeless children and youth within the context of existing schools and, in many cases, in existing programs within the schools. The prevailing philosophy reflected in this approach is that homeless students are similar to all students with one exception: They are temporarily without a permanent home (Stronge & Tenhouse, 1990). Some states, as a matter of public policy, select the mainstreamed, regular education option as the exclusive or preferred mode of service delivery to homeless students. Moreover the 1990 Amendments to the McKinney Act reflect as federal policy a preference for mainstreamed, regular education programming in the delivery of educational services to homeless students: "homelessness alone should not be sufficient reason to separate students from the mainstream school environment" (McKinney Act, 1990, Subtitle VII-B, Sec. 721[3]).

Characteristics that are common among most of the mainstreamed programs include emphasis on accessibility and focus on academic accommodation. These two identifying features will be reviewed in turn.

*Emphasis on accessibility.* Public education provided by a state is primarily a duty imposed on children and their parents for the public good, as well as an individual right afforded them by the state. Unfortunately for homeless students, the delivery of this educational right has historically been restricted to bona fide residents of a given community. Accommodating children with no identifiable or permanent address with access to a free, appropriate public education while acknowledging the tradition of educational provision within the district of residence can be a primary barrier to education. While the McKinney Act explicitly requires that residency barriers be removed (1987, Subtitle VII-B, Section 721 [1,2] located at 42 USC 11431), issues of accessibility can remain in subtle, if not direct, forms. For instance, Jackson (1989) reported that among approximately one third of homeless shelter providers surveyed, instances were known in which homeless children were denied access to education because of residency requirements.

One method of dealing with the residency barrier is to alter existing policy and practices relative to the enrollment of students so that homeless students may be accepted into the schools without unnecessary delays. All mainstreamed programs included in the survey followed this strategy. The Oakland, California, Unified School District Program, in conjunction with the Oakland Salvation Army Shelter, serves as a good example for dealing with this aspect of the accessibility issue. Agreement was reached between the school district and the shelter that children temporarily housed in the shelter could attend the school of their choice within the school district. A special registration process was designed, facilitating immediate enrollment in the public schools and waiving transfer requirements for students living outside a school's attendance zone.

Once residency barriers are removed, another key component to servicing homeless students is that of enhancing awareness of opportunity among both homeless parents and public educators. Project Return of the Portland, Oregon, Public Schools created such a program. Basic objectives of the program are (a) to enroll students who are not enrolled in school and (b) to keep teachers and other school staff members aware of special requirements of homeless students. A key strategy to implementing the objectives is the use of a mobile unit that takes a team of specialists to shelters across the city to identify, assess, and enroll homeless students. The team also provides staff development at the public schools.

*Focus on academic accommodation.* Mainstreamed programs attempt to bring stability to the otherwise disrupted lives of homeless students by providing a structured setting and a familiar routine, if not a familiar place. The staff of most schools, however, recognize the vitality for some programmatic modifications in their efforts to provide a free, appropriate education to homeless students.

Unlike transitional programs, which tend to reflect common characteristics in their methodologies and services, analysis of the mainstreamed programs indicates that diversity characterizes the focus and extent of services delivered. For example, programs like that of the New York City Public Schools offer comprehensive services for homeless students and their families, including identification, placement assistance, transportation, regular and specialized academic services, as well as a wide array of support services such as attendance reporting and monitoring, and interagency social service coordination. Other programs are much more limited in scope and target a specific problem frequently encountered by homeless students, such as the lack of transportation, by providing services exclusively to address the problem (e.g., free bus tokens, adjusted school policies).

Although program diversity prevails in the mainstreamed typology, one unifying characteristic is clear: The greater the frequency and/or density of homeless students to be integrated into the regular school offerings, the more these programs adapt their efforts to specifically accommodate the homeless. This generalization appears to hold true whether several thousand homeless students are spread across the city (as in New York City's case) or a few dozen students are concentrated in one community and attending one public school (Stronge & Tenhouse, 1990). In an effort to make regular education meaningful to homeless students, many mainstreamed programs find it necessary to develop more extensive adaptive services. Thus the programs are transformed to ones that are more integrative in nature, coordinating regular educational offerings with specialized adaptive services.

**Supplemental Support Services**

Programs that provide supplemental support services are characterized by their part-time, beyond-school-hours mode of service delivery. These programs tend to address what are perceived to be the most pressing education-related needs of homeless students and their families in the particular service area and, therefore, are fairly idiosyncratic in nature. Nonetheless, a review of the programs categorized in this typology revealed several common themes for service delivery, including academic support, counseling, cultural enrichment, parental support, personal assistance, and other types of support (Table 13.5).

While some programs focus primarily or exclusively on one type of service, the more common approach is the integration of multiple support services within the program. In addition, the delivery of services is not limited to school premises: Numerous programs are located on the premises of private service providers (e.g., homeless shelters) or public facilities other than schools (e.g., public libraries). Other programs are operated by or in conjunction with temporary housing shelters and private service providers such as the YWCA.

*Academic support services.* Academic support services generally focus on two areas of assistance: (a) helping students with academic work related to their regular school day academic program, and (b) supplemental assistance designed to enhance academic performance in a targeted skill area. Illustrative academic support services include tutoring and remedial assistance, help with homework, provision of a place to study, and preparation assistance for a high school equivalency examination.

The Computer Instruction Teaches Education in Shelters Program (CITES) and Project WORTH (Work Opportunity Readiness for the Homeless) of the Jefferson County, Kentucky, Public Schools offer

**Table 13.5** Supplemental Support Program Areas of Service

| Service Type | Frequency of Programs Offering This Service | Percentage of Programs Offering This Service |
|---|---|---|
| Academic Support | 16 | 84.2 |
| Counseling | 14 | 73.7 |
| Cultural Enrichment | 12 | 63.2 |
| Parental Support | 08 | 42.1 |
| Personal Assistance | 08 | 42.1 |
| Other Support | 11 | 57.9 |

$N = 19$

innovative academic strategies that are designed to supplement the services available through regular public school programming. CITES provides an individualized computer-assisted instructional program for homeless families at selected shelters throughout Louisville. In addition to the on-site instructional program, CITES offers Camp Readiness—a program designed to provide organized preparation for entrance into regular schools at the beginning of the new school year—to homeless parents and their children. The camp, in conjunction with the local Salvation Army's boys and girls summer programs, provides parent workshops dealing with school-related issues and arranges for a medical team to administer physical and eye examinations for all participants.

*Counseling services.* Individual and family counseling is featured in many of the supplemental support programs. The focus for counseling primarily is on socioemotional support, including dealing with such concerns as social acceptance, self-esteem, and stress.

The Kid's Menu Extended Day Program in Fargo, North Dakota, is a good example of counseling services available to homeless children in an after-school program. While the program offers a variety of supervised after-school activities for latchkey children, an important aspect of the program is self-esteem building and cultural awareness activities that are designed specifically for children. Another example of counseling support services is that of the Homeless Student Initiative of the Cincinnati, Ohio, City Schools. This after-school program operates during the school year and includes a component designed to foster a positive self-image and self-awareness among the participating students through the use of instructional materials designed expressly for those purposes.

*Cultural enrichment services.* Cultural enrichment frequently serves the dual purposes of providing students with enrichment and recreational opportunities that they otherwise would be lacking at that point in their lives, while at the same time providing an extended period of supervised activity at times conducive for parents to either work or seek employment. Typical activities include organized play, use of computers, music, and arts and crafts. The Homeless Education Pilot Project of the University of Missouri at Columbia is indicative of the cultural enrichment that is central to most supplemental support programs. In addition to other enrichment services, this project features field trips to area museums and businesses—an opportunity that otherwise would not be available in the lives of the participating children.

*Parental support services.* Numerous programs extend children's support services to their parents, as well as offering family-oriented educational services. The impetus for these services is the knowledge that unless the family environment is supportive, other efforts to improve children's education likely will be futile. The District of Columbia Public Schools' Homeless Children and Youth Technical Assistance Branch offers an example of services within this category: For parents residing in shelters, training programs are provided on topics including budgeting, health, nutrition, and parenting skills. Another prime example of parental support services is the Partners in Progress program in Salisbury, Massachusetts, which provides parent training on how to assist children academically (e.g., how to assist with homework, importance of reading to children), as well as workshops on children's nutrition. Other services typical of support programs include family literacy activities and counseling support for women and children of domestic violence.

*Personal and other support services.* Personal support services include the provision of school supplies, adequate clothing, and snacks (often in conjunction with the operation of after-school activities). Other types of support services include the provision of educational advocacy and educational coordination with various social services.

While numerous supplemental support programs feature personal support as part of their effort, the Pima County, Arizona, Homeless Teen Student Project (PCHTSP) is unique in that personal support provided directly to participating homeless youth is a hallmark of the program. The program is designed specifically to prevent homelessness of middle school and high school youth who find themselves needing permanent shelter outside their parents' homes. To this end, the program provides financial assistance to independent youth through a stipend of $100 per month to help pay rent or to help with the financial stress placed on families who voluntarily take care of these youth. During the 1990-1991 academic year, PCHTSP assisted more than 200 students.

## Conclusions

It is too early in the life of homeless educational programming to make a judgment of worth regarding the various service delivery models that are emerging. To make a determination of worth in terms of outcomes, that is, "a change in quality of life of the client served" (Kettner & Daley, 1988, p. 106), will require more evidence than we currently possess.

It seems ludicrous to contemplate long-term efficacy of homeless education efforts when the best solution would be to eliminate the causes of homelessness and thus eliminate the issue altogether. Unfortunately solutions to the problems posed by homelessness will not come easily. Homelessness is rooted in the broader aspects of society and consequently must be addressed on multiple fronts, including in the classroom. Natriello, McDill, and Pallos (1990) noted that "the problems of disadvantaged students are the results of long-term conditions that are not susceptible to short-term solutions" (p. 1). Nonetheless we have started down the road of providing a free, appropriate public education to homeless children and youth first by recognizing their educational plight and second by initiating service delivery models that offer a promise of success.

## Notes

1. This was a study of extant programs designed for or adapted to meet the unique educational needs of homeless students and was conducted in winter and spring of 1991. Identification of such programs was accomplished through a review of the current literature (ERIC and National Newspaper Index database searches), a survey of homeless education coordinators for state and territorial educational agencies, and contact with 1990 recipients of U.S. Department of Education exemplary grants for the education of homeless children and youth. The study identified 78 separate programs for educating homeless children and youth.

2. While the programs tend to organize within the three identified categories, the organizational typology suggested in this analysis is not a perfect one. Primary attributes noted for one model do exist in other models. Some programs, especially those that are of a more comprehensive nature, tend to encompass more than one service delivery model.

3. The survey that serves as the nucleus for this chapter is a follow-up to the study referenced in Note 1. The 40-program sample reported here reflects the inclusion of transitional, mainstreamed, and supplemental support programs generally in proportion to those identified in the more expansive earlier study.

## References

Felsman, J. K. (1985). *Abandoned children reconsidered: Prevention, social policy, and the trouble with sympathy.* Paper presented at the International Conference on Prevention, University of Montreal, Canada. (ERIC Document Reproduction Service No. 268 457)

Jackson, S. (1989). *The education rights of homeless children.* Cambridge, MA: Center for Law and Education.

Kettner, P. M., & Daley, J. M. (1988). Designing effective programs. *Child Welfare, 67,* 99-111.

Natriello, G., McDill, E. L., & Pallos, A. M. (1990). *Schooling disadvantaged children: Racing against catastrophe.* New York: Teacher's College Press.

Stewart B. McKinney Homeless Assistance Act of 1987. P.L. 100-77, Codified at 42 U.S.C. 11301-11472. (1987, July 22).

Stewart B. McKinney Homeless Assistance Amendment Act of 1990. P.L. 101-645. (1990, November 29).

Stronge, J. H. (1991, April). *Emerging service delivery models for educating homeless children and youth: A sociological perspective.* Paper presented at the Annual Meeting of the American Educational Research Association, Chicago, IL.

Stronge, J. H., & Tenhouse, C. (1990). *Educating homeless children: Issues and answers.* Bloomington, IN: Phi Delta Kappa Educational Foundation.

Tyler, F. B., Tyler, S. L., Echeverey, J. J., & Zea, M. C. (1986). *A preventive psychosocial approach for working with street children.* Paper presented at the Annual Convention of the American Psychological Association, Washington, DC. (ERIC Document Reproduction Service No. 274 887)

# About the Authors

**Joan Alker** is the Assistant Director of the National Coalition for the Homeless, a grass roots advocacy organization in Washington, DC. She specializes in issues relating to homeless families, including educational policy for homeless children. She has authored a number of reports on homelessness and on public policy for the National Coalition, has served on two advisory panels to the U.S. Department of Education on issues related to the education of homeless children, and volunteers with homeless people on the streets of Washington, DC. She received an M.Phil. in Politics at St. Antony's College, Oxford University; and an A.B. with Honors in Political Science from Bryn Mawr College, Bryn Mawr, PA. She can be contacted at the National Coalition for the Homeless, 1621 Connecticut Ave., NW, 4th Floor, Washington, DC 20009.

**E. Anne Eddowes** is Early Childhood Coordinator and Associate Professor in the Department of Curriculum and Instruction at the University of Alabama at Birmingham. She teaches early childhood curriculum and methods of teaching infants, preschool, and primary school children. Her research interests include issues in early childhood programming, the importance of varying play opportunities for young children, and parent education. Her article concerning the problems of educating homeless children appeared in *Childhood Education*. She has served as a consultant with homeless programs, as well as those serving parents and children in lower income housing. She may be contacted at the School of Education, UAB, Birmingham, AL 35294.

**Patricia F. First** is Professor of Educational Leadership and Policy Studies at the University of Oklahoma. Her background includes experience at the national, state, and local levels of educational governance and a National Education Policy Fellowship. Both her teaching and research are in the areas of educational law and policy studies. Articles concerning the access by homeless children to an education have appeared in *West's Education Law Reporter, The School Administrator,* and *Catalyst for Change.* Her books include *Educational Policy for School Administrators* and *School Boards: Changing Local Control,* edited with Herbert Walberg. A continuing research interest is the adequacy of the educational experience. A recent article on this topic appeared in the *Journal of Law and Education.* She may be contacted at the Department of Educational Leadership and Policy Studies, University of OK, Norman, OK 73019.

**María Luisa González** is Associate Professor of Educational Management and Development at New Mexico State University in Las Cruces, where she teaches educational leadership courses. Her publications on homeless children include articles in *Educational Leadership* and the *Phi Delta Kappan.* She was formerly principal of an inner-city school in Dallas that was recognized as one of the 15 exemplary programs in the nation for educating homeless students. She currently serves on the National Advisory Board for the Education of Homeless Children, is a member of New Mexico's 21st Century Commission on Education, and directs the New Mexico Center for Rural Education, where she coordinates a satellite center for a Project LEAD Principal's Institute and a youth aspirations program. She may be contacted at New Mexico State University, Box 30001, Dept. 3N, Las Cruces, NM 88003.

**Doris Helge** is Executive Director of FOR CHILDREN and previous director of the American Council on Rural Special Education (ACRES) and the National Rural and Small Schools Consortium (NRSSC). She has taught a variety of courses regarding special education, at-risk students, and rural education. Her primary research interests include prevention and treatment of at-risk student conditions, related social policy, and strategies for delivering services in rural areas. The results of her research have been disseminated via national television and news programs and in Congressional testimony. She has published widely in books, journals, and preservice curriculum modules concerning at-risk students and has written and directed numerous national projects concerning her areas of expertise. She is a frequent keynote speaker and consultant regarding at-risk student service delivery strategies and rural special education. She may be contacted at Box 4434 Bellingham, WA 98227 or 709 W. Wiser Lake Road, Ferndale, WA 98248.

**Virginia M. Helm** is Professor of Educational Administration and Supervision and Assistant Dean in the College of Education at Western Illinois University in Macomb. She has taught courses in curriculum, school finance, and school law. Her research interests have ranged widely in the area of education law. Early publishing and speaking focused on legal aspects of using technology in the schools (copyright law) and on censorship issues. Later she pursued interests in the legal aspects of personnel evaluation and of educating homeless children and youth. In the latter area she has coauthored with James Stronge a presentation for the American Educational Research Association and an article in the *Journal of Law and Education*. She may be contacted at the Dean's Office, College of Education, Western Illinois University, Macomb, IL 61455.

**Barbara Jaklitsch** has been working with and on behalf of at-risk youth for the past 18 years. Former Director of Family House for runaway, homeless, and troubled youth, in recent years she has been developing, coordinating, and delivering training on adolescent and independent living issues for Cornell University and the City of Philadelphia and New York State. She is author of several articles and curricula, including the Runaway module of the Daniel Memorial, Foster Family System; "Preparing for Independence: Counseling Issues With the Maltreated Youth" and "Understanding Survivors of Abuse: Stories of Homeless and Runaway Adolescents." She currently is an Education Specialist with the Professional Development Program at Rockefeller College, State University of New York in Albany. She may be contacted at SUNY, Albany, Independent Living Center, Rockefeller College, 301 Richardson Hall, Albany, NY 12222.

**Joseph F. Johnson, Jr.,** is Director of Special Projects and State Compensatory Education for the Texas Education Agency. He administers statewide programs designed to meet the educational needs of special populations of children. He was Texas's first State Coordinator for the Education of Homeless Children. While State Coordinator, he served as Founding President of the National Association of State Coordinators for the Education of Homeless Children and Youth and served as editor and primary author of the association's 1990 and 1991 position documents. He served as Chair of the Texas Interagency Council for Services for the Homeless and presently is serving as a Board Member of the National Coalition for the Homeless. He may be contacted at the Texas Education Agency, 1701 N. Congress Ave., Austin, TX 78701.

**Lori Korinek** is Program Coordinator and Associate Professor, Special Education Program, at the College of William and Mary in Williamsburg, Virginia. She teaches characteristics and methods courses in the areas of learning disabilities and behavioral disorders and has made national, state, and local conference presentations related to these specialties. Her research and publications in such journals as *Exceptional Children,* the *Journal of Teacher Education,* and *Preventing School Failure* have focused on curriculum and instruction for students with mild disabilities, collaboration between general and special educators, and service delivery to special education/at-risk students in integrated settings. She may be contacted at the College of William and Mary, School of Education, P.O. Box 8795, Williamsburg, VA 23187-8795.

**Virginia K. Laycock** is Associate Professor in the Special Education Program at the College of William and Mary in Williamsburg, Virginia. She teaches special education courses in curriculum development, interdisciplinary and interagency collaboration, communication skills, and mainstreaming courses in the elementary and secondary education programs. Her current research efforts and recent publications focus on development and evaluation of curriculum for at-risk and gifted students, collaborative service delivery, and collaborative problem-solving processes. She frequently consults with state and local educational agencies on topics related to development and evaluation of programs for students who are at risk or have identified disabilities. She may be contacted at the College of William and Mary, School of Education, P.O. Box 8795, Williamsburg, VA 23187-8795.

**Jane L. Powers** has been a Research Associate at Cornell University's Family Life Development Center since 1985, working on a variety of projects concerned with child abuse and neglect. A specialist in adolescent maltreatment, she directed the research effort for Statewide Teamwork for Abused Runaways (STAR), a federal research and demonstration project concerned with improving services to maltreated runaway and homeless youth in New York State. Currently she is the Project Director for the National Data Archive on Child Abuse and Neglect, a centralized facility that preserves and disseminates high-quality, machine-readable data relevant to the study of child maltreatment. She received her Ph.D. from Cornell University in 1985 in Developmental Psychology from the Department of Human Development and Family Studies. She may be contacted at Cornell University, Family Life Development Center, Ithaca, NY 14853.

**James H. Stronge** is Program Coordinator and Associate Professor, Educational Administration Program Area, at the College of William and Mary in Williamsburg, Virginia. He teaches courses in organizational and administrative theory, educational law, and personnel administration. His primary research interests include personnel issues in education and educational policy analysis. His recent research in the policy area has focused on organizational issues related to educating homeless children and youth. His homeless education research includes publications with the Phi Delta Kappa Education Foundation, the *Journal of Law and Education,* and presentations to the American Educational Research Association. In addition, he has served as consultant and worked on projects related to homeless education issues, including serving as principal investigator for developing state educational policy recommendations for the Illinois State Board of Education. He may be contacted at the College of William and Mary, School of Education, P.O. Box 8795, Williamsburg, VA 23187-8795.

**Cynthia Crosson Tower** is Professor of Human Services, Behavioral Science Department, at Fitchburg State College in Massachusetts. She holds a Masters in Social Work from the University of Connecticut School of Social Work and an Ed.D. in counseling psychology. She has worked as a social worker in the areas of protective services, adoption, foster care, child guidance and corrections, and currently maintains a private practice specializing in adult survivors of child sexual abuse. In addition, she is consultant to several adolescent residential treatment programs in the treatment of juvenile sex offenders. She has had extensive experience in writing and conducting training programs about child abuse and neglect and homeless children, including the development of the National Education Association Child Abuse and Neglect Training Program. She has authored several books, including *Homeless Students, How Schools Can Combat Child Abuse and Neglect, Understanding Child Abuse and Neglect,* and *Secret Scars: A Guide for Survivors of Child Sexual Abuse,* in addition to several chapters and monographs. She may be contacted at Fitchburg State College, 160 Pearl St., Fitchburg, MA 01420.

**Meredith van Ry** is Director of TeenPATH, the Homeless Teen Parent Assistance and Transitional Housing Project at Central Area Youth Association in Seattle for teen parents under the age of 18. Previously she worked as Consultant for Health Care for the Homeless, Seattle Project. She has a Ph.D. in Social Welfare. Her major research has been in the area of programs and policies that impact homeless families. Other research has been in the area of policy practice, programs that deal with homeless mentally ill offenders, and the human costs of unemployment for the individual and the family. She may be contacted at Central Area Youth Association, 119 23rd Ave., Seattle, WA 98122.

**Christine Walther-Thomas** is Assistant Professor, Special Education Program Area, at the College of William and Mary in Williamsburg, Virginia. She teaches courses in teacher collaboration, instructional program planning, and educational integration of students with disabilities and learning disabilities. Her primary interests include collaboration between general and special educators, educational change, and the appropriate integration of students with disabilities into general education classrooms. Her current research focuses on effective use of school resources to meet the needs of students with disabilities and other students who do poorly in school. She has presented nationally on educational planning and appropriate service delivery options for homeless students with disabilities. She may be contacted at the College of William and Mary, School of Education, P.O. Box 8795, Williamsburg, VA 23187-8795.

59129CA FM
5-24-94  32390

]41]  LBC TCI